Language and the Interpretation of Islamic Law

Language and the Interpretation of Islamic Law

Šukrija (Husejn) Ramić

THE ISLAMIC TEXTS SOCIETY

Acknowledgement

Praise be to God Almighty and thanks, and peace be upon the Master of the Messengers Muhammad, his family and followers to the Day of Judgement.

Language and the Interpretation of Islamic Law was first submitted as a Ph.D. thesis at the University of Wales, Lampeter. I am indebted to many people who helped me complete this work. First, I wish to thank Dr. Mawil Izzi Dien, my supervisor, who has been everything to me that a student could ask for in his teacher. May God Almighty reward him for his efforts and high ethics. I will never forget.

I would like to thank also the University of Wales who offered me a place at their distinguished College in Lampeter. Professor Paul Badham, the Head of the Department of Theology and Religious Studies has helped me at a crucial stage of this study. I am also indebted to Mr. Alan Rogers, the Director of Academic Computer Service at the College, who provided me with fonts for the transliteration.

I wish to thank the secretaries at Registry and Theology and Religious Studies departments. They have been kind and helpful.

I am deeply grateful to all my friends in Great Britain and abroad who supported me and encouraged me throughout my studies.

Finally, special thanks to my family, wife Bedrija, daughters Lejla, Esma, Surmeja and sons Ejmen and Muhamed.

Table of Contents

Introduction

The general need for the understanding of *uṣūl al-fiqh*:

The Islamic revival of this century, and the inroads it has made in the last two decades, have placed the Muslim world, its history and culture, back into academic focus. Researchers have been especially interested in Islamic law (*Sharīʿah*),[1] perhaps because, as Hamilton Gibb put it, throughout the centuries it has served not only as the master science but also as the most effective agent of change in the social order and the community life of Muslims. More than any other factor, it has safeguarded the social fabric of Islam through the political vicissitudes of our times.[2] This suggests that if someone wants to understand Muslims, their history and culture, Islamic law is more than a starting point. To understand Islamic law properly, however, we need to understand its structures and foundations (*uṣūl*). Because the methodology of *Sharīʿah* jurisprudence is so unique, secular jurists in particular need to grasp how different it is from other legal traditions.

What is *uṣūl al-fiqh*?

The word *uṣūl* is the plural of *aṣl*, literally, 'root'. In conjunction with the word *fiqh* the phrase − *uṣūl al-fiqh* − refers to a science developed by Islamic scholars. This science represents the theoretical basis of the *Sharīʿah*. *Fiqh* may be defined as the understanding of the principles by which the *mujtahid* derives practical *Sharīʿah* rulings from their particular and valid premises:[3]

——'Principles' includes the absolute propositions (*qaḍāyā kulliyyah*) whose rules may be applied to numerous subjects. One such principle is, 'The absolute order [*amr muṭlaq*] implies duty [*wujūb*].' This is an absolute provision because it may be applied to all absolute commands, such as 'And offer prayers and give alms.'[9] and 'O you who believe! Fulfil [your] obligations.'[10]

These absolute commands ('offer' and 'fulfil') that are not accompanied by any external or internal evidence may be included in the principle by which we may recognise rulings, in this case, with respect to the duty of offering prayers, giving alms and fulfilling obligations.

Another principle is that 'Absolute forbiddance [*nahy muṭlaq*] implies prohibition [*taḥrīm*]'. It also represents an absolute proposition because all absolute forms of prohibition, which are not accompanied by any external or internal evidence, may be included in it. The following verses explain the concept further: 'And do not approach the orphan's property, except to improve it';[11] 'There is no compulsion in religion';[12] 'O you who believe! Let not a nation scoff at another nation, it may be that the latter are better than the former.'[13]

All forms of prohibition (*taḥrīm*) in these verses may be included in that principle by which rulings are recognised. Therefore, in the preceding verses the ban implies the prohibition against mismanagement of orphans' property, the prohibition against forcing non-Muslims to accept Islam and the prohibition against scoffing at other nations.

——'by which a *mujtahid* derives practical *Sharīʿah* rulings' means that these principles are the tools with which a *mujtahid* reaches *Sharīʿah* rulings and derives them from their premises.

——'a *mujtahid*' excludes all those who are not qualified and who have not reached the level of *mujtahid*.[4] This means that only certain kinds of people can undertake legal reasoning (*ijtihād*) and derive legal rulings from valid premises.

——'rulings' (*ḥukm*, pl. *aḥkām*) means here the assertion of something for something. Accordingly the statement: 'The sun has risen or it has not risen' is a ruling, because it contains an assertion about the rising or non-rising of the sun.

The deduction of rulings may be achieved by three general methods:
(1) through reason (*ʿaql*) as in 'the one is half of two', 'the whole is bigger than a part of it'. These rulings are termed as *aḥkām ʿaqliyyah*;
(2) through natural feeling and senses such as knowing that fire burns. These rulings are termed (*aḥkām ḥissiyyah*);
(3) through authoritative texts. These rulings are termed *aḥkām sharʿiyyah*, such as rulings that the prescribed prayers are obligatory, that usury and adultery are forbidden, etc.

The principles of *uṣūl al-fiqh* are concerned with the third kind of rulings. This is restricted by the attribute '*sharʿiyyah*' in order to distinguish it from *aḥkām ʿaqliyyah* and *aḥkām ḥissiyyah*. These principles are established in order to help a *mujtahid* derive *aḥkām sharʿiyyah*[5] from their valid particular premises.

——'from their valid particular premises' – a premise in a particular proof relating to certain questions arising from the verse 'Forbidden to you [for food] are dead animals.'[6] This verse is a premise because it is related to the particular question of eating the flesh of animals who have not been slaughtered according to the rules of the *Sharīʿah* and indicates the ruling that pertains to this question. The premise is valid when it relates to a particular question and is based on the sources of the *Sharīʿah* which are represented in a universal and general proof.[7] The word 'valid' excludes all sources of law which are not based on the Qur'ān and the *Sunnah*.

——'particular' differentiates between specific and general (universal) proofs. From this definition *uṣūl al-fiqh* may be seen as the aggregate of legal proofs which, when acquired properly, guide a *mujtahid* to legal judgements and help him derive legal rulings from their particulars.[8]

The difference between the scholar of *uṣūl al-fiqh* and the scholar of *fiqh*

A scholar of *uṣūl al-fiqh* (*uṣūlī*) studies the Qur'ān, the *Sunnah* and other universal and general proofs. He must determine whether or not they provide general, specific, absolute or qualified indications, commands or prohibitions. A scholar of *uṣūl al-fiqh* must reach certain conclusions and suggest general rules accordingly. For example, when determining the indication of general provisions mentioned in authoritative texts, one may conclude that all unspecified general provisions include all that which is applicable. Thus, the scholar would state the principle that 'The general provisions, when not specified, fully include all that which is applicable'.

Similarly, a scholar of *uṣūl al-fiqh* may study all the commands mentioned in the Qur'ān and the *Sunnah*. If he concludes that these commands, when unaccompanied by any internal or external evidence, imply duty (*wujūb*), he would state the principle: 'The absolute order [*amr muṭlaq*] implies duty [*wujūb*] when unaccompanied by any evidence which might change that implication'.

When the scholar studies the prohibitions mentioned in authoritative texts, he concludes that all prohibitions, if unaccompanied by any internal or external evidence, imply *taḥrīm*. With this conclusion the following principle is deduced: 'The absolute ban [*nahy muṭlaq*] implies prohibition [*taḥrīm*], when unaccompanied by any internal or external evidence that might change that implication'.

This method allows the scholar of *uṣūl al-fiqh* to set forth principles which help the scholar of *fiqh* derive legal rulings from particular premises. When a scholar of *fiqh* wants to know the ruling on a certain matter, he applies the principles of *uṣūl al-fiqh* to particular proofs in order to discover their implications.

For example, if the scholar of *fiqh* wants to know the ruling with respect to prayers, he has first to search for a particular proof relating to prayers. This search must offer many verses and the Prophet's sayings on prayers. It must include the words: 'And offer prayer.' In this verse the scholar must identify the command to perform prayer and apply the *uṣūl al-fiqh* principle: 'The absolute order [*amr muṭlaq*] implies duty [*wujūb*].' In the end he must conclude that the command implies duty (*wujūb*), and therefore rule that prayer is obligatory (*wājib*).

From the previous discussion it is clear that scholars of *uṣūl al-fiqh* study universal and general proofs and deduce from them general rules which help scholars of *fiqh* to deduce legal rulings from particular premises.

Relation of *uṣūl al-fiqh* to other sciences

Because all the Islamic sciences have the same roots and the same objective, they are interdependent, and borrow from and rely upon each other. The science of *uṣūl al-fiqh* is no exception. It is methodologically similar to other classical Islamic sciences. The following are some examples:

(1) The Qur'ānic disciplines are similar in methodology in areas like:
(a) interpretation (*ta'wīl*), as opposed to the obvious or literal meaning of words;
(b) abrogation of legislation (*nāsikh wa mansūkh*);
(c) the non–standard recitations of the Qur'ān and the rules for them.

(2) From the *Sunnah*'s disciplines we may find similarity in methodology for the following subjects:
(a) the transmission of *ḥadīth* and its classification;
(b) the criteria for narrators of *ḥadīth* (*jarḥ wa taʿdīl*).

(3) The disciplines of scholastic theology (*ʿilm al-kalām*) are similar in methodology on the question of whether it is the *Sharīʿah* itself or reason which decides what is right and what is wrong, whether such knowledge can be acquired before revelation.

(4) Among the disciplines of *fiqh*, *uṣūl al-fiqh* offers many examples based on the particulars of *fiqh* (*furūʿ*).[14]

(5) The disciplines of the Arabic language are methodologically similar in the following areas:
(a) the rules basic to language;
(b) the classifications of words as either metaphorical or literal;
(c) etymology, synonymy, generalisation, specification, indication.

Besides these, *uṣūl al-fjqh* benefits and derives much of its elementary output from logic. Moreover, *uṣūl al-fiqh* demands the logical rigour of inductive reasoning for valid conclusions, evidences for claims, the proper method of refuting contrary arguments, the principles by which words convey their meanings.

The importance of *uṣūl al-fiqh* and its development

The importance of the science of *uṣūl al-fiqh* lies in the fact that it represents the foundations upon which the whole structure of Islamic law is built. It is concerned with the rules that are used in 'building' legal rulings from their particulars, i.e. understanding God's judgements concerning human actions and activities.

In the early days of Islam, none of these rules was written down. The first *mujtahid*s exercised *ijtihād* because the pure Arabic language they spoke rested on natural rules. However, the early Islamic scholars felt no great urgency to systematise these rules.

The need for such rules arose when Islam expanded to non-Arabic speak-ing areas and when many non-Arabs entered Islam. It was then that un-grammatical speech appeared. The understanding of Arabic, and, therefore, the understanding of the sources of the *Sharīʿah* of these new Muslims was inadequate and insufficient. Moreover, many people unqualified in legal reasoning (*ijtihād*) began working in that field. All these factors prompted Islamic scholars to systematise the rules that every 'faqih' needed in *ijtihād*. The objective of these rules was to help *mujtahid*s in their deduction of legal rulings from the *Sharīʿah*'s source-texts, to prevent them from errors and to spare them the accusation that the laws they formulated were arbitrary.

Shāfiʿī (d. 204/820) was one of the first scholars to collect[15] and draft rules. After Shāfiʿī, various scholars adopted one of two different approaches to this science. The first approach was that of the Ḥanafīs, who formulated their theory in the light of the practical application of the *Sharīʿah* to rele-vant issues and according to rulings established by previous jurists. The other approach was that of the Shāfiʿī *mutakallimūn*, who based their theories on general proofs (Qurʾān and *Sunnah*), without looking into their application to relevant issues. According to them, every theory supported by a reliable proof was confirmed, whether that theory agreed or disagreed with rulings established by previous jurists.

The real development in *uṣūl al-fiqh* occurred in the fourth century of the Islamic era, when it took its final shape, and when the main authoritative works in the field were written. The books later written were, basically, elaborations of these works.

The branches of *uṣūl al-fiqh*

This science is primarily concerned with Islamic legal logic, its precondi-tions and linguistics. It also focuses on agreed sources of Islamic law, namely, the Qurʾān, the *Sunnah*, consensus and analogy, and the disputed sources of the *Sharīʿah* (istiḥsān, istiṣlāḥ, istiṣḥāb), legal reasoning, indicating preference in cases of apparent conflict between legal proofs, following a specific school of legal thought (*taqlīd*).

The importance of the linguistic principles of *uṣūl al-fiqh*

One of the most important branches of *uṣūl al-fiqh* is the study of language. Linguistics includes principles relating to the way in which words convey their meanings, and to the clarity and ambiguity of words and their interpretation. The knowledge of these principles is essential to the proper understanding of the authoritative texts from which the legal rulings of Islamic law are deduced. Unless these texts are correctly understood no ruling can be deduced from them.

Linguistic principles are especially important when a given text is not self-evident, or when an apparent conflict between texts appears. From these principles a *mujtahid* may distinguish the speculative from the definitive texts and categorise clear and unclear texts (meanings). In cases of disagreement, the preference is for clearer or less ambiguous texts (meaning). A proper implementation of these principles in legal reasoning ensures intellectual rigour in sensitive areas where human beings must uphold the command of God (the only true Lawgiver) and speak in His name. From an Islamic perspective, human reasoning in a system of law which originates in divine revelation, is an arduous, complicated affair. Therefore all precautions need to be taken, and no effort spared in reaching the ruling intended by the Lawgiver. *Uṣūl al-fiqh* linguistic principles are focussed on this difficult process.

The importance of these principles may be summarised as follows:
(a) They are essential to *mujtahid*s for distinguishing between speculative and definitive meanings and for categorising these meanings so that that which is clearer may be given precedence in case of a conflict.
(b) They provide powerful support for the *mujtahid* in his legal reasoning, especially in the case of conflict between legal proofs in Islamic law.
(c) They provide understanding of words whose interpretation is a major cause of disagreement among Muslim jurists (*fuqahā'*).
(d) They help in better understanding the legislation of Islam and Islamic law in general.

The objectives of this research

(1) To show that the deduction of legal rulings from authoritative texts should rely on scientific methods of interpreting these texts, and to show the value of these methods in understanding and maintaining correct Islamic concepts.

(2) To bring to light some 'tools', developed by Islamic scholars, used in deriving *Sharīʿah* laws.

(3) To show the main similarities and differences between the two dominant schools in *uṣūl al-fiqh* (Ḥanafīs and Shāfiʿīs) and their approach to these principles.

(4) To show some of the methods used in Islamic legislation.

(5) To provide English speakers with a better understanding of the sources of Islamic law.

1. In Islam *Sharīʿah* (Islamic law) transcends society. 'In the beginning what Allāh created was a pen [*qalam*], then Allāh *taʿālā* ordered the pen to inscribe everything that could happen until the Day of Judgement' (Abū Dāwūd, *Sunan*, no. 4700); and amongst that which the pen wrote was the *Sharīʿah*. According to Islam the *Sharīʿah* was revealed to messengers before Muḥammad. Muḥammad was the Seal of the Prophets' who received its final form. The main sources of *Sharīʿah* are the Qurʾān and the *Sunnah*. Both were revealed in pure and literal Arabic.

2. Gibb, *Mohammedanism*, pp. 9–11.

3. Khallāf, *ʿIlm Uṣūl al-Fiqh*, p. 12; Khuḍarī, *Uṣūl al-Fiqh*, p. 12; Shaʿbān, *Uṣūl al-Fiqh al-Islāmī*, p. 6.

4. For more details on the subject of *ijtihād* and *mujtahid*, the readers may refer to books of *uṣūl al-fiqh*.

5. The *Sharīʿah* rulings are inherently concerned with all aspects of human life. Their relevance is as follows:

(a) Rulings concerned with human actions and activities like prayer, fasting, trading, religious endowment, writing a will, etc. The rulings related to these activities are called *aḥkām ʿamaliyyah*.

(b) Rulings concerned with beliefs – such as belief in God, His messengers, His books, etc. These rulings are called *aḥkām iʿtiqādiyyah*.

(c) Rulings relating to the purification of human souls – such as the obligation to be truthful and trustworthy, and the prohibition against lying, betrayal, cheating, etc. These rulings are called *aḥkām akhlāqiyyah*.

The science of *uṣūl al-fiqh* is concerned only with rulings on human actions and activities. This is why these rulings are qualified by the attribute *ʿamaliyyah* (practical), thus excluding *aḥkām iʿtiqādiyyah* and *aḥkām akhlāqiyyah*.

6. Qurʾān, V:3.

7. There are universal, general and comprehensive proofs. These include the main sources of the *Sharīʿah*, the Qurʾān, the *Sunnah* and other sources based upon these two main sources like consensus (*ijmāʿ*) and analogy (*qiyās*). These universal proofs may be either general (*ʿāmm*) or specific (*khāṣṣ*); these in turn may be commands (*amr*), prohibitions (*nahy*), absolute (*muṭlaq*) and qualified (*muqayyad*).

8. Rāzī defined *uṣūl al-fiqh* considered per se as the aggregate of legal proofs and evidence. When studied properly, it leads either to a firm grounding for a *Sharīʿah* ruling, or at least a reasonable assumption concerning the manner by which such proofs are deduced and the status of the adducer (*al-Maḥṣūl fī ʿIlm Uṣūl al-Fiqh*, I:1:94).

9. Qurʾān, II:43.

10. Qurʾān, V:1.

11. Qur'ān, VI:152.

12. Qur'ān, II:256.

13. Qur'ān, XLIX:11.

14. Moreover, Ḥanafī methodology derived the rules of *uṣūl al-fiqh* from particulars of *fiqh* (*furū'*).

15. Some may argue that Arabic linguistics cannot be classified as an Islamic science. The fact is that all other Islamic sciences are based on the Arabic language and studies relating to it. In short, Arabic is the main tool of Islam and therefore may be regarded as an Islamic science. Moreover, it is difficult to distinguish between Islamic and non-Islamic sciences because every science which agrees with human nature and which benefits human beings and does not go against natural laws is 'Islamic science'.

The Methods of Textual Indication
On Legal Rulings
(*Ṭuruq Dalālāt al-Alfāẓ ʿalā al-Aḥkām*)

Introduction to the Ḥanafī Approach to the Methods of Textual Indication

Deriving legal rulings from the authoritative texts of the Qur'ān and the *Sunnah* would be impossible without a clear understanding of these texts. It is often difficult to understand the true meaning of an authoritative text because of the shades of meaning that are suggested at different levels.

Every text imparts its meaning through letters, signs and allusions; or by logical implication without which the text would be incomplete. Every meaning indicated by the text[1] must be stated and interpreted.[2] A scholar concerned with the interpretation of a text has the responsibility of uncovering all its possible meanings, and of employing every method of interpretation that is linguistically acceptable. A failure to uncover any of these meanings undoubtedly means that the text cannot be implemented.

This is why scholars of *uṣūl al-fiqh* have been studying the problem of textual indication in legal rulings. They concluded that a text from which rulings can be derived may be understood through methods of indication[3]. Ḥanafī jurists[4] present four of these:

(a) explicit meaning,

(b) meaning indicated by signs and allusions,

(c) meaning arrived at by the logical and juridical purport of the text,

(d) logical and necessary meaning without which the text would remain incomplete and fail to achieve its purpose.

Due to the above reasons, Ḥanafī jurists like Dabbūsī and Bazdawī[5] suggest four types of textual implications: *ʿibārat al-naṣṣ* (the explicit meaning), *ishārat al-naṣṣ* (the alluded meaning), *dalālat al-naṣṣ* (the inferred meaning) and *iqtiḍāʾ al-naṣṣ* (the required meaning). They arrive at these conclusions by dividing a text's indication in a ruling into two categories:

(a) The indication made by words which can be either intended or not. If it is intended by the speaker (i.e. where indication represents the principle or subsidiary theme of the text), it is termed *ʿibārat al-naṣṣ* (the explicit meaning). If it is not directly intended by the speaker, then it is termed *ishārat al-naṣṣ* (the alluded meaning).

(b) The indication which is not derived from the text itself, but is understood either linguistically or legally (according to *Sharīʿah*). When it is understood linguistically it is termed *dalālat al-naṣṣ* (the inferred meaning); when understood legally (according to *Sharīʿah*) it is termed *iqtiṭiḍāʾ al-naṣṣ* (the required meaning).

Ḥanafīs also divide textual expressions in relation to their indication of meanings into four categories:

(a) that which gives explicit indication of meaning,

(b) that which indicates meaning by signs and allusions,

(c) that which indicates meaning according to the logical and juridical purport of the text,

(d) that which indicates meaning according to logical implication, without which the text would be incomplete and fail to achieve its purpose.

The highest level of indication is *ʿibārat al-naṣṣ* (the explicit meaning or immediate meaning). Next is *ishārat al-naṣṣ* (the alluded meaning), which is followed by *dalālat al-naṣṣ* (the inferred meaning). Lastly there is *iqtiḍāʾ al-naṣṣ* (the required meaning). According to this order the higher level of indication is more authoritative and would, in cases of conflict, take precedence over those versions which represent lower levels of implied indications which are detectable in the text. The same ruling has to be applied when two apparently contradictory texts are in question.

Ḥanafī jurists assume that all other indications - like the opposite meaning (*mafhūm al-mukhālafah*) and, in some cases, adopting the qualified (*muqayyad*) from the absolute (*muṭlaq*) - are incorrect.

As we have seen the Ḥanafī *madhhab* classifies texts and their meanings in terms of the method (or manner) of the text's indication of meanings into four types: *ʿibārat al-naṣṣ*, *ishārat al-naṣṣ*, *dalālat al-naṣṣ*. and *iqtiḍāʾ al-naṣṣ*. This division is based on the degree of textual explicitness. The first type is *ʿibārat al-naṣṣ*.

NOTES

1. It is important to note that rulings derived from all these meanings are considered, in the Ḥanafī *madhhab*, as rulings derived from the apparent meaning of the text, not by analogy (*qiyās*). (Sarakhsī, *Uṣūl al-Sarakhsī*, 1:236)

2. Muslim jurists maintain that the application of the explicit meaning of the text and the application of the text's spirit and logical meaning are obligatory duties (*wājib*) (Khallāf, *ʿIlm Uṣūl al-Fiqh*, p. 143).

3. The following methods are intended to encourage rational inquiry in the deduction of legal rulings from authoritative texts. Secondly, they provide Muslim jurists with guidelines as to how one may reach legal rulings from particular premises.

4. Bukhārī, *Kashf al-Asrār*, I:28. Sarakhsī, *Uṣūl al-Sarakhsī*, I:236.

5. Bukhārī, *Kashf al-Asrār*, I:28; Taftāzānī, *Sharḥ al-Talwīḥ ʿalā al-Tawḍīḥ*, I:130.

CHAPTER 1

The Explicit Meaning
(ʿIbārat al-Naṣṣ)

The linguistic definition of ʿibārat al-naṣṣ

ʿIbārah refers to whatever the speaker articulates and the listener hears. It may also refer to a written passage.[1] *Naṣṣ*: explicit, declared, manifest. In the religious sciences of Islam, this is a technical term. The root means 'to raise', 'to elevate something so that it is visible to all'. It also refers to an author's original text. In the technical vocabulary of *uṣūl al-fiqh*, *naṣṣ* refers to the text of the Qurʾān or *ḥadīth* which is adduced as justification for a legal ruling.[2]

In *ʿibārat al-naṣṣ* and other constructions to follow, *naṣṣ* refers to the text of the Qurʾān or *ḥadīth*. In this usage it is more general than just its reference to the apparent or the explained.

The technical definition of ʿibārat al-naṣṣ

Some Ḥanafī scholars have defined *ʿibārat al-naṣṣ* as follows:

Bazdawī stated, 'The argumentation by the explicit meaning (*ʿibārat al-naṣṣ*) is acting according to the apparent meaning that the speech is stated for.'[3] Sarakhsī said, 'The established [ruling] according to the explicit meaning is that ruling which agrees with the context [of the statement]. This [ruling] is normally understood as the subject of that text even without thinking.'[4]

From these definitions and from the examples mentioned by Ḥanafī jurists we may define *ʿibārat al-naṣṣ* as the immediate meaning of the words that is intended to provide such ruling no matter whether it represents the principal theme and purpose of the text or a subsidiary theme or themes. From this definition we can see that the major condition for *ʿibārat al-naṣṣ* is that the expression deliver an immediate meaning or meanings that come to mind without further consideration. Therefore, a single text may contain more than one meaning, and all these meanings may be counted as *ʿibārat al-naṣṣ* whether the meaning represents the principal theme and purpose of the text or a subsidiary theme or themes.[5] The important thing is that the meaning or meanings derived from the text should be apparent. This point is made clear in the examples that follow. Neither the reason for the revelation (*sabab al-nuzūl*), the possibility of specification of meaning (*takhṣīṣ*) or abrogation (*naskh*) play any role in indications (*dalālah*) distinctly from *naṣṣ*, *mufassar* or *muḥkam*.

Examples of ʿibārat al-naṣṣ

Every authoritative text relating to legal rulings is an example of ʿibārat al-naṣṣ, because the Lawgiver has delivered these expressions in order to convey meanings and rulings. Because every text relating to legal rulings has at least one apparent meaning which represents the purpose of the text, examples of ʿibārat al-naṣṣ seem to be numerous. This is all the more obvious if we remember that all apparent meanings of the text represent ʿibārat al-naṣṣ whether they are a principal or subsidiary theme of the text.[6]

(a) The Qur'ān states: 'Allāh has permitted trade and forbidden *ribā*' [usury].'[7]

Two meanings are distinguishable in this verse and both represent a ruling:

(1) Trade is permitted and usury is forbidden.

(2) There is a difference between trade and usury, because the former is permitted and the latter is forbidden.

These two rulings are different from the point of view that the former is subsidiary, while the latter is the principal theme and purpose of the text[8]. Nonetheless, this difference has no effect in relation to ʿibārat al-naṣṣ, and both rulings derived from this text are indicated by ʿibārat al-naṣṣ (the explicit meaning) of the text.[9] This is because both rulings are deduced from the apparent meaning of the text and the deduction does not require any additional effort or *ijtihād*.

(b) The Qur'ān states: 'And if you fear that you shall not be able to deal justly with the orphan-girls, then marry other women of your choice, two or three or four. But if you fear that you shall not be able to deal justly [with them], then only one...'[10]

This verse provides a few apparent meanings:

(1) The legality of marriage, indicated by 'then marry other women'.

(2) Limiting polygamy to a maximum of four wives when there is no fear of injustice. This is indicated by 'then marry other women of your choice, two or three or four'.

(3) Remaining monogamous for someone who fears that polygamy may lead to injustice. This is indicated by: 'But if you fear that you shall not be able to deal justly [with them], then only one'.

All these rulings, as we have seen, are clearly indicated by the apparent meaning of the text. These rulings and meanings, however, are not the whole principal theme and purpose of the text. The reason for revelation (*sabab al-nuzūl*)[11] indicates that the second and third rulings are the purpose for which this verse was revealed, while the first represents a subsidiary meaning. In his discussion on the *sabab al-nuzūl* of this verse, Ṭabarī asserted that some people feared committing injustice against orphans and did not fear committing injustice against women. Therefore, this verse came down as a warning against injustice to women. Men were not to take more than four wives, and if they fear that they may commit an injustice then only one.

Ḥasan and Ḍaḥḥāk held that this verse abrogated the customs of the *jāhiliyyah* and early Islamic period, when men married as many women as they wanted.

Therefore limiting polygamy to a maximum of four wives, and insisting on monogamy if polygamy risked injustice, carried two meanings. These two meanings are the main purpose of the text, while the legality of marriage is the subsidiary and incidental meaning. Despite this difference all three meanings and the rulings are *ʿibārat al-naṣṣ*. This is because all of them are 'apparently indicated' by the text itself and their understanding from the text required no additional effort.

The indication of *ʿibārat al-naṣṣ*

The majority of Ḥanafīs maintain that the indication of *ʿibārat al-naṣṣ* is definite (*qaṭʿī*) if another indefinite indication, based on a reliable proof, does not exist.[12]

Ibn Rahāwayh maintained that *ʿibārat al-naṣṣ* sometimes indicates indefinite meanings (*ẓannī al-dalālah*).[13] This opinion seems to agree with the previous one, because it probably suggests that *ʿibārat al-naṣṣ* indicates indefinite meaning when another meaning based on a proof emerges. This is exactly what the majority of scholars maintain. But, when speaking about indication of *ʿibārat al-naṣṣ*, they mean it in a general sense — i.e. before indefinite indication emerges.

The value of *ʿibārat al-naṣṣ*

The legal adherence to *ʿibārat al-naṣṣ* should be strict obligation (*wājib*) and an implementation of its meaning.[14]

NOTES

1. Fayrūz Ābadī, *al-Qāmūs al-Muḥīṭ*, II:83; *al-Muʿjam al-Wasīṭ*, II:580; Lane, *Arabic-English Lexicon*, II:1938; EI², IV:114; Baʿlabakī, *al-Mawrid*, p. 747.

2. M.L. ʿA., *al-Muʿjam al-Wasīṭ*, II:926; Lane, *Arabic-English Lexicon*, II:2797-9; II:1938; EI², II:1938; VII:1029; Baʿlabakī, *al-Mawrid*, p. 1173.

3. From the explanation of Bukhārī it is clear that he means by 'what the speech was stated for' both the main meaning, which was the reason behind its delivery, and other apparent subsidiary meanings (Bukhārī, *Kashf al-Asrār*, I:68).

4. Sarakhsī, *Uṣūl al-Sarakhsī*, I:236.

5. In *Principles of Islamic Jurisprudence* (p. 125) Kamali considered ʿibārat al-naṣṣ a meaning that represents 'the principal theme and purpose of the text' and excludes subsidiary meanings. This is obvious from his conclusion: 'But the first and the last are subsidiary and incidental, whereas the second and the third represent the explicit themes and meanings of the text, that is, the ʿibārat al-naṣṣ.' It seems that he confused naṣṣ and ʿibārat al-naṣṣ, claiming that ʿibārat al-naṣṣ is related to naṣṣ as the principal theme and purpose of the text. Therefore, his view of ʿibārat al-naṣṣ is inconsistent with the Ḥanafī madhhab. For the Ḥanafī madhhab, all the apparent meanings of the text are regarded as ʿibārat al-naṣṣ, whether they represent the principal theme and purpose of the text or a subsidiary theme. This view is reflected in the statement of Bukhārī, the famous Ḥanafī scholar of uṣūl al-fiqh. 'The indication of words, in relation to the methods by which they imply their meanings, may have three forms:
(1) To indicate a meaning which represents the original purpose [maqṣūd aṣlī] of the text like the number in the following verse: "...then marry [other] women of your choice, two or three, or four..."
(2) To indicate a meaning which does not represent the original purpose [maqṣūd aṣlī] of the text, such as legality of marriage in the previous verse.
(3) To suggest a necessary meaning of affirming something valid despite the statement that the payment is unlawful.
Bukhārī concluded: 'Now that you know [what we have mentioned above], it should be explained that in this case "the purpose" means that the word indicates its meaning unreservedly [muṭlaq], whether it was the original and essential intention or not.' (Bukhārī, *Kashf al-Asrār*, I:68).
Mayhawī confirmed what Bukhārī stated: 'The purpose in this case has a wider meaning than that which is revealed for that particular reason, as in the case of naṣṣ. The purpose in the case of naṣṣ is original and essential intention and purpose, while in the case of ʿibārat al-naṣṣ it can refer to either the original purpose or otherwise. Therefore if someone argues for the legality of marriage by relying on the verse"...then marry [other] women of your choice, two or three, or four...", he would be relying on ʿibārat al-naṣṣ – although it is not naṣṣ [explicit] but ẓāhir [apparent] meaning. It must be clarified, however, that naṣṣ in this verse is the number mentioned.' (Nasafī, *Kashf al-Asrār*, I:374).
According to Kawrānī ʿibārat al-naṣṣ is 'everything' understood from the words of the Qurʾān or Sunnah (Kawrānī, *Sharḥ Mukhtaṣar*, p. 63; Bādshāh, *Taysīr al-Taḥrīr*, I:86-87).

6. Thus, the commands to perform certain prayers, to give alms, to observe the fast during Ramaḍan, to perform pilgrimage, to enforce the prescribed penalties (ḥudūd) for certain offences, etc. – all have indicated those rulings by the method of ʿibārat al-naṣṣ.

7. Qurʾān, II:275.

8. This verse was revealed for the purpose of denying the claim of similarity between trade and usury. It was not revealed in order to explain the ruling of both of them. This is obvious from the verse itself ('That is because they say: trading is just like ribā [usury]') and from the reason for revelation (sabab al-nuzūl) of this verse. (Ibn Kathīr, *Tafsīr al-Qurʾān al-ʿAẓīm*, I:437).

9. This difference would have effect if *wāḍiḥ* were in question. See *ẓāhir* and *naṣṣ* in the second chapter.

10. Qur'ān, IV:3.

11. Bukhārī, *al-Jāmiʿ al-Ṣaḥīḥ*, V:177 (65:1); Ṭabarī, *Jāmiʿ al-Bayān ʿan Tafsīr Āy al-Qur'ān*, VII:536; Qurṭubī, *al-Jāmiʿ li-Aḥkām al-Qur'ān*, V:11-12; Ibn Kathīr, *Tafsīr al-Qur'ān al-ʿAẓīm*, I:597-600.

12. Sarakhsī, *Uṣūl al-Sarakhsī*, I:236-237; Bukhārī, *Kashf al-Asrār*, I:70. It is important to note that Ḥanafī scholars agree that the definite meaning (*qaṭʿī al-dalālah*) has wider significance than its apparent linguistic sense. It means 'non-existence of a possibility based on a proof'. (Taftāzānī, *Sharḥ al-Talwīḥ ʿalā al-Tawḍīḥ*, I:35-36, 130-131.

13. Ibn Rahāwayḥ, *Ḥāshiyat al-Rahāwayḥ*, I:524.

14. Khallāf, *ʿIlm Uṣūl al-Fiqh*, p. 143.

CHAPTER 2

The Alluded Meaning
(*Ishārat al-Naṣṣ*)

The linguistic definition of *ishārat al-naṣṣ*

Ishārah refers to gesture, sign, symbol, signal, indication, hint, allusion. In Arabic rhetoric the word has acquired the technical meaning of 'allusion'.[1] *Naṣṣ* in *uṣūl al-fiqh* refers to either Qur'ān or *ḥadīth* as a text.[2] Therefore, the construction *ishārat al-naṣṣ* has to do with a text from the Qur'ān and the *ḥadīth*.

The technical definition of *ishārat al-naṣṣ*

Ḥanafī scholars have offered similar yet inconsistent definitions of *ishārat al-naṣṣ*. Thus Dabbūsī defined it as 'That which is established by allusion is neither required nor conveyed by the speech context. However, *ishārat al-naṣṣ* is indicated specifically by the apparent [meaning] without increasing or decreasing its meaning.'[3] Bazdawī maintained that *ishārat al-naṣṣ* 'is that which has been composed through language, although it is not in the subject matter of the context or the text. Moreover, it is not apparent in all aspects'.[4] About *ishārat al-naṣṣ* Sarakhsī said: 'What is established by allusion is not the purpose [of the text]. It can, however, be understood by considering the meaning of the word without increasing or decreasing that meaning.'[5]

From these definitions, one may conclude that *ishārat al-naṣṣ* is the word's indication of a ruling which is not intended, and the text was not transmitted for this purpose. The text, therefore, embodies a necessary inference which accompanies the meaning, and this represents the principal theme and purpose of the text. The alluded meaning is not apparent in all aspects. It imparts, however, a rational concomitant meaning which is reached through further analysis of the signs detected in the text. Because this is a necessary though not an intended meaning, the indication of the text's meaning is by allusion (*ishārah*) and not by the explicit method (*'ibārah*)[6] The alluded meaning is sometimes easily detectable in the text. However, sometimes, in order to obtain it, further investigation may be required. Moreover, the scholars who carry out this investigation have different levels of understanding and different abilities to detect alluded meanings. What is discernible to some may not be so to others.[7] This is why disagreements arise whenever alluded meaning is taken as a proof for a ruling.

Some scholars have argued that the alluded meaning cannot be taken as a proof for a ruling.[8] Their opinion is rejected by the majority of scholars, who maintain that the indication of *ishārat al-naṣṣ* is correlated with the apparent meaning. It is acceptable as a proof if the correlation (*al-talāzum*) with *ibārat al-naṣṣ* is evident. Many rulings can be derived and proved by alluded meaning, and searching for the latter should not cause difficulties. Establishing a correlation with the explicit meaning should not tempt the *mujtahid* into exaggerating. Moderation in this kind of study is required, since an exaggeration in the quest for alluded meanings can lead a *mujtahid* in the wrong direction. Islam tends to take the middle ground in everything. The Qur'ān states: 'Thus We have made you a middle nation [justly balanced], that you be witnesses over mankind.'[9] Therefore, a moderate approach to the search for alluded meanings is required as well.

The correlation between the explicit meaning and allusion can either be apparent or hidden. This is why scholars say that understanding *ishārat al-naṣṣ* can sometimes be achieved quickly, and at other times deeper *ijtihād* is necessary.

Examples of *ishārat al-naṣṣ*

(a) The Qur'ān states: 'It is made lawful for you to have sexual relations with your wives on the nights of the fast...'[10] The explicit meaning (*'ibārat al-naṣṣ*) here is that sexual relations with wives in the month of Ramaḍān, from the sunset to daybreak, is permitted. In the same time it indicates by alluded meaning (*ishārat al-naṣṣ*) that if by person is in state of *janābah*, this will not violate his fasting. This follows from the fact that sexual relations are permitted any time at night. Therefore, if a person has intimate relations in the last portion of the night, he will have no time for ritual ablutions before daybreak and would enter the time of fasting in state of *janābah*. Based on this the ruling is that such a person may start fasting in that state, then wash and continue the fast. This ruling is based on textual allusion (*ishārat al-naṣṣ*).

(b) The Qur'ān states: 'The mothers shall give suck to their children for two whole years – those who desire to complete the term of suckling. But the father of the child shall bear the reasonable cost of the mother's food and clothing.'[11] This verse indicates by its explicit meaning (*'ibārat al-naṣṣ*) that the maintenance of mothers and their children is the fathers' duty. The pronoun 'his' (*lahu*) clearly confirms that no one else but 'the father' bears this obligation. This ruling is understood from the apparent meaning of the text. Because the apparent meaning is the reason for which this text was revealed it is termed *'ibārat al-naṣṣ*.[12] However, the textual allusions (*ishārat al-naṣṣ*) of this verse, which are derived through further analysis of the signs detectable within the text, indicate many other rulings. Thus:[13]

(1) The child's descent is solely attributable to the father and the identity is determined with reference to the father. Based on unanimous consensus (*ijmāʿ*), the pronoun 'his' (*lahu*) does not indicate ownership. Therefore, the child is related to the father through descent only.

(2) If the father belongs to a tribe the child follows no matter which tribe the mother belongs to.

(3) Supporting the child is the father's duty alone; no one shares this duty with him because the child is his.

(4) When in dire need, the father may take what he needs from the wealth of his offspring without permission and without any obligation to return it.[14]

(5) The father may not be punished if he commits a crime, for which a *ḥadd* is prescribed, against his child.[15] Therefore, the father would not receive capital punishment if he killed his child,[16] nor would he be punished if he put forward a slanderous accusation of fornication against his child.[17]

All these rulings follow from the fact that a child's descent is solely attributable to the father. These meanings do not represent the principal or subsidiary theme or purpose of the text expressed as *'ibārat al-naṣṣ*. However, they embody a necessary inference and represent meanings which are the inevitable consequence of that attribution by way of *ishārat al-naṣṣ*.

(c) The Qur'ān states: 'So pass over [the Companions' faults] and ask [God] to forgive them, and consult them in affairs.'[18] The explicit meaning (*'ibārat al-naṣṣ*) of the text 'and consult them in affairs' indicates that community affairs must be conducted through consultation (*shūrā*). The alluded meaning, however, requires the creation of a consultative body in society to facilitate the consultation as required by the explicit meaning (*'ibārat al-naṣṣ*) of the text.

(d) The Qur'ān states: 'And We have enjoined on man to be dutiful and kind to his parents. His mother bears him with hardship and she brings him forth with hardship, and his bearing and weaning are thirty months...'[19] Through its explicit meaning (*'ibārat al-naṣṣ*), this verse indicates the favour, grace and kindness of parents towards their children – the context of the verse confirms that indication. At the beginning of the verse God commands children to be kind to their parents because of their kindness to them. Then He explains the reason for kindness to the mother who bears her child with hardship and brings the child forth with hardship.

This verse indicates by textual allusion (*ishārat al-naṣṣ*) that the bearing of a child lasts at least six months, since another verse states that weaning is for two years: 'His mother bore him in weakness upon weakness; and his weaning is in two years – be thankful to Me and to your parents, for unto Me is the final destination.'[20] Therefore, if both the bearing and the weaning are thirty months and the weaning alone is two years, then the bearing lasts six months. This alluded meaning (*ishārat al-naṣṣ*) remained hidden for the majority of the Companions until 'Alī discovered it.[21]

(e) The Prophet said about the poor: 'Give them enough so they will not need to beg on this day.'[22]

From this tradition Sarakhsī deduced a few legal rulings. The first one is based on the explicit meaning (*'ibārat al-naṣṣ*) while others are based on the alluded meaning (*ishārat al-naṣṣ*):[23]

(a) The duty (*wājib*) to give *zakāt al-fiṭr* to the poor on the day of *Eid*. This meaning is explicit and it is the principal theme and purpose of the text. Therefore, it is *'ibārat al-naṣṣ*.

(b) This is the duty of wealthy people, because enrichment cannot come except from someone who is rich himself.

(c) *Zakāt al-fiṭr* should only be given to the needy, because only the needy, not the rich, can be enriched.

(d) *Zakāt* has to be distributed to the poor before going to the *Eid* prayer, so that the needy do not have to beg and can attend the prayer with a clear mind, knowing that family members have enough to eat that day.

(e) The time when donation of *zakāt al-fiṭr* starts is daybreak, because 'the day' is the time between daybreak and sunset.

(f) *Zakāt al-fiṭr* may be offered in any form because the aim is enrichment through any kind of goods. Therefore, money may be given instead of barley, dates, etc.

(g) It is more appropriate for *zakāt al fiṭr* to be given to a single person, because it is easier this way to enrich the poor for a day.

(h) 'On this day' alludes to the *Eid* festival for both the poor and the rich. It is a festival for the poor as well, so long as they are satisfied. They will be happy if they are enriched that day so that they do not need to beg.

Sarakhsī derived all these meanings and rulings from the textual allusion (*ishārat al-naṣṣ*). He concluded that plenty of meanings in this text and other authoritative texts are justified by the following tradition: 'The gift bestowed upon me is comprehensive eloquence...'[24]

The indication of *ishārat al-naṣṣ*

Sarakhsī maintained that the *ishārat al-naṣṣ* alternates between definite (*qaṭ'i*) and indefinite (*ẓannī*), depending on the circumstances and position of the expression. According to Sarakhsī, it alternates between the two only in case when the meaning may be either real or metaphorical; otherwise it is definite.[25] This opinion is accepted by other early scholars like Bazdawī and Bukhārī.[26] Some later scholars maintain that *ishāra* is like *'ibāra* – both have a definite meaning. They considered that cases where *ishārat al-naṣṣ* had indefinite meanings were the only exceptions to the general rule. These exceptions cannot change the general rule because their causes are incidental.[27]

Sarakhsī's opinion seems preferable to that of the Hanafi scholars. Therefore, if *ishārat al-naṣṣ* supposes another meaning based on a reliable proof, its indication would be indefinite (*ẓannī al-dalālah*); otherwise it has a definite meaning (*qaṭ'ī al-dalālah*).

Nonetheless, while Hanafi scholars have agreed that definite meaning (*qaṭ'ī al-dalālah*) means 'the non-existence of a possibility based on a proof' and that the general meaning when restricted becomes indefinite (*ẓannī al-dalālah*),[28] their disagreement on *ishārat al-naṣṣ,* previously mentioned, does seem to be without any influence on legal reasoning (*ijtihād*).

The value of *ishārat al-naṣṣ*

The effect of the textual allusion (*ishārat al-naṣṣ*) is similar to that of the explicit meaning (*'ibārat al-naṣṣ*), because them indicate obligation, unless there is reliable evidence suggesting otherwise. Therefore, legal adherence to *ishārat al-naṣṣ,* according to Islamic law, should be strictly obligatory (*wājib*).[29]

Conflict between *'ibārat al-naṣṣ* and *ishārat al-naṣṣ*

The majority of scholars maintain that *'ibārat al-naṣṣ* indicates a definite meaning, while *ishārat al-naṣṣ* may indicate either definite or indefinite meanings. The fact that *ishārat al-naṣṣ* can be indefinite gives *'ibārat al-naṣṣ* preference in the case of conflict with *ishārat al-naṣṣ*. Moreover, even when both indicate a definite meaning, *'ibārat al-naṣṣ* has priority because its indication is the main or subsidiary purpose of the text in contrast to *ishārat al-naṣṣ*. This is due to the fact that the meaning intended by the speaker is stronger than that which is not intended by the speaker. Therefore, in the event of a conflict between *'ibārat al-naṣṣ* and *ishārat al-naṣṣ* the former would have preference, as in the following example:

The Qur'ān states: 'but the father of a child shall bear the reasonable cost of (the mother's) food and clothing.'[30] This verse impinges on many rulings by both *ʿibārat al-naṣṣ* and *ishārat al-naṣṣ*. By studying the signs detectable in the text, Ḥanafī scholars have derived a number of rulings based on textual allusion.[31] Amongst these rulings is that the father's sole duty is to support his child because the child is his. Consequently, when in dire need, the father has the right to be supported by his son and has preference over other relatives. If the son, for example, cannot support either of his parents, the father has preference over the mother because the father was solely responsible for supporting his son, so that when the father needs support, his need is favoured.

This ruling is derived from textual allusion (*ishārat al-naṣṣ*). However, it is in conflict with the *ḥadīth* where a man asks the Prophet who he should prefer for good companionship. The Prophet replied that he should give his mother the highest priority. The father was given only fourth place. The first three were all reserved for the mother.[32]

This tradition indicates by its explicit meaning (*ʿibārat al-naṣṣ*) that the mother has preference over the father. Since the meaning derived from *ʿibārat al-naṣṣ* is stronger than that derived from *ishārat al-naṣṣ*, giving preference to the ruling is obligatory, based on *ʿibārah* (that the mother has more right to be supported), above the *ishārah* (which suggests that the father should be given preference).[33]

NOTES

1. *al-Muʿjam al-Wasīṭ*, I:499; Lane, *Arabic-English Lexicon*, II:1616; EI², IV:113; Baʿlabakī, *al-Mawrid*, p. 110.

2. The linguistic meaning of *naṣṣ* has been mentioned when *ʿibārat al-naṣṣ* was defined linguistically.

3. Dabbūsī, *al-Asrār fī al-Uṣūl wa al-Furūʿ fī Taqwīm Adillat al-Sharʿ*, I:292.

4. Bukhārī, *Kashf al-Asrār*, I:68, II:210.

5. Sarakhsī, *Uṣūl al-Sarakhsī*, I:236.

6. The important point is that rulings derived from both *ʿibārat al-naṣṣ* and *ishārat al-naṣṣ* are thought to be established by the text (*naṣṣ*), although *ʿibārat al-naṣṣ* is the purpose of the text while the latter is not. The difference between them appears where two rulings conflict and one of them is based on *ʿibārat al-naṣṣ* and the other on *ishārat al-naṣṣ* (Sarakhsī, *Uṣūl al-Sarakhsī*, I:236).

7. For example, ʿAlī detected the shortest time for bearing the child (see second example of *ishārat al-naṣṣ*).

8. Khuḍarī Bak, *Uṣūl al-Fiqh*, pp. 120–1.

9. Qur'ān, II:143.

10. Qur'ān, II:187.

11. Qur'ān, II:233.

12. Ṭabarī, *Jāmiʿ al-Bayān ʿan Ta'wīl Āy al-Qur'ān*, V:43.

13. Bukhārī, *Kashf al-Asrār*, I:71; Sarakhsī, *Uṣūl al-Sarakhsī*, I:237.

14. This ruling is derived from *ishārat al-naṣṣ* and from the tradition where one of the Companions said to the Prophet, 'O Messenger of God, I have wealth and children and my father wants to take from my wealth.' The Prophet replied, 'You and your property belong to your father.' ('Ajlūnī, *Kashf al-Khafā' wa Muzīl al-Ilbās*, I:307; Ibn Mājah, *Sunan Ibn Mājah*, II:769 (no. 2291); Ṭaḥāwī, *Mushkil al-Āthār*, II:230; Albānī, *Irwā' al-Ghalīl*, III:323).

15. He may be punished for some other offences, such as failing to support his child.

16. In addition to the *ishārat al-naṣṣ* of this verse, Islamic scholars proved this ruling by other proofs mentioned in the Prophet's tradition. (Jaṣṣāṣ, *Aḥkām al-Qur'ān*, I:168–169.)

17. Although the father is not punished by *ḥadd* (legally specified punishment in the *Sharī'ah*), because this kind of punishment should be avoided whenever there is doubt, he may be punished by *ta'zīr* (punishment which is not fixed by *Sharī'ah* law but determined by a judge).

18. Qur'ān, III:159.

19. Qur'ān, XLVI:15

20. Qur'ān, XXXI:14

21. It happened that, during the reign of Caliph 'Uthmān, a man was married and his wife gave birth after six months. He went to 'Uthmān and informed him of that. 'Uthmān ordered that the woman be stoned. When 'Alī heard it he asked him: 'Do you read the Qur'ān? Did you not read Allāh's words...' 'Alī recited these two verses and explained the ruling that the shortest time for gestation is six months (Ibn Kathīr, *Tafsīr al-Qur'ān al-'Azīm*, IV:200–1; Zamakhsharī, *al-Kashshāf*, III:520

22. Bayhaqī, *al-Sunan al-Kubrā*, IV:175. Albānī stated that this *ḥadīth* is narrated by Dāraquṭnī, Bayhaqī, Ḥākim in *Ma'rifat 'Ulūm al-Ḥadīth*, and Ibn Zanjawayh in *al-Amwāl*. He categorised this *ḥadīth* as weak (Albānī, *Irwā' al-Ghalīl*, III:332–333).

23. Sarakhsī, *Uṣūl al-Sarakhsī*, I:240–241.

24. Muslim, *Ṣaḥīḥ Muslim*, I:371 (no. 523).

25. Sarakhsī, *Uṣūl al-Sarakhsī*, I:236–237.

26. Bukhārī, *Kash al-Asrār*, I:70.

27. Mullā Khusro, *Mirqāt al-Wuṣūl*, I:77.

28. Taftāzānī, *Sharḥ al-Talwīḥ 'alā al-Tawḍīḥ*, I:35–36, 130–131.

29. Kawrānī, *Sharḥ Mukhtaṣar al-Manār*, p. 64.

30. Qur'ān, II:233

31. Bukhārī, *Kashf al-Asrār*, I:71; Sarakhsī, *Uṣūl al-Sarakhsī*, I:237.

32. Bukhārī, *al-Jāmi' al-Ṣaḥīḥ*, VII:69. (78:2); Muslim, *Ṣaḥīḥ Muslim*, IV:1974 (no.2548).

33. In fact, there are three opinions on this issue in the Ḥanafī *madhhab* (Marghīnānī, *al-Hidāyah*, II:46; Kāsānī, *Badā'i' al-Ṣanā'i'*, IV:36; Ibn 'Ābidīn, *Ḥāshiyat Ibn 'Ābidīn*, II:763).

CHAPTER 3

The Inferred Meaning
(*Dalālat al-Naṣṣ*)

The linguistic definition of *dalālat al-naṣṣ*

Dalālah refers to sign, indication, mark, denotation, notion; word significa-tion or indication of meaning which may be of three kinds: a) complete correspondence (*muṭābaqah*) (thus *insān* indicates an animal endowed with reason); b) partial inclusion (*taḍammun*) (thus *insān* indicates a being endowed with reason); c) a necessary idea attached to the meaning, in the mind (*iltizām*) (thus *insān* indicates a being capable of knowledge).[1]

The technical definition *of dalālat al-naṣṣ*

Ḥanafī scholars have defined *dalālat al-naṣṣ* as follows. Bazdawī offered his definition while referring to its meaning. He defined *dalālat al-naṣṣ* in this fashion: 'What the inferred meaning establishes is obtained by the linguistic meaning of the text, and not by legal reasoning or deduction.'[2] Sarakhsī offered a similar definition: 'What the inferred meaning establishes it does so linguistically by the composition's meaning not by rational deduction.'[3] Bukhārī offered a more specific definition of *dalālat al-naṣṣ*: '*Dalālat al-naṣṣ* is understanding the unpronounced from the pronounced by the context and purpose of speech.'[4]

From these definitions one may conclude that *dalālat al-naṣṣ* is the indi-cation of the text that the ruling is valid for another instance, because both of these instances have a common effective cause ('*illah*). This may be explained as follows.

Linguistically, speech sometimes indicates a ruling on an instance the effective cause of which calls for such a ruling. The effective cause of this instance is so simple and the ruling so obvious that their comprehension does not depend on study and legal reasoning (*ijtihād*). However, there is another instance about which God offers no ruling, but where the same effective cause, which was the reason for the first legislation, exists in the second instance too. Under these circumstances the suggestion comes to mind that the ruling for the second instance, about which the Legislator was silent, is the same as for the instance for which the ruling was originally intended. This suggestion, is not the result of legal reasoning or analogy, but of linguistic understanding. This suggests that the same ruling covers both instances – what is pronounced and that about which the text is silent.[5]

In contrast to the explicit meaning (*ʿibārat al-naṣṣ*) and the alluded meaning (*ishārat al-naṣṣ*), which are both indicated through words and signs in the text, the inferred meaning (*dalālat al-naṣṣ*) is derived from identification with the effective cause of the ruling (*ʿillat al-ḥukm*), common to both the explicit meaning (*ʿibārat al-naṣṣ*) and the meaning derived through inference (*dalālat al-naṣṣ*). The same ruling is extended because both instances share a common meaning (an effective cause) which is obviously *manāṭ al-ḥukm*.

As previously mentioned, this shared meaning should be so obvious (i.e., linguistically understandable) that anyone who understands the language should understand it without recourse to legal reasoning (*ijtihād*) or further reflection. It would be *dalālat al-naṣṣ*, whether the unpronounced (*maskūt ʿanh*) is equivalent or preferable (*awlā*) to that which is pronounced (*manṭūq*).

Therefore, when the explicit meaning (*ʿibārat al-naṣṣ*) indicates a ruling, and from the same meaning one understands that that same ruling is valid for another instance that has not been mentioned, this indication is called *dalālat al-naṣṣ*.

A ruling based on *dalālat al-naṣṣ* may be established linguistically, rather than on legal grounds through *ijtihād* or through deduction. This is due to the fact that the comprehension of the effective cause in an unpronounced (*maskūt ʿanh*) ruling is based on the knowledge of the language only.[6]

Examples of *dalālat al-naṣṣ*

(a) The Qur'ān states: 'And your Lord has decreed that you worship none but Him. And that you be good to your parents. If one of them or both attain old age in your lifetime, say not to them a word of disrespect, nor chide them but address them in terms of honour. And lower unto them the wing of submission through mercy, and say: My Lord, bestow on them Your mercy, as they brought me up when I was small.'[7]

By the explicit meaning (*ʿibārat al-naṣṣ*) this text obviously forbids utterance of the slightest disrespect to parents ('Say not to them a word of disrespect'). By its explicit meaning it places a duty upon a child to treat his parents kindly with high respect and honour – 'but address them in terms of honour. And lower unto them the wing of submission through mercy.'

From the perspective of the Arabic language, the effective cause for the prohibition against uttering the slightest word of disrespect to parents is the avoidance of offending them, and the need to cherish and respect them. If such a slight offence as speaking with disrespect is forbidden, the inferred meaning (*dalālat al-naṣṣ*) suggests that other forms of offensive behaviour – like beating, cursing etc. – are implicit in the text and, therefore, specifically forbidden. They are forbidden because the effective cause for the prohibition applies to them equally.[8] The fact that all forms of abusive words and acts which offend the parents are forbidden may be inferred from the previous text by anyone who understands the language, although other offences are not specifically mentioned. This because the inferred meaning (*dalālat al-naṣṣ*) is so obvious that it is understood without recourse to legal reasoning and reflection.[9]

(b) The Qur'ān states: 'And divorced women shall wait for three menstrual periods [before remarriage] and it is not lawful for them to conceal what God has created in their wombs, if they believe in God and the last day.'[10]

This verse indicates by its explicit meaning (*'ibārat al-naṣṣ*) that a period of waiting before remarriage is obligatory for a divorced woman. However, from the viewpoint of the Arabic language, the effective cause for this ruling is establishing whether the woman carries a child from her former husband or not. In this way paternity will not be confused when she remarries.[11] This effective cause exists in every kind of separation between husband and wife, whether the divorce is by *khul'*[12] or the death of the husband. In all these cases women have to wait the prescribed period, like the divorced wife mentioned in the verse – the text indicates this ruling by its inferred meaning (*dalālat al-naṣṣ*). All cases of separation share this effective cause, as indicated by the explicit meaning (*'ibārat al-naṣṣ*) of the previous verse.

(c) The Qur'ān states: 'Verily, those who unjustly eat up the property of orphans, eat up only fire for their bellies, and they will be burnt in a blazing Fire!'[13]

The explicit meaning of this verse is that the unjustified 'eating up' of the property of orphans is forbidden (*ḥarām*). It forbids guardians and executors from using orphans' property for their own personal gain. The effective cause of this prohibition (the protection of orphans' property and fear for its ruin and waste) may be understood by anyone who understands the language. By way of inference, this ruling is extended to other situations where the effective cause for protecting orphans' property is identified. An example of this is financial mismanagement that involves no personal benefit and yet causes the loss and destruction of orphans' property. Although the previous verse does not indicate different ways in which destruction may be caused, these ways are nevertheless equally forbidden. Therefore, any act which causes the destruction or loss of orphans' property falls under the same prohibition.

(d) The Qur'ān states: 'Forbidden to you [for marriage] are your mothers, your daughters, sisters, father's sisters, mother's sisters, brother's daughters, sister's daughters.'[14]

The explicit meaning of this verse clearly indicates that marriage with one's sister, one's father's sister, one's brother's daughter, one's sister's daughter, etc. is forbidden. The cause for the ruling holds for other relatives not mentioned in the verse – e.g., grandmother and grandchildren. They are even closer relatives than the children of one's brothers and sisters. Therefore, the previous text forbids marriage with the sisters of one's father and mother by explicit meaning (*ʿibārat al-naṣṣ*) and forbids marriage with grandmothers by inferred meaning (*dalālat al-naṣṣ*). Also, the children of one's brothers and sisters are forbidden by explicit meaning (*ʿibārat al-naṣṣ*) and grandchildren are forbidden by inferred meaning (*dalālat al-naṣṣ*).

The indication of *dalālat al-naṣṣ*

Early Ḥanafī scholars like Bazdawī and Sarakhsī[15] did not consider whether the indication of *dalālat al-naṣṣ* is definite (*qaṭʿī*) or indefinite (*ẓannī*), but explained the difference between *dalālat al-naṣṣ* and *qiyās*. Sarakhsī discussed this very issue. For example, in the case of *dalālat al-naṣṣ*, understanding the effective cause common to both what is pronounced (*manṭūq*) and what is not unpronounced (*maskūt ʿanh*) depends entirely on knowledge of the language. In analogy, however, understanding the effective cause common to an original case (*maqīs ʿalayh*) and a subsidiary (a new) case (*maqīs*) requires certain specialised abilities from the *mujtahid*. This difference means that the effective cause, in the case of *dalālat al-naṣṣ*, can be understood by scholars who possess legal knowledge (*fuqahā'*) and others with a knowledge of the language only; while in the case of analogy the effective cause can be understood only by scholars with legal knowledge.

Some later Ḥanafī scholars,[16] however, considered whether the indication of *dalālat al-naṣṣ* is definite (*qaṭʿī*) or indefinite (*ẓannī*). On this ground they divided *dalālat al-naṣṣ* into *qaṭʿī* and *ẓannī*.

(1) *Dalālat al-naṣṣ* as definite (*qaṭʿī*) indication is when the intended meaning is known with certainty. Its certainty comes from the positive indication of the ruling, in a literal sense, and in this respect known with certainty. Thus, this ruling is valid for the instance which has not been mentioned, if both instances have a common cause. Therefore, the common meaning between what is pronounced and what is not is known with certainty. This is clear from the following example.

The Qur'ān states: 'Among the People of the Book is he who, entrusted with a *qinṭār*,[17] will readily pay it back; and among them there is he who, entrusted with a single silver coin, will not repay it unless you constantly stand demanding.'[18]

The first part of this verse certainly indicates, although it is not a literal utterance, that the trustworthy repays whatever he is entrusted with. This conclusion is based on the fact that trustworthiness is the intended meaning in 'paying back'. There is no doubt that someone who is trustworthy with a great amount is trustworthy with a small amount; he will pay it back when required. The inferred meaning, in this case, is certain because the intended meaning (trustworthy) is common to what is pronounced (*manṭūq*) and what is not pronounced (*maskūt ʿanh*).

The second part of the verse makes the same reference to treachery. A treacherous person will betray even with a small amount. This meaning has a literal utterance. If he betrays trust with a small amount, no doubt he will do it with a greater amount also. This is indicated with certainty by the verse, although it is not a literal utterance. This inferred meaning is certain, because the intended meaning (treachery) is certain to be common to what is pronounced and what is not pronounced.

(2) *Dalālat al-naṣṣ* gives indefinite indication (*ẓannī al-dalālah*) when the effective cause of the ruling literally uttered is not known with certainty, or because the effective cause does not exist, in a certain way, in what is unpronounced, since another meaning may be intended.

Therefore, the common meaning (the effective cause) between the pronounced and that which is not pronounced is not known for certain because another meaning is possible, too. This is clear from the following example.

Abū Hurayrah narrated that a man came to the Prophet and said: 'I am ruined, O Prophet of God!' The Prophet asked: 'Why?' The man answered: 'I had sexual relations with my wife during a day of Ramaḍān.' 'Can you afford to free a slave?' The man replied: 'No.' 'Can you fast two months continuously?' 'No.' 'Can you afford to feed sixty poor people?' The man's answer was again negative. Then he sat down and the Prophet brought him a stem of a date and said: 'Give this in charity.' The man exclaimed: 'Is there any one poorer than me to give charity to? By God, there is no house in greater need than ours anywhere in the vicinity.' The Prophet smiled widely, his back teeth visible, and said to him, 'Go and feed your family.'[19]

The explicit meaning (*ibārat al-naṣṣ*) of this tradition is that penance is obligatory for someone who deliberately has sexual relations during a day of Ramaḍān, because the Prophet clearly ordered the person who did so to pay penance. Behind this ruling was a serious offence against fasting and an omission of its basic element (*rukn*) through sexual relations. Eating and drinking during the day in the month of Ramaḍān are also serious offences and give rise to the same ruling as for sexual relations (a ruling based on the explicit meaning), since eating and drinking violate the basic element (*rukn*) of fasting.

The second conclusion is based on the inferred meaning Therefore, the same penance is obligatory for someone who has sexual relations in the day and who deliberately breaks his fasting in other ways, such as by eating or drinking, etc.[20] The first ruling is based on the explicit meaning (*ʿibārat al-naṣṣ*), while the second is based on the inferred meaning (*dalālat al-naṣṣ*).

The effective cause for the obligation of penance, as previously mentioned, is violating the basic element (*rukn*) of fasting – namely, abstinence from anything that may spoil the fasting. However, this conclusion is not certain, since the Prophet may have ordered the man to do that particular penance because he had violated the basic element in that particular way, i.e. sexual relations.[21] This is why the effective cause in this example is indefinite (*ẓannī*). Therefore, the inferred meaning, which suggests that the penance is obligatory in this case, is indefinite (*ẓannī*). This fact, however, does not prevent this meaning from being the inferred meaning (*dalālat al-naṣṣ*) or the ruling being derived from it. This is because the main condition for the inferred meaning is for it to be achievable through knowledge of the language without the need for further thinking and investigation.

One may conclude that this certainty is based on the fact that the effective cause, which is common to both what is pronounced and what is not pronounced, is certainly known. In the case of *ẓannī al-dalālah*, the effective cause is not known with certainty, because another meaning is also supposed to be the effective cause.

Legislating punishments and penances according to *dalālat al-naṣṣ*[22]

Both the legislation and execution of punishments in *Sharīʿah* are sensitive issues. They are considered to be the sole prerogative of the Divine. Being so, they must be based on authoritative texts that are sound and clear, and cannot be carried out if there is the slightest doubt about their legal validity, or if they lack requisite conditions. Ibn al–Mundhir stated: 'There is a consensus amongst all the scholars I know that punishments [*ḥudūd*] are averted by doubts.'[23] The well-known rule amongst Muslim judges is that 'a wrongful non-punishment is better than a wrongful punishment'.

In general, the Ḥanafī *madhhab* legislates punishments and penances by *dalālat al-naṣṣ*.[24] However, when the indication of the inferred meaning is indefinite, scholars differ about the ruling based on such a proof. The following are some examples which bring to light the differences between different schools of law and even within these schools of law.

(a) The Qur'ān states: 'The women and men guilty of illicit sexual relations flog each of them a hundred times.'[25] This verse indicates by the explicit meaning (*ʿibārat al-naṣṣ*) the ruling which states that adulterous men and women should be flogged.[26] Moreover, it indicates by the inferred meaning (*dalālat al-naṣṣ*) that the same punishment applies to sodomy.

Ḥanafī scholars themselves, however, disagree about the ruling on sodomy. Abū Ḥanīfah maintains that the punishment for homosexuals is *taʿzīr*, while his disciples Abū Yūsuf and Muḥammad b. al-Ḥasan al-Shaybānī maintain that their punishment would be the same as that for adulterers. This, too, is the opinion of Shāfiʿī.[27]

Abū Yūsuf and Muḥammad established the ruling on homosexuals by *dalālat al-naṣṣ*. They argued that the effective reasoning for prohibiting adultery is that it involves 'putting the sperm into a forbidden and desired place'. This meaning is even more true of sodomy, because the latter implies 'an abnormal place' and its inviolability is all the more important. The only difference between the two is the name of the place, which does not prevent sodomy from sharing the same meaning (the effective cause) with adultery.

Abū Ḥanīfah differentiated between *zinā* and sodomy on the grounds of effective cause. In *zinā* he sees activity that distracts man both in practice and result. To him, adultery unlike sodomy can produce illegitimate children with almost no status. They have no lineage or supporting father. In sodomy, such a result (effective cause) does not exist, since no children can result.

As previously mentioned, both the legal rulings and the verification of their punishments are viewed in *Sharīʿah* as very delicate matters. Therefore, the rulings supported by inferred meaning, when its indication is indefinite, rest on a weak proof.

This is why those scholars, who extended the punishment for adulterers to homosexuals, supported their opinion, besides the inferred meaning, by other proofs. They normally mention the verses which rebuke sodomy and inform about the punishments of homosexuals in older times.[28] They also invoked traditions[29]: 'If the man approaches the man they are adulterers'; and 'Kill those whom you find acting like the people of Lūt[30] both the active and passive.' In another narration this tradition contains: 'and stone that which is active and that which is passive.'

It seems that scholars do not regard the inferred meaning (*dalālat al-nass*), when its indication is indefinite as a strong proof by which the ruling for homosexuals can be established. This is probably why they would rather support their opinion by other reliable proofs.

One may observe that the inferred meaning, when it gives an indefinite indication, is not a proof which can establish punishments. This is inferred from the fact that the prescribed punishments (*ḥudūd*) are precluded by the slightest doubt relating to any requisite condition. This is supported by the fact that the inferred meaning (*dalālat al-naṣṣ*) when its indication is indefinite, carries such a suspicion.

(b) Regarding penance, the Qur'ān explains the case of a believer who kills another believer in error: 'And whosoever finds this [the penance of freeing a slave] beyond his means, he must fast for two consecutive months in order to seek repentance from God.'[31]

The Muslim schools of law[32] disagree about the effective cause in the penance for manslaughter. Shāfiʿīs maintain that the effective cause for this ruling is the restraint and the prevention of killing. This meaning is more appropriate in the case of murder. Therefore, penance in this case is established by the inferred meaning. Shāfiʿīs argue that if the penance is obligatory in the case of manslaughter, where there is no intention of killing, it is worthier and more deserving for such a penance to be introduced and obligatory in the case of murder where there is such an intention.[33] This ruling is consistent with and appropriate to restraining someone from killing another.

Ḥanafīs, Mālikīs and Ḥanbalīs maintain that the effective cause in the case of manslaughter, indicated by the explicit meaning, is correcting the carelessness displayed by the person who committed the error which led to the death of a human being protected by the law. The penance was not prescribed in order to prevent or restrain people from killing because a person who has committed an error is not considered a person who has committed a sin. The Prophet stated, 'God has, indeed, disburdened from my followers errors, forgetfulness and that which they were forced to do against their wishes.'[34]

The majority of scholars, therefore, have concluded that the effective cause present in manslaughter is not present in murder, because murder is a major sin and its crime is greater than manslaughter. Moreover, putting carelessness to rights by penance in minor crimes does not mean that such a penance is appropriate for a greater crime. Therefore, penance as expiation for murder may not be established.

The value of *dalālat al-naṣṣ*

The effect of the inferred meaning (*dalālat al-naṣṣ*) corresponds to the effect of the textual allusion (*ishārat al-naṣṣ*). This means that both indicate the definite (*qaṭʿī*) meaning if there is no proof which suggests otherwise. The only difference between them emerges in cases of conflict.[35] Therefore, the adherence to *dalālat al-naṣṣ* should be obligatory.

Conflict between *dalālat al-naṣṣ* and *ishārat al-naṣṣ*

The inferred meaning and the textual allusion seem to be at the same level of strength and value, because both have a definite indication if a reliable proof does not suggest otherwise. In both, the indication is taken from the understandable meaning of the text, its spirit and notion by relying on linguistic knowledge, rather than on legal reasoning and deduction.

Despite this equality, the textual allusion has priority in the event of conflict with the inferred meaning.[36] This is because in the case of alluded meaning the ruling is indicated by the word itself by way of compliance. In the case of the inferred meaning the ruling is based on acquaintance with the effective cause, which was the motive for the ruling. Although this acquaintance relies on knowledge of the language, and the indication is given by the text itself (as in the case of the alluded meaning), they are not the same. This is because in the alluded meaning the indication comes through the meaning which was a motive for the ruling in the explicit meaning and through acquaintance with its realisation in that which is not mentioned (*maskūt ʿanh*).

Therefore, the alluded meaning is indicated directly by way of compliance and the inferred meaning is indicated through a medium which is the effective cause. And what is indicated without a medium is stronger than what is indicated through the medium. This is why the alluded meaning is preferable to the inferred meaning in cases of conflict.

An example of this conflict is the legislation of penance for murder. The Qur'ān states: 'And whosoever finds this [the penance of freeing a slave] beyond his means, he must fast for two consecutive months in order to seek repentance from God.'[37] By the inferred meaning of this verse Shāfiʿīs, as mentioned before, established the duty of the penance for murder. They argued that if this penance is ordered for manslaughter, it is even more appropriate for murder.

The Ḥanafīs responded that this inferred meaning is opposed by the alluded meaning indicated by the following verse: 'And whoever kills a believer intentionally, his recompense is Hell to abide therein, and the wrath and the curse of God are upon him, and a great punishment is prepared for him.'[38] This verse indicates by the alluded meaning that no penance is obligatory for the murderer because it is not mentioned in the explanation of punishment.

In this example, therefore, the *dalālat al-naṣṣ* (which establishes the penance) disagrees with the *ishārat al-naṣṣ*. Priority belongs to the latter, because its indication is stronger, as previously explained, and the penance is not established in the case of murder.

NOTES

 1. *al-Muʿjam al-Wasīṭ*, I:294; Lane, *Arabic-English Lexicon*, I:901: EI[2], II:101–102; Baʿlabakī, *al-Mawrid*, p. 458.
 2. Bukhārī, *Kashf al-Asrār*, I:73

3. Sarakhsī, *Uṣūl al-Sarakhsī*, I:241.

4. Bukhārī, *Kashf al-Asrār*, I:73.

5. The first ruling is indicated by the explicit meaning (*ʿibārat al-naṣṣ*), the second by inferred meaning (*dalālat al-naṣṣ*).

6. Since the ruling in the case of *dalālat al-naṣṣ* is taken from the meaning of the text and not from its words, this indication is called 'dalālat al-dalālah' or 'fahwā al-khiṭāb'. In the Shāfiʿī *madhhab* it is termed 'mafhūm al-muwāfaqah' because the indication of the words, in the instance pronounced, corresponds to its indication in the instance which has not been pronounced. Therefore *ʿibārat al-naṣṣ* and *dalālat al-naṣṣ* agree with each other when the cause for a ruling is in question. (Bukhārī, *Kashf al-Asrār*, I:73; Taftāzānī, *Sharḥ al-Talwīḥ ʿala al-Tawḍīḥ*, I:133).

7. Qur'ān, XVII:23–24.

8. The prohibition of something in a small amount implies its prohibition in a great amount.

9. Because of this clarity some scholars refer to the inferred meaning (*dalālat al-naṣṣ*) as clear analogy (*qiyās jalī*). They consider it to be a kind of analogy. These scholars include Shāfiʿī himself, who stated, 'This is [the kind of knowledge] of which nobody is allowed to be ignorant or indefinite [as to its certainty]' (Shāfiʿī, *al-Risālah*, p. 289). The majority of scholars disagree with this opinion. They say that the inferred meaning is different from analogy because the effective cause (*ʿillah*) in the case of the inferred meaning is established by language only and can be understood by anyone who understands the language. The derivation of the effective cause in analogy, however, requires a proper *ijtihād* and can be understood only by qualified scholars. Therefore, the mere knowledge of the language is not enough when analogy (*qiyās*) is in question. (Shaʿban, *Uṣūl al-Fiqh al-Islāmī*, p. 303).

10. Qur'ān, II:228.

11. Islamic scholars normally mention only this effective cause for the waiting period. One may observe that in this case other reasons may be regarded as the effective cause for the legislation of the waiting period – for example, the need for rest and relief from the stress which normally accompanies separation; physical, emotional and mental preparation for a new life; resolving important matters before a divorcee can remarry; etc. If detection of pregnancy is the only effective cause, one may argue that nowadays there are medical techniques by which pregnancy or lack thereof can be accurately detected. The length of the *ʿiddah* ruling is therefore questionable. However, to my knowledge no Muslim scholar seems to have discussed this matter. This may be because they are of the opinion that there are other reasons which count as effective causes of the ruling.

12. *Khulʿ* is separation based on the wife's request, whereby she receives divorce in return for monetary compensation for her husband.

13. Qur'ān, IV:10.

14. Qur'ān, IV:23.

15. Bukhārī, *Kashf al-Asrār*, I:73–74; Sarakhsī, *Uṣūl al-Sarakhsī*, I:241

16. Such as ʿAbd al-ʿAzīz al-Bukhārī and Kamāl b. al-Humām (Bukhārī, *Kashf al-Asrār*, I:73; Ibn Amīr al-Ḥājj, *al-Taqrīr wa al-Taḥbīr*, I:113–115).

17. This is a measure of capacity. One *qinṭār* has 100 *raṭl*s (EI², VI:117).

18. Qur'ān, III:75.

19. Bukhārī, *al-Jāmiʿ al-Ṣaḥīḥ*, II:235–236 (30:31); Muslim, *Ṣaḥīḥ Muslim*, II:781 (no. 1111).

20. This is the opinion of Mālik and his followers, Abū Ḥanīfah and his followers, Thawrī and other scholars. (Ibn Rushd, *Bidāyat al-Mujtahid*, I:302–303; Ibn Qudāmah, *al-Mughnī*, III:115; Sarakhsī, *al-Mabsūṭ*, III:79; Ibn al-Humām, *Fatḥ al-Qadīr*, II:68–70)

21. This is one reason why scholars like Shāfiʿī, Ibn Ḥanbal, Ẓāhirīs and others maintained that penance is obligatory only in the case where fasting is deliberately spoiled by sexual relations, not by eating, drinking or something else. They maintained that the basic rule is

against penance except in areas clearly mentioned by the *Sharīʿah*. Here, the *Sharīʿah* mentions sexual relations only. These scholars maintained that the effective cause (*ʿillah*) is the violation of the basic element (*rukn*) of fasting in this particular way, i.e., sexual relations. Deliberate eating and drinking cannot be analogised with sexual relations because of essential differences between them (Ibn Rushd, *Bidāyat al-Mujtahid*, I:302–303; Ibn Qudāmah, *al-Mughnī*, III:115; Shīrāzī, *al-Muhadhdhab*, I:182).

22. Marghīnānī, *al-Hidāyah*, II:102, IV:159; Ibn Qudāmah, *al-Mughnī*, VIII:186–187; Dassūqī, *Ḥashiyat al-Dassūqī ʿalā al-Sharḥ al-Kabīr*, IV:314; Sarakhsī, *Uṣūl al-Sarakhsī*, I:242–244; Ibn Amīr al-Ḥājj, *al-Taqrīr wa al-Taḥbīr*, I:113.

23. Ibn Qudāmah, *al-Mughnī*, VIII:184. There are many traditions which support this opinion. Tirmidhī, *al-Jāmiʿ al-Ṣaḥīḥ*, IV:25 (no.1424); Ibn Mājah, *Sunan*, II:850 (no.2545).

24. Nasafī stated that the legislation for punishments and penances by the inferred meaning is correct. It would be incorrect if it were based on analogy (*qiyās*), because analogy is based on reasoning, which normally contains doubt. Therefore, *qiyās* cannot be the ground for legislation of punishment, which should be free of all doubt (Nasafī, *al-Asrār*, I:386).

25. Qurʾān, XXIV:2.

26. This ruling is for the unmarried. For those adulterers who are married, the punishment is stoning to death (Marghīnānī, *al-Hidāyah*, II:98).

27. Ibn Qudāmah, *al-Mughnī*, VIII:186–187; Dassūqī, *Ḥashiyat al-Dassūqī ʿalā al-Sharḥ al-Kabīr*, IV:314

28. See the following verses: XI:77–83; XVI:61–77; XXVI:160–175; LVI:32–39.

29. Ibn Mājah, *Sunan*, II:856 (no. 2561, 2562); Ibn Qudāmah, *al-Mughnī*, VIII:188; Marghīnānī, *al-Hidāyah*, II:102.

30. In the act of homosexuality.

31. Qurʾān, IV:92.

32. Ibn ʿAbd al-Shakūr, *Fawātiḥ al-Rahamūt*, I:409; Ibn Amīr al-Ḥājj, *al-Taqrīr wa al-Taḥbīr*, I:113; Nasafī, *Kash al-Asrār*, I:257–258.

33. It would be an additional punishment for the murderer because the main punishment for him is death. If any of the heirs of the deceased forgive him, he would pay only *diyah* (blood money) which may be forgiven, too. According to Shāfiʿīs, even if blood money is forgiven, the murderer has still to fulfil this penance.

34. Ibn Mājah, *Sunan*, I:659 (no.2043, 2045).

35. Nasafī, *Kashf al-Asrār*, I:385.

36. Nasafī, *Kashf al-Asrār*, I:385–386.

37. Qurʾān, IV:92

38. Qurʾān, IV:93.

CHAPTER 4

The Required Meaning
(*Iqtiḍā' al-Naṣṣ*)

The linguistic definition of *iqtiḍā' al-naṣṣ*

Iqtiḍā' refers to need, necessity, exigency, requirement, request; from *iqtaḍā* to call for, require, demand, need, (e.g. *iqtaḍā al-dayn*, he required the debt).[1]

The technical definition of *iqtiḍā' al-naṣṣ*

Unlike the previous three kinds of indications, *iqtiḍā' al-naṣṣ* is not indicated by the text or its meaning but by the requirement that a meaning be presumed in order to make the text truthful or valid in *Sharīʿah* and mind.

Ḥanafī scholars differ on the issue of whether or not *iqtiḍā' al-naṣṣ* includes omitted and concealed words (*maḥdhūf* and *muḍmar*). It seems that early Ḥanafīs made no distinction between *iqtiḍā' al-naṣṣ* and *maḥdhūf*. Dabbūsī defined *iqtiḍā' al-naṣṣ* as 'an addition to the text without which the meaning of the text cannot be fulfilled'.[2] In this definition he included *maḥdhūf* by making that which has to be presumed as one section. From the examples he provided it is clear that he does not differentiate between *iqtiḍā' al-naṣṣ* and *maḥdhūf*. He presented as an example for *iqtiḍā' al-naṣṣ* the following verse: 'And ask the town where we have been and the caravan in which we returned.'[3] He explained that it means: 'Ask the people of the town' and not the town itself, because the aim of the question is to be answered. Therefore this speech requires that the object of the question provides an answer. Here, the presumed object would be 'the people' in order to make the speech truthful.[4] As we will see, this example is normally mentioned by those who distinguish between *iqtiḍā' al-naṣṣ* and *maḥdhūf* as an example for *maḥdhūf*.

Later Ḥanafī scholars distinguished between *iqtiḍā' al-naṣṣ* and *maḥdhūf*. They maintained that the meaning which must be presumed in order to make the text correct and valid in *Sharīʿah* is called *muqtaḍā*, and the meaning which must be presumed in order to make the text truthful and correct in the mind is said to be omitted (*maḥdhūf*) or implicit (*muḍmar*).

Sarakhsī defined *iqtiḍā' al-naṣṣ* as 'an addition to that which is laid down in the text'.[5] From his further comments[6] it is clear that he considered that *iqtiḍā' al-naṣṣ* indicated a meaning upon which depended the truthfulness of speech or its validity in the *Sharīʿah*. He excluded the omitted and the implicit and maintained that those who included them in *iqtiḍā' al-naṣṣ* did so by mistake because what is omitted is different from what is required (*muqtaḍā*). It is the custom of *ahl al-lisān* to omit some words in order to shorten speech, when the rest of the speech indicates the sense. Sarakhsī provided examples by making a clear distinction between *muqtaḍā* and *maḥdhūf*.[7]

Dispute about this question led to a long debate between the two opposing groups of scholars. The majority do not acknowledge the distinction, while the second group of scholars, who seem in the minority, restrict *iqtiḍā' al-naṣṣ* to what has to be presumed in order to make speech correct and valid for *Sharīʿah*, not language or mind. The majority's opinion is sounder because the arguments of the minority are easily overturned.[8]

According to the majority of scholars who do not distinguish between *iqtiḍā' al-naṣṣ* and *maḥdhūf, iqtiḍā' al-naṣṣ* must be the presumed indication of the text. Upon it depend the correctness of that text and its validity in the *Sharīʿah* and mind (*sharʿ* and *ʿaql*). This indication is not rooted in the text. The text itself contains no word of indication; however, the truthfulness of the text and its correctness require such a presumption.

Presumed and supposed meanings

Scholars of *uṣūl al-fiqh* generally speak about three kinds of meanings which must sometimes be presumed in order to make speech truthful or valid in *Sharīʿah* and the mind.

(a) That which must be presumed in order to make speech truthful. Example: The Prophet stated: 'God has indeed disburdened my followers their errors, forgetfulness and whatever they were compelled to do against their wishes.[9] This tradition literally means that Muslims do not have error, forgetfulness or coercion, since they were 'disburdened of them'. On the surface the meaning seems to be wrong and untruthful, because the followers of the Prophet commit errors and forget, and these deeds, which have already happened, cannot be undone. However, Muslims believe that the Prophet always speaks the truth because he is infallible (*maʿṣūm*).[10] For that reason omitted words would be presumed here, such as 'sin' or 'ruling'. Therefore the tradition means: 'God has indeed disburdened the sin on my followers for their errors, forgetfulness and that which they were forced to do against their wishes.' With this presumption the tradition becomes consistent with reality. The indication of 'God has indeed disburdened' for 'sin' is established by way of *iqtiḍā' al-naṣṣ*, because the truthfulness of the speech depends on the presumption of this word.

(b) That which must be presumed in order to make a speech acceptable in terms of rational reason. The Qur'ān states: 'And ask the town where we have been and the caravan in which we returned.'[11] The apparent meaning of this verse is logically unacceptable without the presumption of 'people'. This phrase has to be presumed because it is yet to be answered. The question cannot be directed at the buildings (of the town) which cannot speak, but to the people of the town. Therefore the verse would mean: 'And ask [the people] of the town.'

(c) That which must be presumed in order to make speech legally acceptable by the *Sharī'ah*. This may be illustrated by the following example. If one real estate owner says to another: 'Give in charity the value of one thousand pounds from your estate, on my behalf', this is a command to the owner of the estate to give part of it in charity on behalf of the one giving the command. In Islamic law one may not act as an agent in a similar situation if the one commanding does not possess the object of his command. Therefore, in order to make this command acceptable in Islamic law, the missing part of the speech which indicates the owner's possession would have to be presumed. The reason for possession in this case is in terms of the purchase. It is implicitly indicated by the word 'one thousand pounds'. Accordingly, the meaning of the command is: 'Sell me for the value of one thousand pounds some of your estate and give it in charity on my behalf, acting as my agent.' The presumed meaning is based on the indication provided by *iqtiḍā' al-naṣṣ*.

Examples of *iqtiḍā' al-naṣṣ*

(a) The Qur'ān states: 'It is for the poor emigrants, expelled from their habitations and their possessions, who seek bounty from God and to please Him.'[12] In this verse the Qur'ān refers to the emigrants as 'poor'. This term normally describes someone who possesses no wealth. However, these emigrants were far from poor in this sense, because in Mecca they had owned estates and money and taken part in commerce. Some were very wealthy. To call them 'poor' could be seen as incorrect. However, because this was uttered by God who, according to Islamic beliefs, cannot err, it is bound to be correct. In line with this assumption scholars would normally assume another meaning which is more likely to agree with the intention of the Lawgiver. In this example the presumption is that ownership of their belongings in Mecca ended by their migration, and the ownership was taken over by their enemies in Mecca. The indication of the word 'poor' on this ruling is by *iqtiḍā' al-naṣṣ* because its truthfulness and correctness in Islamic law are dependent on this presumption.[13]

(b) The Qur'ān states: 'Forbidden to you are your mothers, your daughters, your sisters.'[14] This verse explains the prohibited degrees of relations in marriage. It does not mention explicitly the word 'marriage'. Nonetheless, that word has to be read into the text to complete the meaning.[15]

(c) The Qur'ān states: 'Forbidden to you are carrion, blood, the flesh of swine.'[16] Although this verse does not mention the word 'for consumption', this must be presumed in order to complete the meaning of the text.[17]

(d) The Prophet stated: 'There is no fast [*lā ṣiyāma*] for anyone who has not intended to fast from the night before.' It is clear that the meaning of this tradition is incomplete and that an element is missing. Islamic scholars have presumed the completing element, but have had differing views of it. Some, like the Ḥanafīs, presumed that the missing element is the word 'incomplete'. Therefore, the tradition would mean that fasting is incomplete for anyone who had not made the intention to do so the night before. Others, like the Shāfiʿīs, presumed that the missing element is the word 'invalid'. Therefore, the tradition would mean that there is no valid fast for anyone who had not made the intention to do so the night before. Due to these differences among the schools of law, legal decisions and rulings differed too.[18]

The indication of *iqtiḍā' al-naṣṣ*

Here we discuss two points related to the indication of *iqtiḍā' al-naṣṣ*. The first point is related to cases where *iqtiḍā' al-naṣṣ* assumes more than one indication. The second is related to the generalisation of the required meaning (*ʿumūm al-muqtaḍā*).

(a) In some cases of *iqtiḍā' al-naṣṣ* a few meanings are presumed. In such situations a *mujtahid* would choose the meaning which he considers most appropriate. This is illustrated in the tradition related by Ḥasan b. Samurah where the Prophet says: 'The hand has a duty for what it took until it returns it back.'[19] This text mentions a certain duty which must be fulfilled. That duty, however, is not clearly known. In order to obtain a useful and clear meaning, the missing part of the text has to be presumed. Upon closer examination the tradition contains several meanings that may be presumed: keeping, protection, liability and return. The last meaning is dismissed by Islamic scholars because the tradition has made it an objective of the ruling and something cannot be an objective of itself. Therefore, by *iqtiḍā' al-naṣṣ* this tradition may indicate keeping, protection or liability. Some scholars presumed keeping and protection. This led to the legal ruling by which pledgee and borrower are not liable to pay compensation to the owner if what they took or borrowed is lost or has been destroyed. On the other hand, those who presumed liability obliged the pledgee and borrower to compensate the owner.[20]

(b) Generalisation of the required meaning (*'umūm al-muqtaḍā*) is a question about which scholars are not unanimous. They do not disagree when *muqtaḍā* (the indication of *iqtiḍā' al-naṣṣ*) is specific — as in the verse: 'Forbidden to you are carrion, blood, the flesh of swine.'[21] This is because the prohibition is related to specified food and the first idea which comes to mind is that what is forbidden is eating the food mentioned in the verse.

Since *muqtaḍā* includes many separate themes, Islamic scholars have disagreed on whether or not to include them all. Some like Shāfiʿī maintain that *muqtaḍā* (the presumed indication) in these situations continues to be general and includes all subjects. They argue that the *muqtaḍā* which is presumed is on the same level as *naṣṣ*. This is supported by the fact that a ruling based on it is considered as strong as a ruling which is based on *naṣṣ* and not as a ruling which is based on *qiyās*. Therefore, its indication can be generalised when it includes many subjects, as in the case of *naṣṣ*.

The majority of Ḥanafī scholars and many others, like Ghazālī, have maintained that *muqtaḍā* cannot be generalised. They argue that *muqtaḍā* is established out of necessity and according to the legal maxim *al-ḍarūrah tuqaddar bi qadariha*, where necessity is assessed according to need (i.e., the minimum, irreducible need).[22] Therefore, if the text properly conveys meaning without generalisation, no generalisation would be allowed. An example of this is the permission that *Sharīʿah* grants concerning the consumption of a killed animal if this is necessary. Someone in dire need would be allowed to eat only the amount necessary for survival. The law forbids a person to eat more than that or to store it. In the case of *iqtiḍā' al-naṣṣ*, necessity is only one legitimate meaning; when it is confirmed no other meaning follows. Therefore, scholars maintain that a single meaning, which makes the general, enables the text to provide a proper and useful meaning which may be correctly understood. The Prophet stated: 'God has indeed disburdened from my followers their errors, forgetfulness and that which they were compelled to do against their wishes.'[23]

Removing errors, forgetfulness and coercion, after they have occurred, is logically impossible. If the explicit meaning of this text is taken as its meaning, this would mean that it is untrue. Accordingly, the word 'ruling' is presumed and the sentence would be: 'God has indeed disburdened from my followers the ruling relevant to their errors, forgetfulness and that which they were compelled to do against their wishes.'[24] However, the word 'ruling' is general and includes the ruling related to this world, whether it is acceptable or not in Islamic law; and it includes the ruling related to the Hereafter, whether or not the action deserves punishment.

In this example the scholars who generalise *muqtaḍā* argue that the apparent meaning of the text precludes error, forgetfulness and coercion. Since this meaning is impossible, the speech would have to be shifted to the nearest and most suitable metaphorical meaning. This meaning denies all consequences in this world and the next.

Those who do not generalise *muqtaḍā* maintain that the necessity is fulfilled with the presumption of the one meaning only, thanks to *al-ḍarūrah tuqaddar bi qadariha*. Because the ruling related to the Hereafter is agreed upon, they presume only that meaning.

Disagreement on this question has led to many differences in legal rulings. The following examples illustrate this point.

(a) Islamic scholars differ on the ruling about someone who speaks during prayer through error or forgetfulness.[25] Those who maintain that *muqtaḍā* does not include all its possible meanings claim that the prayer would be invalid and the worshipper must start his prayer again. Based on this approach to *iqtiḍā' al-naṣṣ*, they argue that the tradition indicates the removal of 'sins' accountable in the Hereafter only. Therefore, the tradition does not indicate that speaking unknowingly or inadvertently during the prayer is excusable and that such a prayer is valid and correct in this world. On the contrary, those who maintain that *muqtaḍā* includes all its possible meanings say that the prayer during which a person has spoken in error or negligence is valid and that the person need not start his prayer again. They argue that the tradition suspends the ruling relating to this world and the Hereafter. Therefore, a few extraneous comments made during the prayer, in error and negligence, do not invalidate the prayer and demand no retribution in the Hereafter.

(b) Islamic scholars have disagreed on whether or not coercive divorce[26] is legally valid and thus has any legal effect. In the course of this disagreement *ʿUmūm al-muqtaḍā* has exacerbated the disagreement and has been used for support by both sides. We will see that some scholars based their argumentation on *ʿumūm al-muqtaḍā* and on the previously mentioned tradition where the Prophet informs his followers that God has disburdened them of what they were forced to do against their will.[27]

The Ḥanafīs and some scholars like Nakhaʿī, Ibn al-Musayyib and Thawrī maintained that if a husband is compelled to divorce his wife, this divorce is valid and takes full legal effect. They argue that the intention (*niyyah*) is not a condition for the validity of the divorce.[28] They reached this conclusion by comparing coercive divorce with divorce pronounced in jest. The following tradition of the Prophet states: 'Three things are serious even if said in jest: marriage, divorce and remarriage with one's divorced wife.'[29] Therefore, if the divorce pronounced without serious intention was legally valid, the coercive divorce would be, too. What is common to both is that the divorce was pronounced and neither intended its meaning.

These scholars supported their opinion with other proofs like the general and unrestricted meanings of some verses in this domain: 'O Prophet! When you divorce women, divorce them at their *'iddah* [prescribed periods]'[30] and the tradition where the Prophet says, 'Every divorce is permitted except that of the boy and the mentally deranged.'[31]

The majority of scholars, Mālikīs, Shāfi'īs, Ḥanbalīs, Ẓāhirīs – and some Companions of the Prophet like 'Umar, 'Alī and Ibn 'Abbās – maintain that coercive divorce is invalid and has no legal consequences. They supported their opinion with many arguments. The main argument is based on the same tradition used by the first group: 'God has indeed disburdened from my followers error, forgetfulness and what they were compelled to do against their wishes.' They maintain that the ruling taken from this tradition relates to both this world and the next. Therefore, God has removed responsibility, in these three circumstances, in both this world and the next.

Most scholars have provided other proofs in their favour. 'Ā'ishah narrated that the Prophet said, 'There is no divorce and freeing slave in *ighlāq*[32,33]. 'Aṭā' argued that coercive divorce is invalid. He based his argumentation on the verse: 'Whoever disbelieved in God after believing, except he who is forced thereto and whose heart is at rest with faith.'[34] His view was that disbelief is more dangerous than divorce. Accordingly, if coercive disbelief is not considered valid by God, a divorce is more appropriately invalid under such circumstances. It has been narrated that in the time of 'Umar a man climbed up a rope to reach some honey. While he was hanging from the rope his wife arrived. She held the rope and asked him to divorce her, if not, she would cut the rope. He begged her to desist but she refused. In the end he divorced her three times. Afterwards, the man went to 'Umar and informed him of what had happened. 'Umar said to him: 'Go back to your wife. It is not a divorce.' Ibn Ḥazm and Ibn Qudāmah related the same opinion from 'Alī, Ibn al-Zubayr and Ibn 'Abbās.[35]

In addition to these proofs, Ibn Ḥazm regarded such a divorce as an action without intention (*niyyah*). Therefore, the consequences of that divorce are not obligatory because the Prophet said: 'To every person that which he intends.'[36] According to this tradition every action without a proper intention is invalid. There is no doubt that coercive divorce lacks the intention. Therefore, it is invalid and has no legal status or consequences.

The Ḥanafis, for their part, tried to dismiss these proofs. They said that the tradition of the Prophet is a proof by *iqtiḍā' al-naṣṣ*. If 'ruling' is presumed, it is incorrect to include the ruling relating to this world and the Hereafter, but it should be limited to one of them – since this presumption is due to necessity and necessity cannot to be exceeded. In this case the necessity would be fulfilled if it is applied to either world, therefore only one world can be presumed. Bearing in mind that all scholars agree that the ruling relates to the Hereafter, and that there is disagreement about this world, the former is taken as the probable and correct version. Therefore, the meaning of the tradition would be: 'God has indeed disburdened [the sins] from my followers for their error, forgetfulness and what they have been forced to do.' Accordingly, this tradition cannot prove their opinion, because *ʿumūm al-muqtaḍā* is not acceptable.

Based on analogy, their proof is not right because of the difference between *aṣl* and *farʿ*. This difference is reflected clearly in the fact that a jester has free choice, while a man who is forced to make a coercive divorce has no such choice. Therefore, the analogy is incorrect.

From this argumentation it is obvious that the scholarly disagreement about *ʿumūm al-muqtaḍā* had a great impact on disagreement about coercive divorce and from there on many legal issues related to divorce.

The majority of scholars have stated their preference for the second opinion and maintained that coercive divorce is legally invalid. It would seem that they are right for three reasons.

(1) The coercive divorcee was unjustly forced to accept it, and the Islamic law does not allow the implementation of an injustice. The Qurʾān is explicit: 'And when you judge between people, judge with justice.'[37] 'Verily, God enjoins justice and good deeds and assistance to kith and kin; and He forbids indecency, dishonour, and insolence.'[38] The basic rules extracted from Islamic law and ethics suggest it clearly. 'No damage or retaliation for damage is allowed in Islam'[39], 'Harm should be removed.'[40], 'Action is by intention.'[41]

(2) The proofs from the Qurʾān and the *Sunnah* clearly suggest that coercive divorce is invalid. These proofs are stronger and more explicit than proofs which suggest otherwise.

(3) This is the opinion of the great majority of the Prophet's Companions and of Islamic scholars.

The value of *iqtiḍāʾ al-naṣṣ*

The effect of the required meaning is similar to that of the three previously mentioned meanings. Sarakhsī discussed all four indications under the title: 'The explanation of rulings based on the apparent meaning of the text, not the analogical or the mental'.[42] According to this, *iqtiḍāʾ al-naṣṣ* is a definite meaning, if no proof suggests otherwise. The ruling based on *iqtiḍāʾ al-naṣṣ* has the same treatment as that based on the explicit, alluded or inferred meaning. The only difference among them arises in conflict.[43] Therefore, adherence to *iqtiḍā' al-naṣṣ* should be a strict obligation (*wājib*).[44]

Conflict between *iqtiḍā' al-naṣṣ* and the other three kinds of indications

As previously mentioned, these four kinds of indications are not all equal in strength. The weakest is *iqtiḍā' al-naṣṣ*, due to the fact that it is not indicated by the text itself, or by its meaning, but by necessity – in order to make the text correct and acceptable. Therefore, in case of conflict between *iqtiḍā' al-naṣṣ* and any of the three other indications, the latter would prevail over it.

The following example illustrates a conflict between *iqtiḍā' al-naṣṣ* and *dalālat al-naṣṣ*.[45] The Prophet instructed ʿĀ'ishah regarding washing the blood of menstruation by saying: 'Scrub it off, then wash it with water, then wring it.'[46] This tradition indicates by *iqtiḍā' al-naṣṣ* that one is not allowed to wash the impure object with any liquid but water. This indication is inferred from the fact that the Prophet has ordered that the washing should be with water. It requires that washing with something else is not allowed. This text, however, indicates by *dalālat al-naṣṣ* (the inferred meaning) that the washing can be carried out by any clean liquid because the aim of washing is cleaning – which is achievable with any clean liquid.[47] The inferred meaning has preference over the required meaning. Therefore, one is allowed to wash dirt using anything that removes its traces.

The next example is about the conflict between *iqtiḍā' al-naṣṣ* and *ʿibārat al-naṣṣ* and relates to the punishment for manslaughter. This example complies with the opinion of those who claim that *iqtiḍā' al-naṣṣ* includes all its possible indications.[48] There is the tradition of the Prophet: 'God has indeed disburdened from my followers error, forgetfulness and what they were forced to do against their wishes.' This tradition indicates by *iqtiḍā' al-naṣṣ* that a person who commits manslaughter in this fashion is pardoned for the deed; there is punishment neither in this world nor the Hereafter. On the other hand, there is the verse: 'If any slays a believer by error, then let him set free a believing slave, and blood money is to be paid to his family unless they forgo it freely.'[49] This verse indicates by the explicit meaning (*ʿibārat al-naṣṣ*) that a specified punishment should be meted out to such a person. Because the explicit meaning has preference over the required meaning, a person who commits manslaughter should be punished in the way mentioned in the verse.

Conclusion

From what has been discussed, we may hold that the meaning of an authoritative text is indicated by the words of the text, its signs and allusions; by inference and the addition of a missing element. In interpretation, these may be applied individually or in combination. Furthermore, Ḥanafī scholars divided indication into four kinds. Briefly, an authoritative legal text may be interpreted through application of any of these four kinds of textual implications. They carry the text to its proper and logical meaning. They also indicate a definite meaning if a reliable proof does not suggest otherwise. Therefore, these meanings have to be implemented.

Every method assumes that meanings are indicated by the text (*naṣṣ*) and that the text is their proof. The meaning taken from the text's *ʿibārah* is the intended meaning indicated by its actual words. The meaning taken from the text's *ishārah* is a necessary indication of the meaning of its *ʿibārah* in such a way that they cannot be separated. It is considered an indication by way of compliance. The meaning taken from its *dalālah* is a meaning indicated by its spirit and rational reason. The meaning taken from its *iqtiḍāʾ* is a necessary meaning required by the text for truthfulness and validity in the *Sharīʿah*. The strongest indication is that of *ʿibārah*, then that of *dalālah*, *ishārah* and, finally, *iqtiḍāʾ*. Logically, in the case of conflict between these indications the stronger prevails over the weaker one.

NOTES

1. *al-Muʿjam al-Wasīṭ*, II:743; Baʿlabakī, *al-Mawrid*, p. 147.

2. Dabbūsī, *al-Asrār fī al-Uṣūl wa al-Furūʿ fī Taqwīm Adillat al-Sharʿ*, I:305.

3. Qurʾān, XII:82.

4. Dabbūsī, *al-Asrār fī al-Uṣūl wa al-Furūʿ fī Taqwīm Adillat al-Sharʿ*, I:305–306. It is interesting that scholars of *uṣūl al-fiqh* very frequently use the first part of this verse ('And ask the town where we have been') as an example when they speak about metaphor (*majāz*) or *iqtiḍāʾ al-naṣṣ*. Yet they ignore the second part ('and the caravan in which we returned'), although it has the same application.

5. Sarakhsī, *Uṣūl al-Sarakhsī*, I:248.

6. Sarakhsī, *Uṣūl al-Sarakhsī*, I:251.

7. Sarakhsī, *Uṣūl al-Sarakhsī*, I:251–252.

8. See the discussion on this question in Sarakhsī, *Uṣūl al-Sarakhsī*, I:248–254; Nasafī, *Kashf al-Asrār*, I:293–398; Bukhārī, *Kashf al-Asrār*, I:75–78, II:237–252; Taftāzānī, *Sharḥ al-Talwīḥ ʿalā al-Tawḍīḥ*, I:137–140; Ibn ʿAbd al-Shakūr, *Fawātiḥ al-Raḥamūt*, II:412.

9. Ibn Mājah, *Sunan*, I:659 (no. 2045).

10. Muslims believe that the Prophet committed some minor errors later corrected through divine revelations. He is like other human beings in being prone to error. The only difference is that God has saved him from committing the great sins, and that He has corrected his errors through revelation. For example, the Prophet erred by asking forgiveness for his uncle

Abū Ṭālib and he was corrected by the revelation: 'It is not [proper] for the Prophet and the believers to ask God's forgiveness for polytheists, even though they be near kinsmen.' (Qur'ān, IX:113). He was also corrected in the case of a blind man who came to ask him a question and the Prophet refused to pay attention to him, because he was too busy with tribal chiefs (Qur'ān, LXXX:1–10)

11. Qur'ān, XII:82.

12. Qur'ān, LIX:8.

13. Scholars like Sarakhsī and Bazdawī regarded this indication as *ishārat al-naṣṣ*, not as *iqtiḍā' al-naṣṣ* (Sarakhsī, *Uṣūl al-Sarakhsī*, I:236; Bukhārī, *Kashf al-Asrār*, I:69). Nonetheless, it seems that this indication is *iqtiḍā' al-naṣṣ*, not *ishārat al-naṣṣ*, because in the latter the necessary meaning is belated and the correctness of speech depends on it. There is no doubt that the necessary meaning for 'poor' in this verse is 'end of ownership'. The latter term necessarily precedes the correct understanding and should be presumed if the exact meaning of the word 'poor' is to be understood. Therefore it is *iqtiḍā' al-naṣṣ* and not *ishārat al-naṣṣ*.

14. Qur'ān, IV:23

15. Khān and Hilālī (p. 127) translate this verse of the Qur'ān as follows: 'Forbidden to you [for marriage] are your mothers, your daughter.' Arberry (p. 75) and Pickhtall (p. 81) did not mention the omitted 'marriage', probably because that meaning seems obvious. This is probably why Ibn Kathīr did not give this explanation (Ibn Kathīr, *Tafsīr al-Qur'ān al-ʿAẓīm*, I:623).

16. Qur'ān, V:3

17. Khān and Hilālī (p. 164) translate this verse of the Qur'ān as follows: 'Forbidden to you [for food] are.' Therefore, this missing section is supplied in order that the verse may convey a complete meaning.

18. Marghinānī, *al-Hidāyah*, I:118; Ibn Rushd, *Bidāyat al-Mujtahid*, I:293–294; Ibn Qudāmah, *al-Kāfī*, I:350–351

19. Tirmidhī, *al-Jāmiʿ al-Ṣaḥīḥ*, III:566 (no. 1266); Ibn Mājah, *Sunan*, II:802 (no. 2400).

20. See chapters which deal with *ḍamān al-ʿāriyyah wa al-rahn* in books of *fiqh*.

21. Qur'ān, V:3.

22. Bukhārī, *Kashf al-Asrār*, II:237; Taftāzānī, *Sharḥ al-Talwīḥ ʿalā al-Tawḍīḥ*, I:137. It is interesting that ʿĀmidī who followed the Shāfiʿī *madhhab* did not mention this opinion, but maintained that *muqtaḍā* could be generalised. (ʿĀmidī, *al-Iḥkām fī Uṣūl al-Aḥkām*, II:363).

23. Ibn Nujaym, *al-Ashbāh wa al-Naẓā'ir*, p. 86; Lubnānī, *Sharḥ al-Majallah*, p. 30.

24. Ibn Mājah, *Sunan*, I:659 (no. 2045).

25. Marghinānī, *al-Hidāyah*, I:61; ʿĀbidīn, *al-Hadiyyah al-ʿAlā'iyyah*, p. 87; Khaṭīb, *Mughnī al-Muḥtāj*, I:430. In their argumentation about these matters both sides provided some other proofs too.

26. Here coercive means divorce which is legally wrong. However, proper coercive divorce, when a judge concludes and passes such a judgement on the basis of the *Sharīʿah*, is approved by all scholars.

27. Normally, scholars have used various arguments beside this tradition and *ʿumūm al-muqtaḍā* as proofs.

28. When speaking about the *arkān* of divorce, Kāsānī mentioned only the utterance of the explicit word of divorce. He did not mention the intention (*niyyah*) as a *rukn*. According to him the intention is stipulated when the word 'divorce' is implicit (*kināyah*). Kāsānī, *Badā'iʿ al-Ṣanā'iʿ*, III:100–101.

29. Abū Dāwūd, *Sunan*, II:259 (no. 2149); Ibn Mājah, *Sunan*, I:658 (no.2039).

30. Qur'ān, LXV:1.

31. Tirmidhī, *al-Jāmiʿ al-Ṣaḥīḥ*, III:496 (no.1191).

32. The word *ighlāq* has been interpreted as coercion (Ibn Qudāmah, *al-Mughnī*, VII:118).

33. Abū Dāwūd, *Sunan*, II:258–259 (no. 2193); Ibn Mājah, *Sunan*, I:660 (2046).

34. Qur'ān, XVI:106.

35. Shawkānī, *Nayl al-Awṭār*, VI:250; Ibn Ḥazm, *al-Muḥallā*, X:202–204; Ibn Qudāmah, *al-Mughnī*, VII:118.

36. Bukhārī, *al-Jāmiʿ al-Ṣaḥīḥ*, I:2 (1:1); Abū Dāwūd, *Sunan*, II:262 (no. 2201); Ibn Mājah, *Sunan*, II:1413 (no. 4227).

37. Qur'ān, IV:58.

38. Qur'ān, XVI:90.

39. Lubnānī, *Sharḥ al-Majallah*, p. 29.

40. Ibn Nujaym, *al-Ashbāh wa al-Naẓā'ir*, p. 85; Lubnānī, *Sharḥ al-Majallah*, p. 29.

41. Ibn Nujaym, *al-Ashbāh wa al-Naẓā'ir*, p. 38; Lubnānī, *Sharḥ al-Majallah*, p. 17–18.

42. Sarakhsī, *Uṣūl al-Sarakhsī*, I:236.

43. Nasafī, *Kashf al-Asrār*, I:398.

44. Isnawī, *al-Tamhīd*, p. 242.

45. Some scholars claimed that a proper example of the conflict between the two may not be found. Mayhawī rejected this claim, stating that it showed insufficient research (Nasafī, *Kashf al-Asrār*, I:398).

46. Bukhārī, *al-Jāmiʿ al-Ṣaḥīḥ*, I:62–63; Muslim, *Ṣaḥīḥ Muslim*, I:240 (no. 291).

47. Today we may speak about other methods of cleaning (e.g. dry cleaning). Any kind of cleaning which removes traces of dirt may be taken into consideration.

48. In this case it would include the ruling related to this world and the Hereafter. This example does not comply with the opinion that does not accept ʿumūm al-muqtaḍā, because if only the Hereafter is presumed, there is no conflict between these two texts. The first one would be related to the Hereafter and the second one to this world.

49. Qur'ān, IV:92.

Introduction to the Shāfiʿī Approach to the Methods of Textual Indication[1]

The Shāfiʿīs' approach to textual indication (*dalālat al-naṣṣ*) is different from that of the Ḥanafīs. While this difference seems more technical than real, it would be interesting to discuss this approach in further detail.

In contrast to the Ḥanafīs, who classified textual indication as being of four types, the Shāfiʿīs divided it into two: pronounced meaning (*dalālat al-manṭūq*) and implied meaning (*dalālat al-mafhūm*). Both these indications are derived from the text and its words.

Pronounced meaning (*dalālat al-manṭūq*) is derived from the obvious text and it is divided into two types: *ṣarīḥ* and *ghayr al-ṣarīḥ*. *Ṣarīḥ* includes the explicit meaning (*ʿibārat al-naṣṣ*) mentioned by the Ḥanafīs. *Ghayr al-ṣarīḥ* is divided into three types: the required meaning (*dalālat al-iqtiḍāʾ*) gestured meaning (*dalālat al-īmāʾ*) and the alluded meaning (*dalālat al-ishārah*). From this division it appears that *ghayr al-ṣarīḥ* includes two types regarding the indications mentioned by the Ḥanafīs: the alluded meaning (*ishārat al-naṣṣ*) and the required meaning (*iqtiḍāʾ al-naṣṣ*).

Implied meaning (*dalālat al-mafhūm*) is derived through the logical and juridical construction of the text and it is divided into two kinds: opposite meaning (*mafhūm al-mukhālafah*) and harmonious meaning (*mafhūm al-muwāfaqah*). The latter corresponds to the inferred meaning (*dalālat al-naṣṣ*) of the Ḥanafīs.[2]

NOTES

1. Āmidī, *al-Iḥkām fī Uṣūl al-Aḥkām*, III:63; Ījī, *Mukhtaṣar al-Muntahā*, II:171; Ibn Amīr al-Ḥajj, *al-Taqrīr wa al-Taḥbīr*, I:111; Shawkānī, *Irshād al-Fuḥūl*, p. 156.

2. Abū Zahrah stated that all four Ḥanafī divisions of *dalālah* may be classified under *dalālat al-manṭūq* (Abū Zahrah, *Uṣūl al-Fiqh*, p. 116). However, it would be more accurate to say that some divisions are derived from *mafhūm*, just as the inferred meaning (*dalālat al-naṣṣ*) and *mafhūm* are derived from *manṭūq*.

CHAPTER 5

The Pronounced
(*al-Manṭūq*)

The linguistic definition of *manṭūq*

Manṭūq refers to pronounced, uttered, said; text, wording.[1]

The technical definition of *manṭūq*.[2]

Shāfiʿī scholars have offered some definitions of *manṭūq* which are very similar to each other. ʿĀmidī defined *manṭūq* as 'what is undoubtedly understood with certainty from the word's indication'. Ījī defined *manṭūq* as 'what has been understood with certainty from the text's words'. Ibn al-Subkī defined it as 'that which the text indicates by its words'. The same definition for *manṭūq* is provided by Shawkānī. From these definitions it may be concluded that *manṭūq* is the certain indication of the text.

Subdivision of *manṭūq*

When *manṭūq* is not amenable to *ta'wīl*, it is considered as *naṣṣ*. When it is, it is considered *ẓāhir*.

Naṣṣ is divided into two types: frank (*ṣarīḥ*) and unclear (*ghayr al-ṣarīḥ*). The former is when the text indicates the ruling by complete correspondence (*muṭābaqah*) or by partial inclusion (*taḍammun*); the latter is when the text indicates the ruling through a necessary idea attached to the meaning in the mind (*iltizām*). In the case of *ghayr al-ṣarīḥ*, the text does not yield a particular ruling, but that ruling is necessary for the meaning of the text. *Ghayr-al-ṣarīḥ* is further divided into three types: required meaning (*dalālat al-iqtiḍā'*), gestured meaning (*dalālat al-imā'*) and alluded meaning (*dalālat al-ishārah*).

The scholars arrived at these conclusions by dividing the necessary indication into two categories.[3]

(a) When the text's necessary indication on a ruling intended by the speaker is indicated by the wording itself.

(b) When the text's necessary indication on a ruling not intended by the speaker is indicated by the wording itself.

The former case may be further divided into two:

(1) When the correctness of the text in one's mind and its rational and legal validity (*ʿaql* and *sharʿ*) depend on its presumption, it has *dalālat al-iqtiḍāʾ*.

(2) When the correctness of the text in the mind and its validity does not depend on its presumption, it has *dalālat al-imāʾ*.

When the text's necessary indication on a ruling is not intended by the speaker, it is *dalālat al-ishārah*.[4]

One may conclude that *manṭūq* is the text's indication on a ruling mentioned in the text and pronounced by complete correspondence (*muṭābaqah*), partial inclusion (*taḍammun*), or a necessary idea attached to the meaning in the mind (*iltizām*).

Examples of *manṭūq*

(1) Examples of *manṭūq ṣarīḥ*

(a) The Qurʾān states: 'Forbidden to you [for food] are carrion, blood, the flesh of swine, what has been consecrated to anything other than God, the beast strangled, the beast bludgeoned, the beast fallen to death, the beast gored.'[5] This verse explicitly pronounces that carrion, blood, etc. are forbidden to Muslims. Therefore it is classified as *manṭūq ṣarīḥ*.

(b) The Qurʾān states: 'God has permitted trade and forbidden usury.'[6] Linguistically, this verse clearly states that trading is allowed and usury forbidden. Since the ruling relates to both trading and usury, its plainly pronounced ruling is considered *manṭūq ṣarīḥ*.

(c) The Qurʾān states: 'Forbidden to you are [...] the stepdaughters in your care, [born] of your wives whom you have entered.'[7] In this verse men are not allowed to marry the stepdaughters begotten by the women they marry and with whom they consummated marriage. This indication is *manṭūq ṣarīḥ*.

(2) Examples of manṭūq ghayr al-ṣarīḥ

It was mentioned previously that *manṭūq ghayr al-ṣarīḥ* is divided into three types. The following are examples of these.

(a) *Dalālat al-iqtiḍāʾ*: When the correctness of the text and its rational and legal validity (*ʿaql* and *sharʿ*) depend on the presumption of a meaning intended by the speaker. The Qurʾān states: 'O you who believe! Fasting is prescribed for you as it was prescribed for those before you, that you may remain God-fearing. For a certain number of days; and if any of you is ill, or on a journey, then the same number [should be fasted] on other days.'[8]

This verse apparently means that when someone is ill or goes on a journey he must fast on other days, even if he does not break the fast and continues fasting. This apparent meaning is understood since the Qur'ān clearly states: 'Then the same number [should be made up] from other days.' The majority of Islamic scholars, however, presumed the concealed word to be 'and he did not fast'. Therefore, the meaning of the verse is, 'and if any of you is ill, or on a journey [without fasting], then the same number [should be fasted] on other days.'[9]

(b) *Dalālat al-imā'*: When correctness of the text and its rational and legal validity do not depend on the presumption of a meaning intended by the speaker.

The Qur'ān states: 'And the thief, male or female: cut off his hands, in recompense for what they have earned and an exemplary punishment from God.'[10] The ruling announced in this verse includes an intended explanation and justification that the speaker offers for the ruling. It clearly affirms that theft was the reason for the introduction of this ruling. This is the actual meaning of the sentence, although the ruling begins after the '*fa*' conjunction, which in Arabic indicates continuation (*ta'qīb*), not justification (*ta'līl*).[11] Since the sentence does not indicate the justification, the association between the ruling (cutting of the hand) and the thief would be unreasonable, because there would be no consistency or harmony between them.

(c) *Dalālat al-ishārah*: When correctness of the text and its rational and legal validity do not depend on the presumption of a meaning which is not intended[12] by the speaker.

The Qur'ān states: 'And We have enjoined on man to be good to his parents. His mother bears him with hardship and she brings him forth with hardship, bearing him and weaning him in thirty months.'[13] This verse indicates by alluded meaning that the child is carried for at least six months, because another verse states that the weaning period is two years only: 'His mother bore him in weakness upon weakness, and his weaning is in two years – give thanks to Me and to your parents; unto Me is the final destination.'[14] Therefore, if the total period for both bearing and weaning the child is thirty months and the weaning alone is two years, one may conclude that the gestation period alone is at least six months. This meaning is indicated by the verse even if its correctness and validity, rationally and legally, do not depend on the presumption of that meaning which, presumably, was not intended by the speaker.

Restriction of meaning of *manṭūq* by *mafhūm*

The meaning of *manṭūq*, according to the majority of scholars,[15] is restricted by both types of *mafhūm*: agreement (*muwāfaqah*) and disagreement (*mukhālafah*). In *Iḥkām* ʿĀmidī stated that he did not know whether any scholar disagreed in this matter.[16] We have found, however, that Rāzī disagreed, maintaining that such a restriction is not allowed, because it would give preference to a weaker *mafhūm* over ʿ*āmm manṭūq*, which is stronger.[17]

An example of restriction of *manṭūq* by *mafhūm al-muwāfaqah*

The Shāfiʿī scholars suggested an example for the above restriction without mentioning the authoritative texts. They maintain that it is illustrated by the example of the house owner who orders a doorkeeper to attack anyone who enters his house and afterwards tells him: 'If Zayd comes in, do not be disrespectful to him.' This indicates by *mafhūm al-muwāfaqah* that the doorkeeper is not allowed to attack Zayd and that Zayd is excluded from the general order delivered by what was pronounced (*manṭūq*).

Examples of restriction of *manṭūq* by *mafhūm al-mukhālafah*

(a) The Prophet gave a general command for *zakāh* to be offered for animals.[18] According to some traditions, however, he stated that *zakāh* should be paid only for grazing animals. In one of them he says: 'For grazing sheep and goats *zakāh* is prescribed.'[19] From this tradition we construe, by opposite meaning (*mafhūm al-mukhālafah*), that *zakāh* is not obligatory for stall-fed animals, because this tradition restricts the absolute meaning, and excludes from the absolute order animals which are stall-fed.[20]

(b) The Prophet said, 'Indeed, water cannot be sullied except by what changes its smell, taste or colour.'[21] This general meaning is restricted by the *mafhūm* of the tradition: 'When the amount of water reaches *qullatayn* it cannot be sullied.'[22] The water mentioned in the first tradition is taken in a general sense. It includes that which exceeds *qullatayn* and that which is less. The first tradition indicated by the *manṭūq* is that water, no matter how much it is, does not became dirty if something dirty falls into it. The second indicates that it would be sullied if it is less than *qullatayn*.

The indication of *manṭūq*

Based on what has been discussed so far, I have concluded[23] that *manṭūq ṣarīḥ* provides a definite (*qaṭʿī*) meaning, because it is a clear indication declared by the apparent meaning of the text. On the other hand *manṭūq ghayr al-ṣarīḥ* can provide both definite (*qaṭʿī*) and probable (*ẓannī*) meaning, depending on the type, as follows.

(a) *Dalālat al-iqtiḍāʾ* provides a definite meaning when only one meaning can be presumed, and a reliable proof does not suggest otherwise. When more than one meaning can be presumed, there is probable (*ẓannī*) meaning.

(b) *Dalālat al-imā'* provides probable meaning because it cannot be certain that the attributes mentioned represent the actual reason for the ruling that precedes it.

(c) *Dalālat al-ishārah* would provide a probable meaning when the meaning supposes reality and metaphor. If it supposes reality only, it would provide definite (*qaṭʿī*) meaning.

The value of *manṭūq*

For Muslims, adherence to the *manṭūq* and implementation of its meaning are obligatory, whether it is *manṭūq ṣarīḥ* (which provides a definite meaning) or *manṭūq ghayr al-ṣarīḥ* (which provides indefinite meaning). This is because indefinite meanings are also valid and should be implemented[24] until other reliable proofs suggest otherwise.

NOTES

1. *al-Mujām al-Wasīṭ*, II:931; Baʿlabakī, *al-Mawrid*, p. 1124 (see etymology of the word *manṭūq* in EI², VI:442).

2. Āmidī, *al-Iḥkām fī Uṣūl al-Aḥkām*, III:63; Ījī, *Mukhtaṣar al-Muntahā*, II171; Ibn Amīr al-Ḥājj, *al-Taqrīr wa al-Taḥbīr*, I:111; Shawkānī, *Irshād al-Fuḥūl*, p. 156.

3. Ījī, *Mukhtaṣar al-Muntahā*, II:171; Anṣārī, *Ghāyat al-Wuṣūl*, p. 36; Ibn Amīr al-Ḥājj, *al-Taqrīr wa al-Taḥbīr*, I:111; Shawkānī, *Irshād al-Fuḥūl*, p. 156.

4. Therefore, both *dalālat al-iqtiḍā'* and *dalālat al-imā'* are necessary meanings intended by the speaker while *dalālat al-ishārah* is the necessary meaning not intended by the speaker.

5. Qur'ān, V:3.

6. Qur'ān, II:275.

7. Qur'ān, IV:23.

8. Qur'ān, II:183–184

9. The fasting during sickness or while travelling is a question on which Islamic scholars have differed. The majority maintain that a person who is ill or goes on a journey has permission (*rukhṣah*) to either fast or not to fast. If he fasts he is not obliged to make up any days. They argued this position through prior presumption, which indicates that fasting on other days is an obligation for someone who did not fast. This presumption is supported by some traditions of the Prophet, which indicate that fasting while travelling is permissible and therefore valid. ʿĀ'ishah narrated that Ḥamzah b. ʿAmr al-Aslamī, who fasted regularly, asked the Prophet, 'Shall I fast on a journey?' The Prophet answered, 'If you like you can fast, and if you like you may eat and drink' (Bukhārī, *al-Jāmiʿ al-Ṣaḥīḥ*, II:237 [30:33]; Muslim, *Ṣaḥīḥ Muslim* II:789 [no. 1121]). Though this tradition may imply that the fast was not obligatory, the narration mentioned by Muslim suggests that al-Aslamī had asked about fasting in Ramaḍān, because the Prophet answered, 'It is a permission [*rukhṣah*] from God. He who takes it is good; he who likes to fast will not sin. The use of the word 'permission' indicates that the question was related to the obligatory fasting of the month of Ramaḍān, because on other days one does not have to fast. Those who argue in favour of this opinion mention other proofs which appear to be strong. The Ẓāhirīs had a different view. They held that

fasting while travelling is not allowed because the verse apparently stated that he who travels should fast on other days. This is supported by the tradition where the Prophet said, 'fasting while travelling is not an act of piety,' The opposite of piety is sin and committing sins is forbidden; and if a person is going to commit a sin by fasting it will not be accepted as a good deed (ʿAsqalānī, *Fatḥ al-Bārī*, IV:156–159; Shawkānī, *Nayl al-Awṭār*, IV:235–238; ʿId, *Iḥkām al-Iḥkā*, II:17; Ṭaḥāwī, *Sharḥ Maʿānī al-Āthār*, I:333; Ibn Ḥazm, *al-Muḥallā*, VI:243).

10. Qurʾān, V:38.

11. According to this all rulings in the Qurʾān or Sunnah which follow the 'fa' conjunction – which sometimes may even be implicit (*muqaddar*) – are modifiers of the adjectives that interpret and justify them. The same situation arose when someone came to the Prophet and asked him a question and received an answer in the form of a ruling. That ruling is considered proper for that particular question, as in the case of a man who said to the Prophet that he lay with his wife one day of Ramaḍān, and the Prophet ordered him to pay a certain amount of ransom. This conclusion, however, is indefinite (*ẓannī*) because the 'fa' conjunction in Arabic originally indicates continuation (*taʿqīb*) and does not indicate justification (*taʿlīl*). Accordingly, the rulings deduced from these proofs are indefinite and could be challenged by other appropriate proofs, bearing in mind that the Qurʾānic texts would have preference over Sunnah in the case of an apparent conflict.

12. This is what we suppose and, accordingly, it may be incorrect.

13. Qurʾān, XLVI:15.

14. Qurʾān, XXXI:14.

15. Āmidī, *al-Iḥkām fī Uṣūl al-Aḥkām*, II:529; Aṣfahānī, *Sharḥ al-Minhāj*, I:418–420.

16. Āmidī, *al-Iḥkām fī Uṣūl al-Aḥkām*, II:529.

17. Rāzī, *al-Maḥṣūl*, I:3:159–160.

18. For example, he ordered Muʿadh, whom he had dispatched to Yemen, to take a year-old calf from every thirty cows without mentioning whether they should be grazing livestock or not (Tirmidhī, *al-Jāmiʿ al-Ṣaḥīḥ*, III:20 [no. 623]; Nasāʾī, *Sunan*, V:26 [no. 2453])

19. Bukhārī, *al-Jāmiʿ al-Ṣaḥīḥ*, II:124 (24:38).

20. The general order is regarded as ʿāmm (general in meaning), while the traditions where stall-fed animals are excluded are regarded as specific (*khāṣṣ*). According to a rule in *uṣūl al-fiqh* the specified meaning is preferred to the general meaning.

21. Ibn Mājah, *Sunan*, I:172 (no. 521).

22. Ibn Ḥanbal, *Musnad*, VI:276 (no. 4605); Ibn Mājah, *Sunan*, I:172 (no. 517).

23. Some Islamic scholars, however, hold different opinions on certain aspects. In order to shorten this elaboration I have not discussed their opinions.

24. There are no differences on this point among Islamic scholars.

CHAPTER 6

The Implied (*al-Mafhūm*)

Introduction

Mafhūm is the implicit meaning reached by way of inference, and is not indicated by the word's apparent indication. *Mafhūm* is accepted by the majority of Islamic scholars as a way of reaching legal rulings based on the authoritative legal texts. Ibn Ḥazm seems to be the only scholar who entirely rejected *mafhūm*. He maintained that *mafhūm* is a kind of analogy (*qiyās*), which is rejected entirely in the Ẓāhirī *madhhab*.[1] Ibn Ḥazm's position, however, is rejected by the majority of Islamic scholars. Even the founder of Ẓāhirī *madhhab* Dāwūd al-Ẓāhirī, who rejected analogy in general, recognised some kinds of *mafhūm*, i.e., clear analogy (*qiyās jālī*), otherwise known as *mafhūm al-muwāfaqah*.[2]

Therefore, the majority of Islamic scholars did not just search for meanings confined to the apparent sense of the words. They went beyond this, searching for meanings which can be understood from the spirit of Islamic law, and implicit meanings of the authoritative texts (but bound by the rules of Arabic). Using this method of Islamic law, they were able to produce adequate rulings suitable for ever new instances and cases. The Ḥanafī scholars, as we have seen, did not differentiate between the indication reached through inference and that reached through the apparent meaning of the text. In their opinion the inferred meaning has the same legal value as the apparent meaning. Āmidī mentioned that scholars were unanimous that *mafhūm al-muwāfaqah* (agreed meaning) is a legal proof. He mentioned the dissent of Dāwūd al-Ẓāhirī, but he did not count this as either a valuable or effective disagreement, or one that could affect the unanimity of other scholars who recognised it.[3] *Mafhūm* can be divided into two types:

(a) *mafhūm al-muwāfaqah* (agreed meaning);
(b) *mafhūm al-mukhālafah* (divergent meaning).

a) *Mafhūm al-Muwāfaqah*
(the Agreed Meaning)

The linguistic definition of *mafhūm al-muwāfaqah*

Mafhūm al-muwāfaqah is composed of two words: *mafhūm* and *muwāfaqah*.[4] *Mafhūm* refers to understood, known, implied, implicit, tacit; notion, connotation; the meaning, or sense in which the word is understood.[5] *Muwāfaqah* refers to correspondence, agreement, conformity, coincidence, compatibility, consistence, accordance, harmony.[6]

The technical definition of *mafhūm al-muwāfaqah*

On closer examination, it appears that Āmidī gave a definition of *mafhūm al-muwāfaqah* in two places in his *Iḥkām*. The first is: 'Where the ruling of the unpronounced agrees with the ruling of the pronounced.'[7] The second is a slightly different definition: 'It is the implicit indication which agrees with the pronounced indication.'[8]

Shawkānī defined *mafhūm al-muwāfaqah* in a similar fashion to Āmidī's first definition: 'Where the unpronounced agrees with the pronounced.'[9]

Taking into consideration these definitions, the following analysis and contemplation of the scholars in respect of the agreed meaning, (*mafhūm al-muwāfaqah*)[10] may be proffered: 'It is an implicit meaning about which the text is silent, but it nonetheless agrees with the pronounced meaning of another text, [the meaning] of which is equivalent or superior to it.'

Therefore *mafhūm al-muwāfaqah* is the indication of the text that a certain meaning (ruling) within it is equivalent or superior to the pronounced meaning (ruling)[11] within another text, because both instances share an effective cause (*ʿillah*).[12] Accordingly, the implicit indication takes the ruling of the pronounced. The understanding of that effective cause is so simple that it does not depend on study and legal reasoning (*ijtihād*). An example of *mafhūm al-muwāfaqah* is the Qur'ānic command to children regarding their parents: 'Say not *ʿuff* to them [in disrespect], nor shout at them.'[13] From this verse anyone who knows the language may immediately infer that the reason for this legislation is the prohibition of behaviour offensive in any way to parents. The agreed meaning (*mafhūm al-muwāfaqah*) suggests that other forms of offensive behaviour, like beating, cursing etc., are also forbidden because the effective cause for the prohibition applies to them equally or with even more reason. If another form of offensive behaviour (such as any other word similar to *ʿuff*) is equal to that stated in the text, it would be termed *laḥn al-khiṭāb* (parallel meaning). If it is more offensive, like beating and cursing, it would be termed *faḥwā al-khiṭāb* (superior meaning).[14]

Types of *mafhūm al-muwāfaqah*[15]

In the examples of *mafhūm al-muwāfaqah*, we see that this implicit meaning is not always equivalent to the pronounced (*manṭūq*), but is sometimes superior to it. On this basis some Shāfiʿī scholars divided the *mafhūm al-muwāfaqah* into two types: *laḥn al-khiṭāb* (parallel meaning) and *faḥwā al-khiṭāb* (superior meaning).

If the implicit meaning is equivalent to the pronounced meaning (*manṭūq*), *mafhūm al-muwāfaqah* is termed as *laḥn al-khiṭāb* (parallel meaning) and if it is superior to the pronounced meaning, it is termed as *faḥwā al-khiṭāb* (superior meaning).[16]

Some Shāfiʿī scholars like Ghazālī and Rāzī[17] maintain that the superiority of the implicit meaning to the pronounced meaning is not a condition for *mafhūm al-muwāfaqah*. It is sufficient that the effective cause, which is a reason for legislation (*manāṭ al-ḥukm*), is equivalent to the pronounced (and no less appropriate or adequate), and that this shared meaning (the effective cause) is so obvious (and linguistically understandable) that anyone who understands the language will understand it without further thought or legal reasoning (*ijtihād*). Therefore, according to them, the agreed meaning is sometimes equivalent and sometimes superior to the pronounced meaning.

In their argument they use the fact that the ruling of what is pronounced is sometimes extended to the unpronounced, although the unpronounced is not more entitled to that ruling than the pronounced. This is because it is easy and simple to understand the reason for the legislation (*manāṭ al-ḥukm*), a reason which is common to the pronounced and the unpronounced – e.g., the question regarding orphans' property. The Qur'ān prohibits guardians from unjustly using up the property of orphans.[18] This ruling, however, is extended to all other forms of mismanagement producing the same result e.g., waste and destruction of their property. The extension of this ruling is based on the agreed meaning, or more precisely on its type that is called parallel meaning (*laḥn al-khiṭāb*).

According to Hindī, the majority of scholars maintain that the implicit meaning has to be superior in order to be considered the agreed meaning. This opinion is ascribed to Shāfiʿī himself.[19]

They argue that if the unpronounced is superior to the pronounced (because the meaning of the unpronounced is more adequate for that than ruling of the pronounced) it is certain that they share the same ruling. This is because it is less likely that the ruling of the pronounced is prescribed for *ta'abbud* worship,[20] since the unpronounced is more appropriate for that ruling than the pronounced.

When they are equal, the possibility of *ta'abbud* in establishing the ruling by the pronounced is actual and therefore its ruling cannot be extended to the unpronounced. Its extension would be by way of analogy, not by the agreed meaning (*mafhūm al-muwāfaqah*).

This argument seems unfounded if we keep in mind that the shared meaning (the effective cause) in *mafhūm al-muwāfaqah* ought to be clear and simple to observe for anyone who understands the language, without a need for analysis or legal reasoning (*ijtihād*). If the method for inferring the shared effective cause is not simple, that question[21] will not have any connection with *mafhūm al-muwāfaqah*, and therefore will not be related to previous disagreements.

The argument that the reason for legislation in both the pronounced (*manṭūq*) and the unpronounced (*mafhūm*) is discerned simply by understanding and knowledge of the language, denies the possibility of *ta'abbud* in establishing a ruling by the pronounced.

Therefore, for *mafhūm al-muwāfaqah* it is sufficient that the effective cause of the unpronounced be equivalent to that of the pronounced, not less. This is the opinion of the majority of Islamic scholars, both Ḥanafīs and Shāfi'īs.

The resulting practical application does not reflect a scholarly difference, but is rooted in the difference of the nature of *mafhūm al-muwāfaqah* and *qiyās*. This practical application appears in cases where the unpronounced is equivalent to the pronounced. Under these circumstances, the first group of scholars maintains that the application represents *mafhūm al-muwāfaqah*; the second maintains that it represents analogy (*qiyās*). If a ruling is based on *mafhūm al-muwāfaqah*, this means that it is directly derived from the text[22] as something distinct from the ruling based on analogy and mediated by analogy (*qiyās*). The ruling based on the text may be extended to other instances through *qiyās*. In other words, it is the original subject (*aṣl*), whereas the ruling based on *qiyās* cannot be *aṣl*. Moreover, in the case of conflict between the two, the *mafhūm al-muwāfaqah* is stronger than the *qiyās* because the former is taken directly from the text while the latter is derived through a mediator.

The indication of *mafhūm al-muwāfaqah*

Shāfi'ī scholars divided *mafhūm al-muwāfaqah* into two types: definite (*qaṭ'ī*) and indefinite (*ẓannī*).[23] This division resembles that of later Ḥanafī scholars who divided *dalālat al-naṣṣ* into definite and indefinite. However, the Shāfi'īs understood and defined these two types differently. The main difference lies in the fact that the Shāfiʿīs stipulated for *mafhūm al-muwāfaqah*, both definite and indefinite, the superiority of implicit indication (*mafhūm*) to the pronounced indication (*manṭūq*).[24] The Ḥanafīs stipulated only the definitive existence of the effective cause of the pronounced in the unpronounced.[25]

(a) *Mafhūm al-muwāfaqah* would provide a definite indication if the justification (*taʿlīl*) determined by the linguistic meaning, and the superiority of implicit indication to the pronounced indication are both definite – e.g., the command about one's parent 'say not to them '*uff*' [in protest] nor shout at them'.[26] From this verse any Arabic speaker would definitely understand that the reason (justification) for this legislation (*manāṭ al-ḥukm*) is the prohibition of any offensive behaviour towards parents. Moreover, it would be definitely understood that more offensive behaviour, such as beating and cursing them is 'superior', i.e., more deserving to be applied than the pronounced meaning (the utterance of the word '*uff*').

(b) *Mafhūm al-muwāfaqah* would provide indefinite indication if justification (*taʿlīl*), determined by the linguistic meaning, and the superiority of implicit indication (*mafhūm*) to the pronounced indication are indefinite. This is exemplified by the penance in the case of murder where the justification is not definite. The Qurʾān states: 'And whosoever kills a believer by mistake, [it is ordained that] he must set free a believing slave, and compensate by 'blood-money' the deceased's family, unless they remit it.'[27] By its pronounced meaning this verse indicates that in cases of manslaughter penance should be paid. At the same time it suggests, by its implicit indication, that a similar penance should be paid for murder because it more deserving of punishment, which is seen as both justification and reason for the legislation (*manāṭ al-ḥukm*) for the prescribed penance.

This conclusion, however, is not definite, because there is the possibility that the reason (*manāṭ al-ḥukm*) for the penance in the case of manslaughter is not punishment but warning about the carelessness which caused the death of an innocent person. The Prophet stated: 'God has indeed disburdened from my followers their error, forgetfulness and that which they were compelled to do against their wishes.'[28]Moreover, there is the question of whether such a penance is a punishment or a form of worship. If it is a punishment, then in the case of murder it is superior to that of manslaughter. If it is worship then they are equal.[29] This indefinite indication caused disagreement among Islamic scholars concerning this and many other legal questions which are based on the indefinite form of *mafhūm al-muwāfaqah*. Accordingly, in the case where *mafhūm al-muwāfaqah* is indefinite, disagreement is possible and acceptable.

The method of indication of *mafhūm al-muwāfaqah*[30]

Islamic scholars generally disagree on whether the indication of *mafhūm al-muwāfaqah* is arrived at directly from the text's words or by use of analogy.[31] The majority of scholars of both *madhhab*s maintain that *mafhūm al-muwāfaqah* is the actual text's implicit indication understood from the text's words. They clearly stated that *mafhūm al-muwāfaqah* is an implicit (*mafhūm*) and not a pronounced (*mantūq*) meaning or analogy (*qiyās*). This is why they viewed a ruling on the basis of *mafhūm al-muwāfaqah* (i.e. *dalālat al-nass* in the Hanafī *madhhab*) as a ruling based on the text, not on analogy. They produced several arguments in support.

(a) The indication of *mafhūm al-muwāfaqah* is stronger than that of analogy because the former is reached by knowledge of the language only,[32] while the latter is not. Sarakhsī[33] pointed out this difference very clearly. He maintained that in the case of *dalālat al-nass* understanding the effective cause, which is common between that which is pronounced and that which is not pronounced (*maskūt 'anh*), depends entirely on knowledge of the language; and that in analogy understanding the effective cause, which is common between *maqīs* and *maqīs 'alayh*, requires further abilities and skills in a *mujtahid*. This difference means that the effective cause, in *dalālat al-nass*, is understood by scholars who possess legal knowledge (*fuqahā'*) and by others who possess the knowledge of the language only. In the case of analogy the effective cause is understood only by scholars who possess legal knowledge.

(b) *Mafhūm al-muwāfaqah* existed before the rules for analogy were set in Islamic law. The Arabs used such expressions to indicate meaning implicitly and more eloquently than they could directly through words. For example they would say, 'This mare cannot catch the dust of that mare.' This expression is more powerful than 'This mare is faster than that mare.' Therefore the indication of *mafhūm al-muwāfaqah* is stronger than that of analogy.

(c) While analogy cannot be based on a new subject (*far'*), *mafhūm al-muwāfaqah* can.

Some scholars, however, maintain that the indication of *mafhūm al-muwāfaqah* is achieved through analogy, not directly from the text's vocabulary. They call that analogy 'analogy of the superior'(*qiyās awlā*)[34] or 'analogy of equals' (*qiyās musāwī*).[35] Both terms are part of clear analogy (*qiyās jalī*), whereby the common effective cause is equally or more evident in a new subject, with respect to an original subject. The equation between the original subject and the new subject is obvious; their discrepancy is dispelled by the evidence. They argue that it is well known in the case of *mafhūm al-muwāfaqah* that the extension of the ruling of the pronounced to the unpronounced depends on an understanding of the effective cause. In order to understand it a form of reasoning is required. That reasoning is nothing but analogy. In the example of: 'say not to them "*uff*", nor shout at them'[36], the original subject is understood to be 'slightest disrespect', and the new subject the beating. Their common effective cause is the prevention of any kind of harm.

This reasoning is in fact an analogy. If no such analysis is undertaken in this case, no legislation would say that beating parents is forbidden. Because this deduction is simple to understand and deduce, it is called clear analogy (*qiyās jalī*). The founder of *uṣūl al-fiqh*, Shāfiʿī, clearly indicates in the first book ever written in this field that *mafhūm al-muwāfaqah* is a clear analogy: 'Analogy is of various kinds, and all are included under the term "analogy". They differ from one to another in the antecedence of the analogy of either one of them, or its source, or the source of both, or the circumstance that one is clearer than the other. The strongest kind [is the deduction] from an order of prohibition by God or the Apostle involving a small quantity. This makes equally strong or stronger an order of prohibition involving a great quantity, owing to the [compelling] reason in the greater quantity. Similarly, the commendation of a small act of piety implies the presumably stronger commendation of a greater act of piety; and an order of permission involving a great quantity renders permissible something involving a smaller quantity.'[37] The examples he cited confirm that he regards *mafhūm al-muwāfaqah* as *qiyās jalī*.[38]

Examples of *mafhūm al-muwāfaqah*

In our discussion of the types of *mafhūm al-muwāfaqah* (and *dalālat al-naṣṣ* in the Ḥanafī *madhhab*) we have offered some illustrations. Here are a few more which indicate that the Companions themselves used *mafhūm al-muwāfaqah* to understand a text.

(a) The Qurʾān states: 'And know that among you there is the Messenger of God. If he were to obey you in most matters, you would surely be in trouble.'[39] Abū Saʿīd al-Khudrī recited this verse and offered his interpretation of the verse[40]: 'This is [an example of] your Prophet to whom revelation was coming and who was accompanied by the best of your leaders. Had he obeyed them [i.e. those who were the best amongst you] in many matters, they could have been in trouble. What about you today [when you cannot equal his Companions]?'[41] From his explanation of the verse it is obvious that al-Khudrī deduced more meanings from the verse than the verse's apparent meaning. He used the agreed meaning because he said that if the first Companions (and amongst them were the best leaders) were not always competent in their advice to the Prophet, how could people do so today, when no one can equal the great leaders and imāms who accompanied the Prophet.

(b) The Qur'ān states: 'So whosoever does an atom's weight of good will see it then, and whosoever does an atom's weight of evil will see it then.'[42] The pronounced apparent meaning is clear. The Muslims have, however, understood from these verses that people will also see the good they did that exceeded an atom's weight, as will those who do evil see more than an atom's weight.[43] This understanding is deduced through *mafhūm al-muwāfaqah*.

(c) The Prophet states: 'He who steals a staff [walking stick] from his brother must return it.'[44] From this tradition it is understood that any stolen good that is more valuable should be returned, too.

The value of *mafhūm al-muwāfaqah*

Adherence to *mafhūm al-muwāfaqah* for Muslims is strictly obligatory, as is implementation of its meaning until another reliable proof suggests otherwise. There is unanimous agreement between Islamic scholars that *mafhūm al-muwāfaqah* is a *ḥujjah* (legal proof) that must be adhered to.[45]

b) *Mafhūm al-Mukhālafah* (Divergent Meaning)

Linguistic definition of *mafhūm al-mukhālafah*

Mafhūm al-mukhālafah is composed of two words: *mafhūm* and *mukhālafah*.[46] *Mafhūm* refers to understood, known, implied, implicit, tacit; notion, connotation; the meaning, or sense, in which a word is understood.[47] *Mukhālafah* refers to opposite, divergent, varying, different; inconsistent, incompatible, contradictory.[48]

The technical definition of *mafhūm al-mukhālafah*

Most Ḥanafī scholars[49] rejected *mafhūm al-mukhālafah*[50] as a method for interpreting authoritative texts and their implications on rulings, unlike the Shāfiʿīs, who accepted it under certain conditions.[51] Āmidī defined *mafhūm al-mukhālafah* as an implicit indication which is opposite to the pronounced indication.[52] Qarrāfī defined *mafhūm al-mukhālafah* as follows: 'Establishing for an unpronounced a ruling opposite to the pronounced.'[53]

In the light of these definitions and the following considerations of the Shāfiʿīs, *mafhūm al-mukhālafah* may be defined as an implicit meaning which indicates that the ruling of the unpronounced is opposite to the ruling of the pronounced.

Disagreement between *Hanafīs* and *Shāfiʿīs*[54]

As mentioned, these two main *madhhabs* of *uṣūl al-fiqh* have disagreed on whether the divergent meaning is acceptable or not.

Hanafīs argued that the divergent meaning should not be applied to authoritative texts because this would lead to distortion. For example, the Qurʾān states: 'Verily, the number of months with God is twelve months [in a year], so God ordained on the Day when He created the heavens and the earth; of them four are sacred: that is the right religion, so do not wrong yourselves therein.'[55] This verse indicates through explicit meaning that four months are sacred, and during these months injustice should be avoided. The divergent meaning, therefore, indicates that injustice is allowed in the rest of the year.[56] This meaning, however, obviously contradicts the purpose of this verse, because *ẓulm* or injustice is always forbidden, regardless of the month in which it is committed. There are many similar examples which may be cited in support of the Hanafīs.

The Shāfiʿīs offered several arguments in support of their views:

(1) The Qurʾān states: 'And whoever of you has not the means to wed free, believing women, may [wed] believing girls from among those [captives and slaves] whom your right hands possess.'[57] The explicit meaning of this verse indicates the ruling that the marriage of a free man with a slave girl is not valid if he has the means to wed free women. Shāfiʿīs argue that Islamic scholars have maintained that the validity of such marriage is stipulated by the inability to marry a free woman. This stipulation is deduced from this verse by the divergent meaning. Therefore, the divergent meaning (*mafhūm al-mukhālafah*) is valid and may be used as a proof.

(2) The Prophet has ordered *zakāh* to be paid on grazing animals: 'for grazing sheep and goats *zakāh* is prescribed.'[58] From this tradition we can understand by the divergent meaning (*mafhūm al-mukhālafah*) that for stall-fed animals, *zakāh* is not obligatory; the verse is restricted to 'grazing' animals. This ruling is accepted by the majority of scholars. They maintain that there is no *zakāh* on stall-fed animals. This opinion is even accepted by Hanafīs who reject *mafhūm al-mukhālafah*.

(3) These restrictions were not mentioned in vain. They were certainly mentioned for a purpose. Therefore, if there is no other reason – or other use like invitation (*targhīb*), intimidation (*tarhīb*), indebtedness (*imtinān*), explanation of the current situation, etc. – than to establish the opposite ruling to the unpronounced, then that indication should be taken into consideration. Accordingly, if the validity of a ruling is dependent on certain

restrictions or attributes attached to the ruling, it would be invalid if that restriction or attribute were lacking. Therefore, whoever maintains a contrary opinion to this principle is indirectly claiming that these restrictions were mentioned in vain and without purpose. However, no Islamic scholar would ever claim this.

It seems to me that divergent meaning (*mafhūm al-mukhālafah*) may be used to deduce legal rulings. The Shāfiʿīs' arguments seem convincing, and their superiority to the arguments of the Ḥanafīs are clearer in the light of the conditions they offer for divergent meaning. These conditions represent, at the same time, a sufficient reply to Ḥanafī scepticism about the divergent meaning in respect of the distortion of authoritative texts. Therefore, divergent meaning may be considered in legal reasoning, but only under the strict guidelines of the Shāfiʿīs.

The conditions for *mafhūm al-mukhālafah*[59]

Shāfiʿī scholars formulate certain conditions for divergent meaning. It becomes acceptable, as a way of deducing legal rulings, only if these conditions are fulfilled.

(1) The non-existence of any particular proof for the actual ruling on a certain matter. If such a proof exists the divergent meaning would not be taken into account because *mafhūm* cannot oppose *manṭūq*. An example of this may be seen in the following verse: 'And when you go forth in the land, it is no sin for you to curtail [your] worship if you fear that the disbelievers may attack you.'[60]

This verse establishes the explicit ruling that Muslims may shorten their prayers if they fear an attack. The divergent meaning of this verse suggests that they may not curtail their worship if there is neither danger or fear.

This divergent meaning, however, is opposed by the pronounced ruling especially related to this matter. The Prophet was asked by ʿUmar about shortening the prayers when there is no danger or fear of an enemy. He replied that shortening is a charity (*ṣadaqah*) from God to the Muslims, and they should accept His charity.[61] Therefore, the divergent meaning may not be considered in this and similar cases for which a particular proof may be found, because it would violate explicit rulings.

(2) Divergent meaning does not exceed the scope of the pronounced meaning. This is illustrated by the following verse: 'And your Lord has decreed that you worship none but Him, and that you be dutiful towards your parents. When one of them or both attain old age in your lifetime, say not to them '*uff*' [in disrespect], nor shout at them, but address them in terms of honour.'[62] 'Say not to them '*uff*' [in disrespect], nor shout at them' may indicate, through divergent meaning, that other kinds of abuse are permis-

sible. The divergent meaning, however, exceeds the scope of the pronounced[63] and is therefore not acceptable.

(3) The text containing a restriction should be independent. If the text is mentioned incidentally (*tabaʿiyyah*) it would not provide the divergent meaning as in the following verse: 'And do not engage in sexual relations with [your wives] while you are in *iʿtikāf* in the mosques.'[64] From the restriction 'in the mosques' one may understand, by the divergent meaning, that *iʿtikāf* in other places does not preclude sexual relations. This restriction, however, does not justify the divergent meaning, since the phrase 'in the mosques' is mentioned incidentally.[65]

(4) The restriction in the given text has no other use except to establish the ruling opposite to the unpronounced. 'Another use' may be anything that indicates that the ruling is unconnected with the restriction and is, therefore, mentioned for another reason like invitation (*targhīb*), intimidation (*tarhīb*), indebtedness (*imtinān*), or to explain a current situation. An example for this condition might be seen in the following verse: 'O you who believe! Eat not *ribā* (usury) doubled and multiplied.'[66] The divergent meaning of this verse suggests that taking usury which is not doubled and multiplied is lawful. This divergent meaning, however, is not acceptable because the restriction 'doubled and multiplied' was mentioned only in order to make repulsion for and establish deterrence from such trading as existed at that time, and which was leading to the loss of all the property of those who were indebted.[67] The proof which supports this claim is found in the verse: 'But if you repent, you shall have your capital sums. Deal not unjustly [by asking more than your capital sums], and you shall not be dealt with unjustly [by receiving less than your capital sums].'[68] In this verse all usury is forbidden, not just that which is doubled and multiplied.

(5) The restriction in the given text is left unmentioned because it represents a common practice, as in the following verse: 'Forbidden to you [for marriage] are: your step daughters under your guardianship.'[69]In this verse the restriction 'under your guardianship' is mentioned only because it was commonplace at the time for the step-daughter to be under the guardianship of her stepfather, and to live in the same house. Therefore, the divergent meaning indicating that the step-daughter under someone else's guardianship is allowed to marry her stepfather is unacceptable. This divergent meaning may not be considered in legal reasoning.

Examples of *mafhūm al-mukhālafah*

Further examples will help us explain the forms of *mafhūm al-mukhālafah*. These forms are the result of restrictions in the pronounced ruling, which affect *mafhūm al-mukhālafah*. Because they are variegated, *mafhūm al-mukhālafah* may appear in different forms. In view of this, Shāfiʿīs mentioned a few forms of *mafhūm al-mukhālafah*.[70] They are:

(1) Indication of the attribute (*ṣifah*). This is an indication of the word, restricted by an attribute, suggesting that an opposite ruling is established in the case of the unpronounced, when the unpronounced is not restricted by the same attribute. An example of this indication may be seen in the following verse: 'O you who believe, if an evil person [*fāsiq*] comes to you with news, verify it, lest you harm people with ignorance and later you become remorseful as regards what you have done.'[71] This verse indicates by its divergent meaning that if the carrier of the news is not an 'evil person', the news he carries must not be verified.

(2) Indication of the condition (*sharṭ*). This is an indication of the word which depends on a condition, such that an opposite ruling may be established in a case of the unpronounced when that condition is not fulfilled. An example of this indication is: 'Lodge them [the divorced women] where you dwell, according to your means, and do not treat them so harshly that they are oppressed. And if they are pregnant, then spend on them till they deliver.'[72] This verse indicates by its words that a man should spend on his divorced wife if she is pregnant. The divergent meaning indicates that if the condition of pregnancy is not fulfilled, the husband is not required to provide maintenance for the wife he finally divorces.

(3) Implication of the extent (*ghāyah*). This is an indication of the text with a ruling the scope of which is demarcated by the text itself, such that an opposite ruling may be established beyond this scope. This indication is illustrated by the following verse: 'They ask you concerning menstruation. Say: that is a hurt, therefore keep away from women during menses and go not unto them until they have purified themselves.'[73]

The pronounced ruling in this verse indicates that the husband should avoid sexual relations with his wife during the menstrual period. This prohibition, however, is limited by the scope (*ghāyah*) 'until they have purified themselves'. The divergent meaning indicates that beyond this scope the ruling would be opposite and the husband may go unto his wife.

(4) Implication of the stated number (*ʿadad*). This is an indication of the text with a ruling restricted by a specific number, such that an opposite ruling may be established in the absence of that specific number. This indication is illustrated by the following verse: 'And those who accuse chaste women without producing four witnesses, flog them eighty times.'[74] This verse on the punishment for slanderous accusation clearly stipulates eighty strikes. The divergent meaning indicates that it is not permissible either to increase or decrease the stated number of strikes.

The value of *mafhūm al-mukhālafah*

As we have seen, Islamic scholars have disagreed on whether or not *mafhūm al-mukhālafah* is acceptable as a way of deducing legal rulings. If one must choose between the two opinions, I would submit that the divergent meaning may be used in deduction, but it must be treated very carefully and under the strictest guidelines and conditions proposed by scholars. If *mafhūm al-mukhālafah* accords with general Islamic rules, it may be a useful method in legal reasoning. Otherwise, the indication of 'divergent meaning' would be indefinite (*zannī al-dalalah*), and that implies disagreement among scholars.

Comparison between the Ḥanafī and the Shāfiʿī approaches to textual indication

A careful examination of the Ḥanafī and Shāfiʿī approaches reveals that, despite some scholarly differences, they have many common characteristics.

Ḥanafī jurists termed the intended indication[75] of the text the explicit meaning (*ibārat al-naṣṣ*), and called non-intended, yet logical and necessary meaning,[76] the alluded meaning, (*ishārat al-naṣṣ*). Both these indications, the explicit and the alluded meaning, are regarded by Ḥanafīs as the pronounced, i.e. that which is indicated by the texts' words.

The Ḥanafīs termed the indication of the text - which is not understood from the text's words but can be understood from the meaning provided by the text's words – as the inferred meaning (*dalālat al-naṣṣ*).[77] This indication is 'what has been understood' (*mafhūm*) from the spirit of the text (or the text's indications), and not what has been explicitly mentioned and pronounced (*manṭūq*).

The indication represents a logical and necessary meaning without which the text is incomplete and fails to achieve its purpose. The Ḥanafīs termed this the required meaning (*iqtiḍāʾ al-naṣṣ*), which may be classified neither as that which is understood from the text's meaning (*mafhūm*) nor as the explicit and pronounced meaning (*manṭūq*).

All these indications are regarded by the Ḥanafīs as the clear (*wāḍiḥ*) indications of the text, which, as we will see, should be followed when there is no reliable proof to the contrary. Moreover, they considered the legal rulings based on these indications to be indicated by the apparent meaning (*ẓāhir*) of the text, and not deduced from the text by way of analogy.

The Shāfiʿī approach to textual indication is different from that of the Ḥanafīs. They divided it into two: the pronounced meaning (*dalālat al-manṭūq*) and the implied meaning (*dalālat al-mafhūm*). The former consists of two types: frank (*ṣarīḥ*)[78] and not frank (*ghayr al-ṣarīḥ*). *Ghayr al-ṣarīḥ* consists[79] of three types: required meaning (*dalālat al-iqtiḍāʾ*), gestured meaning (*dalālat al-īmāʾ*) and alluded meaning (*dalālat al-ishārah*).

The pronounced meaning of the Shāfiʿīs, therefore, includes all three: explicit meaning, alluded meaning and required meaning. These have all been mentioned by the Ḥanafīs.[80] The latter one consists of the agreed meaning (*mafhūm al-muwāfaqah*), which corresponds to the inferred meaning (*dalālat al-naṣṣ*) of the Ḥanafīs, and the divergent meaning (*mafhūm al-mukhālafah*), which the Ḥanafīs reject.

Therefore, the real difference between the two *madhhabs* exists only when the divergent meaning (*mafhūm al-mukhālafah*) is in question. The remaining differences seem more technical than real.

While the Ḥanafī classification of the methods of indication seems more accurate, the approach of the Shāfiʿīs seems to me to be easier to comprehend.

NOTES

1. Ibn Ḥazm, *al-Iḥkām fī Uṣūl al-Aḥkām*, VII:2–4, 53–59.

2. Ibn ʿAbd al-Barr, *Jāmiʿ Bayān al-ʿIlm wa Faḍlih*, II:55–69; Āmidī, *al-Iḥkām fī Uṣūl al-Aḥkām*, IV:272–286; Ibn Qayyim al-Jawziyyah, *Iʿlām al-Muwaqqiʿīn*, I:197; Shawkānī, *Nayl al-Awṭār*, IV:129; Unlike these scholars, Āmidī appears to overlook Dāwūd al-Ẓāhirī's use of a kind of *mafhūm* because he remarked that he did not consider it as a proof (*ḥujjah*). (Āmidī, *al-Iḥkām fī Uṣūl al-Aḥkām*, III:64–65).

3. Āmidī, *al-Iḥkām fī Uṣūl al-Aḥkām*, III:64–65.

4. In Arabic this construction in known as genitive construction (*iḍāfah*), where the first word is the adjunct or governed word (*muḍāf*) and the second is the governing noun of the genitive construction (*muḍāf ilayh*).

5. M.L.ʿA, *al-Muʿjam al-Wasīṭ*, II:704; Lane, *Arabic-English Lexicon*, II:2454; Baʿlabakī, *al-Mawrid*, pp.1084–1085.

6. M.L.ʿA, *al-Muʿjam al-Wasīṭ*, II:1046; Baʿlabakī, *al-Mawrid*, pp.1136.

7. Āmidī, *al-Iḥkām fī Uṣūl al-Aḥkām*, III:466.

8. Āmidī, *al-Iḥkām fī Uṣūl al-Aḥkām*, III:63

9. Shawkānī, *Irshād al-Fuḥūl*, p. 156.

10. This in the Ḥanafī *madhhab* is known as inferred meaning (*dalālat al-naṣṣ*).

11. In a positive or negative sense.

12. This was the reason for the legislation (*manāṭ al-ḥukm*) of the pronounced ruling (*manṭūq*).

13. Qurʾān, XVII:23.

14. Therefore, the prohibition of something in small amounts implies its prohibition in greater amounts.

15. Anṣārī, *Ghāyat al-Wuṣūl*, 37; Ibn Amīr al-Ḥājj, *al-Taqrīr wa al-Taḥbīr*, I:112; Shawkānī, *Irshād al-Fuḥūl*, p. 156.

16. Some scholars of *uṣūl al-fiqh* have disagreed about the difference between *laḥn al-khiṭāb* (parallel meaning) and *faḥwā al-khiṭāb* (superior meaning) (Anṣārī, *Ghāyat al-Wuṣūl*, 37; Ibn Amīr al-Ḥājj, *al-Taqrīr wa al-Taḥbīr*, I:112; Shawkānī, *Irshād al-Fuḥūl*, p. 156).

17. Moreover, Zarkashī mentioned that this is the opinion of the majority of Shāfiʿī scholars. This is opposed by Hindī's comments that the majority stipulated that the implicit is superior to the pronounced (Shawkānī, *Irshād al-Fuḥūl*, p. 156). Beside Shāfiʿī scholars, the Ḥanafīs do not stipulate its superiority. Their opinions are discussed under the title 'Dalālat al-Naṣṣ'.

18. 'Verily, those who unjustly eat up the property of orphans eat up only fire into their bellies, and they will be burnt in a blazing Fire!' (Qur'ān, IV:10).

19. Shawkānī, *Irshād al-Fuḥūl*, p. 156.

20. That is, a religious obligation for which the reason for legislation (*manāṭ al-ḥukm*) has not been discovered.

21. Proving the extension of the pronounced ruling to the unpronounced.

22. This is the reason why the Ḥanafī scholars termed it the inferred meaning of the text (*dalālat al-naṣṣ*).

23. Ījī, *Mukhtaṣar al-Muntahā*, II:173.

24. In definite *mafhūm al-muwāfaqah*, this superiority is certain and definite, while in indefinite *mafhūm al-muwāfaqah* it is uncertain and indefinite.

25. In definite *mafhūm al-muwāfaqah*, this existence is certain and definite, while in indefinite *mafhūm al-muwāfaqah* it is uncertain and indefinite because there is the possibility that another effective cause is intended.

26. Qur'ān, XVII:23.

27. Qur'ān, IV:92.

28. Ibn Mājah, *Sunan*, I:659 (no. 2045).

29. This is important because some would not consider it *mafhūm al-muwāfaqah* if they were equal.

30. This question is very important for some legal schools when prescribed legal punishments and penance are in question. The Ḥanafī school, for example, does not establish *ḥudūd* and *kaffārāt* through analogy but through *mafhūm al-muwāfaqah*. Moreover, the meaning reached by *mafhūm al-muwāfaqah* may be an original subject (*aṣl*) for a new subject (*farʿ*); while the meaning reached by analogy cannot be an original subject. Early scholars of the Ḥanafī *madhhab*, like Bazdawī in *Kashf al-Asrār* (I:73–74) and Sarakhsī in *Uṣūl al-Sarakhsī* (I:241–242), tried to explain the difference between *dalālat al-naṣṣ* and *qiyās*. Sarakhsī discussed this matter extensively. He recommended that because of these differences Ḥanafī scholars establish punishments and penances by *dalālat al-naṣṣ*, and not analogy. For other schools, however, this question was less important because it did not affect their legal reasoning. For example, the Shāfiʿī *madhhab* determined punishments and penances through both analogy and *mafhūm al-muwāfaqah*. Therefore, the difference did not affect them at all. This is probably the reason why some Shāfiʿī scholars declared that it was more verbal (literal) than real. (Bunānī, *Ḥāshiyat al-Bunānī ʿalā Jamʿ al-Jawāmiʿ*, I:245). However, they were incorrect in this, because this difference made a great impact on legal reasoning in the Ḥanafī *madhhab*.

31. Bukhārī, *Kashf al-Asrār*, I: 73–74; Sarakhsī, *Uṣūl al-Sarākhsī*, I:241; Āmidī, *al-Iḥkām fī Uṣūl al-Aḥkām*, III:65–66; Subkī, *Jamʿ al-Jawāmiʿ*, I:242; Ījī, *Mukhtaṣar al-Muntahā*, II:173.

32. Cf. above examples.

33. Sarakhsī, *Uṣūl al-Sarākhsī*, I:241

34. The effective cause in this analogy is more evident in the new case than in the original case.

35. The effective cause in this analogy is equally effective in both the new and the original case.

36. Qur'ān, XVII:23.

37. Shāfiʿī, *al-Risālah*, pp. 387–388.

38. Shāfiʿī, *al-Risālah*, pp. 388–389.

39. Qur'ān, XLIX:7.

40. Tirmidhī, *al-Jāmiᶜ al-Ṣaḥīḥ*, V:362–363 (no. 3269).

41. Therefore, you also should not be obeyed.

42. Qur'ān, XCIX:7–8.

43. See the interpretation of these verses in *Tafsīr Ibn Kathīr* and other relevant books which deal with the interpretation of the Qur'ān.

44. Tirmidhī, *Sunan*, IV:402 (no.2160).

45. Āmidī, *al-Iḥkām fī Uṣūl al-Aḥkām*, III:64.

46. This is the genitive construction (*iḍāfah*) where the first word is the adjunct or governed word (*muḍāf*) and the second is the governing noun of a genitive construction (*muḍāf ilayh*)

47. M.L.ᶜA, *al-Muᶜjam al-Wasīt*, II:704; Lane, *Arabic-English Lexicon*, II:2454; Baᶜlabakī, *al-Mawrid*, pp. 1084–1085.

48. M.L.ᶜA, *al-Muᶜjam al-Wasīt*, II:251; Wehr, *Arabic-English Dictionary*, p. 258.

49. Bukhārī, *Kashf al-Asrār*, II:253.

50. They reject it only when authoritative texts are in question (Ibn Amīr al-Ḥājj, *al-Taqrīr wa al-Taḥbīr*, I:177).

51. Ghazālī, *al-Mustaṣfā*, p. 264; Qarrāfī, *Sharḥ Tanqīḥ al-Fuṣūl*, p. 270; Āmidī, *al-Iḥkām fī Uṣūl al-Aḥkām*, III:67.

52. Āmidī, *al-Iḥkām fī Uṣūl al-Aḥkām*, III:67.

53. Qarrāfī, *Sharḥ Tanqīḥ al-Fuṣūl*, p. 55.

54. Bukhārī, *Kashf al-Asrār*, II:253; Qarrāfī, *Sharḥ Tanqīḥ al-Fuṣūl*, p. 55.

55. Qur'ān, IX:36.

56. At the same time, this would mean that oppression was forbidden because of the time in which it was committed. This is entirely wrong.

57. Qur'ān, IV:25.

58. Bukhārī, *al-Jāmiᶜ al-Ṣaḥīḥ*, II:124 (24:38).

59. Ījī, *Mukhtaṣar al-Muntahā*, III:173; Tilmisānī, *Miftāḥ al-Wuṣūl*, p. 66; Shawkānī, *Irshād al-Fuḥūl*, 179.

60. Qur'ān, IV:101.

61. Ibn Kathīr, *Tafsīr al-Qur'ān al-ᶜAẓīm*, I:723.

62. Qur'ān, XVII:23.

63. Because physical abuse, hitting, punching, etc imply greater abuse than a word of disrespect.

64. Qur'ān, II:187.

65. Which apparently has no intended bearing on the meaning.

66. Qur'ān, III:130.

67. Ibn Kathīr, *Tafsīr al-Qur'ān al-ᶜAẓīm*, I:536.

68. Qur'ān, II:279; Ibn Kathīr, *Tafsīr al-Qur'ān al-ᶜAẓīm*, I:442.

69. Qur'ān, IV:23.

70. Āmidī, *al-Iḥkām fī Uṣūl al-Aḥkām*, III:67–69; Qarāfī, *Sharḥ Tanqīḥ al-Fuṣūl*, p. 55–61.

71. Qur'ān, XLIX:6.

72. Qur'ān, LXV:6.

73. Qur'ān, II:222.

74. Qur'ān, XXIV:4.

75. The intended indication represents the principle or secondary theme and purpose of the text.

76. Which necessarily accompanies the meaning that represents the intended meaning (the principle or secondary theme).

77. Some of them called it 'the indication of the indication' (*dalālat al-dalālah* or *faḥwā al-khiṭāb*) or agreed meaning (*mafhūm al-muwāfaqah*).

78. *Ṣarīḥ* includes the explicit meaning (*ʿibarāt al-naṣṣ*) mentioned by the Ḥanafīs.

79. From this division it appears that *ghayr al-ṣarīḥ* includes two types of indications mentioned by the Ḥanafīs: alluded meaning and required meaning.

80. Abū Zahrah stated that the fourfold Ḥanafī division of *dalālāt* can be classified under *dalālat al-manṭūq* (Abū Zahrah, *Uṣūl al-Fiqh*, p. 116). However, it would be more accurate to say that some of them are derived from *mafhūm* – such as the inferred meaning (*dalālat al-naṣṣ*) – and *mafhūm* is derived from *manṭūq*.

PART II

Clarity and Ambiguity in Words
(*al-Wuḍūḥ wa'l-Ibhām fī'l-Alfāẓ*)

Introduction

A *mujtahid* who approaches an authoritative text must examine it thoroughly in order to discern as accurately as possible the author's intention and to derive the intended legal rulings. To assist him in this task, scholars have developed scientific rules for the disciplines of *ʿulūm al-Qurʾān*, *ʿulūm al-ḥadīth*, *uṣūl al-fiqh*, etc. These rules facilitate legal reasoning (*ijtihād*) and minimise error. In this piece of research we are basically concerned with the linguistic rules developed by scholars of *uṣūl al-fiqh*. A study of the text and the application of these rules are one stage in the process of legal reasoning.

When the *mujtahid* reads an authoritative text he either understands it or he does not. If he understands it well and has no doubts about what he understands, the text is said to be clear (*wāḍiḥ*). If he has doubts, the text is said to be ambiguous and unclear (*mubham*). Accordingly, scholars have classified words into two main categories: clear and unclear words. The former convey meanings which are clear and intelligible, requiring no interpretation (*taʾwīl*)[1] beyond their obvious import. The rulings deduced from authoritative texts that provide this kind of clear meaning constitute the basis of obligation. They are obligatory and, according to Islamic belief, should be implemented until a reliable proof suggests otherwise. Unclear words, on the other hand, have meanings which are incomplete, ambiguous, and require further explanation and clarification to be understood. These words cannot on their own justify obligation but need further clarification and explanation from other reliable sources.

NOTES

1. We will see that some of the words (categories), while relatively clear, may be open to interpretation if there is a reliable proof for it.

Introduction to the *Ḥanafī* Approach to Clear (*wāḍiḥ*) Words

What the *mujtahid* understands from *wāḍiḥ* does not exhibit uniform clarity. This is because the meaning of clear words may be subject to:

(a) specification of meaning (*takhṣīṣ*),

(b) interpretation beyond the obvious import (*ta'wīl*),

(c) abrogation (*naskh*)

(d) and a different reason for revelation from the ruling deduced from the text which directly affects the clarity of textual indications.

Based on their degree of textual clarity, Ḥanafī scholars have classified the explicit into four categories: *ẓāhir*, *naṣṣ*, *mufassar* and *muḥkam*.

These distinguish how clear words may be interpreted according to their obvious sense (*ta'wīl*) and determine whether or not they are susceptible and open to abrogation. Furthermore, they provide the *mujtahid* with guidelines for resolving possible conflicts between the various categories of words. Next we will attempt to explore these categories, their degrees of clarity and their effect on the deduction of legal rulings (*istinbāt al-aḥkām*) from the authoritative texts. The first category is *ẓāhir*.

CHAPTER 7

The Apparent
(al-Ẓāhir)

The linguistic definition of *ẓāhir*

Ẓāhir refers to apparent, plain, manifest, evident; *ẓahara ẓuhūr*, to appear and become clear and evident after being concealed; *ẓāhiran*, outwardly and apparently;[1] *fī'l-ẓāhir*, in appearance.[2]

The technical definition of *ẓāhir*

Ḥanafī scholars have proffered various definitions of *ẓāhir*. Dabbūsī defined *ẓāhir* as 'whatever becomes apparent to a listener by his hearing only'.[3] Bazdawī concentrates on the 'wording' (*bi ṣīghatih*) as the defining element. He said, 'It is a name for any speech the aim of which became apparent to a listener by its wording.'[4]

Sarakhsī excludes from his definition the use of 'reason' and analysis in the definition of *ẓāhir*: 'What can be understood by pure hearing without thinking. It precedes the mind because it reflects the meaning by which it is employed.'[5]

According to Nasafī, *ẓāhir* is the name for speech whose aim is apparent to a listener by its wording.[6] While to Ibn al-Humām *ẓāhir* shows its linguistic meaning autonomously.[7]

These definitions resemble each other. At first glance, the Ḥanafī scholars appear to have the same opinion about *ẓāhir*. However, when we consider how they relate *ẓāhir* and *naṣṣ*, it becomes clear that they are different in their approach to *ẓāhir*.

On these definitions and the Ḥanafī principle that *ẓāhir* is open to a specification of meaning (*takhṣīṣ*), interpretation beyond the obvious meaning (*ta'wīl*) and abrogation (*naskh*), we can formulate the following definition: '*ẓāhir* is an expression with clearly stated meaning which requires no internal [textual] or external evidence [*qarīnah*], with a possible interpretation beyond the obvious import [*ta'wīl*],[8] and abrogation [*naskh*][9].' Therefore, *ẓāhir* has a clear meaning and yet is open to an alternative interpretation. This is mainly because its clear literal meaning is not harmonious with the context in which it occurs -because *ẓāhir* is not the principal theme of the text.

Examples of *ẓāhir*

(a) The Qur'ān states: 'Those who consume *ribā* [usury] will not stand [on the Day of Resurrection] except like a person who has been beaten by Satan. That is because they say: "Trading is just like usury", whereas God has permitted trading and forbidden usury.'[10] The apparent (*ẓāhir*) meaning of this verse indicates that usury is forbidden. This meaning is clear, but it is not the principle theme of the verse.

The purpose for which this verse was revealed is to deny what some people claimed, that trading and usury are alike.[11] Although this verse was not revealed to give a legal ruling (*ḥukm*) on the two, but to deny their similarity, the apparent (*ẓāhir*) meaning of 'God has permitted trading and forbidden *ribā*', clearly indicates that trading is permitted and usury forbidden. This indication is deducible from the text without further thought and without use of any internal textual, or external evidence (*qarīnah*). It is *ẓāhir* because it is clear and its apparent meaning is not the main purpose of the verse.

(b) The Qur'ān states: 'And if you fear that you shall not be able to deal justly with the orphan-girls, then marry [other] women, of your choice, two or three, or four. But if you fear that you shall not be able to deal justly [with them], then only one or [the captives and the slaves] that your right hands possess. That will better prevent you from committing injustice.'[12]

This verse has an apparent meaning which relates to legitimate marriage ('then marry [other] women'). This is the apparent (*ẓāhir*) meaning because its meaning is clear. Understanding this meaning does not depend on textual or external evidence (*qarīnah*), and the verse was not revealed for the purpose indicated by the apparent meaning, but to explain other matters.[13]

(c) The Qur'ān states: 'O Prophet! When you divorce women, divorce them at their ʿ*iddah* [prescribed periods], and count [accurately] their ʿ*iddah* [periods].'[14] According to the *ḥadīth* this verse was revealed in order to explain the period during which wives may be legally divorced.[15] This verse, however, carries another apparent instruction for Muslim not to divorce more than once. This legal ruling is deduced from the apparent meaning, which is not the main purpose of the verse. Therefore, it is *ẓāhir*.

The value of *ẓāhir*

Adherence to *ẓāhir* should be a strict obligation (*wājib*), and its obvious indications must be followed in legal reasoning because it provides definite indication.[16] This adherence would be obligatory until another reliable proof indicates otherwise. The basic rule is that the apparent meaning of the word should not be dismissed except by a reliable proof[17] that suggests an alternative interpretation beyond the obvious sense (*ta'wīl*) which appears in greater harmony with the intention of the Lawgiver.

NOTES

1. *Uṣūl al-fiqh* draws no parallel between *ẓāhir* and *bāṭin*. The parallel is always between *khafī* and *ẓāhir*. The term *bāṭin* (essence, interior nature) is normally found in *ʿilm al-kalām*.

2. M.L. ʿA, *al-Muʿjam al-Wasīṭ*, II:578; Lane, *Arabic-English Lexicon*, II:1926–30; EI², I:1039, I:1099; Baʿlabakī, *al-Mawrid*, p. 736.

3. Dabbusi, *al-Asrār fī al-Uṣūl wa al-Furūʿ fī Taqwīm Adillat al-Sharʿ*, I:260.

4. Bukhārī, *Kashf al-Asrār*, I:46.

5. Sarakhsī, *Uṣul al-Sarakhsī*, I:164

6. Nasafī, *Kashf al-Asrār*, I:205. This means that there is no need for analysis to understand its meaning, and no textual or external evidence (*qarīnah*) was added to the text. However, the listener has to be fluent in the language (*min ahl al-lisān*). (Mayhawī, *Sharḥ Nūr al-Anwār ʿalā al-Manār*, :205–206).

7. Ibn Amīr al-Ḥājj, *al-Taqrīr wa al-Taḥbīr*, I:146; Bādshāh, *Taysīr al-Taḥrīr*, I:136.

8. This means that a) its literal meaning may be abandoned in favour of metaphorical meaning, which seems to be closer to the intention of the lawgiver; b) when *ẓāhir* provides a general indication it may be specified; c) when *ẓāhir* is the absolute (*muṭlaq*) it may be qualified.

9. According to the Islamic beliefs abrogation was possible during the time of the revelation only.

10. Qur'ān, II:275.

11. Ibn Kathīr, *Tafsīr al-Qur'ān al-ʿAẓīm*, I:437.

12. Qur'ān, IV:3.

13. The principal themes of this verse are a limit of four wives and a prohibition against men marrying more than one woman if they fear they cannot deal with them justly. These rulings are considered *naṣṣ* because they are clear and represent the main purpose of the text. The proof that they represent the main purpose of the text is in the *ḥadīth* narrated by ʿUrwah b. al-Zubayr, who asked ʿĀʾishah regarding God's words: 'if you fear that you shall not be able to deal justly with the orphans.' She said, 'O son of my sister! An orphan girl used to be under the care of a guardian with whom she shared property. Her guardian, being attracted by her wealth and beauty, may intend to marry her without giving her a just *mahr*. Guardians are forbidden to marry, unless they can act justly with girls and give them the maximum *mahr* their peers might get. God commands them, therefore, to marry the women who seem good to them, rather than those orphans girls.' (Bukhārī, *al-Jāmiʿ al-Ṣaḥīḥ*, V:177 (65:4:1).

14. Qur'ān, LXV:1.

15. It was narrated by ʿAbdullāh b. ʿUmar that, when the Prophet was still alive, he

divorced his wife while she was menstruating. ʿUmar b. al-Khaṭṭāb asked the Prophet about this. The Prophet replied, 'Command [your son] to take her back and keep her until she is clean and then wait until her next period when she will be clean again. If he wishes to stay with her, he may; if he wishes to divorce her he may do so before the marriage is consummated. This is the prescribed period which God has fixed for the women meant to be divorced.' (Bukhārī, *al-Jāmiʿ al-Ṣaḥīḥ*, VI:163 [68:1].

16. Hence, the verification of *ḥudūd* and *kaffārāt* by *ẓāhir* is valid, because *ẓāhir* is only open to the possibility of metaphor (*majāz*). However, some scholars maintain that although the apparent meaning should be followed, the legal ruling which rests on *ẓāhir* is not definite (*qaṭʿī*) because *ẓāhir* accepts *taʾwīl* (*takhṣīṣ*, *taqyīd*, *majāz*) and *naskh*. They argue that these possibilities are far fetched and do not rest on valid proofs (*adillah sharʿiyyah*). Consequently, the apparent meaning is not considered valid. (Taftāzānī, *Sharḥ al-Talwīḥ ʿalā al-Tawḍīḥ*, I:126; Mayhawī, *Sharḥ Nūr al-Anwār ʿalā al-Manār*, I:206). In my opinion this disagreement has no practical effect, because all agree on the duty to implement the indefinite indications (*ẓunūn*), which cannot be beneath that level.

17. Ibn Nujaym, *al-Ashbāh wa al-Naẓāʾir*, p. 145; Lubnānī, *Sharḥ al-Majallah*, p. 24.

CHAPTER 8

The Explicit
(*al-Naṣṣ*)

The linguistic definition of *naṣṣ*

Naṣṣ refers to explicit, declared, manifest; a religious legal term. The root means 'to raise', especially 'to elevate the thing to make it visible to all'. *Naṣṣ* is also the author's original text. In the technical vocabulary of *uṣūl al-fiqh*, the term refers to either the Qur'ān or the *ḥadīth* text.[1]

The technical definition of *naṣṣ*

The Ḥanafī scholars offered similar definitions of *naṣṣ*: Dabbūsī defined *naṣṣ* in the following terms: 'It clarifies *ẓāhir* further when compared with it.'[2] Nasafī: '*Naṣṣ* is that which is clearer than *ẓāhir* by virtue of the meaning of speech, not the text itself.[3]

Bazdawī emphasises the meaning given by the speaker: '*Naṣṣ* is that which is clearer than *ẓāhir* because of the meaning conveyed by the speaker, not by the text itself.'[4] Like Bazdawī, Sarakhsī defines *naṣṣ* from the perspective of the speaker's evidence. 'It is what becomes more explicit through the evidence (*qarīnah*) given by the speaker.'[5]

Naṣṣ refers to the speaker's purpose, whereas *ẓāhir* is not what the speaker means. This condition is widely acknowledged amongst Ḥanafī scholars,[6] who stipulate (*yashtariṭūn*) that a *naṣṣ* be stated for the purpose of its literally apparent meaning,[7] and that *ẓāhir* not be stated for the purpose of the text's apparent meaning. For example, someone may say: 'The people came to me.' This is a *naṣṣ* about their coming. On the other hand, the statement 'I saw so-and-so when the people came to me', is a *naṣṣ* about seeing someone or something, because it is the principal theme of the text; and it is *ẓāhir* about the people who came, because this is not the main purpose of the text.

According to Ḥanafī scholars, who stipulate that the indication of *naṣṣ* is the principal theme of the text,[8] a proper and comprehensive definition of *naṣṣ* would be that it is 'an expression which provides a clear meaning representing the principal theme of the text; yet it is susceptible and open to the possibility of interpretation beyond the obvious import[9] and abrogation.[10]

Examples of *naṣṣ*

(a) The Qur'ān states: 'That is because they say: "Trading is only like *ribā* [usury],' whereas God has permitted trade and forbidden *ribā* [usury].'[11] This verse is *naṣṣ* in its denial that trade and usury are alike in respect of lawfulness and prohibition,[12] because this is what it clearly means and it was revealed for that purpose. It was revealed in response to those people who claimed that trade and usury are alike, by saying 'Trading is only like *ribā*'. So *naṣṣ* surpasses the clarity of *ẓāhir* (the lawfulness of the trading and the prohibition of usury) by the meaning given by the Lawgiver – that additional meaning is the purpose (*sabab al-nuzūl*) for which the verse was revealed[13] not by the text itself.

(b) The Qur'ān states: 'And divorced women shall hold themselves back [for marriage] for three menstrual periods.'[14] This text is *naṣṣ* in regard to the period (*ʿiddah*) during which a divorcee[15] is not allowed to remarry. It is *naṣṣ* because this apparent meaning of the verse is the purpose of the Lawgiver and it represents its principal theme.[16]

(c) The Qur'ān states: 'And if you fear that you shall not be able to deal justly with the orphan–girls, then marry [other] women of your choice, two or three, or four; but if you fear that you shall not be able to deal justly [with them], then marry only one, or [the captives and the slaves] that your right hands possess. That will better prevent you from doing injustice.'[17]

As previously mentioned, this verse contains the apparent meaning which relates to legalising the marriage of women ('then marry [other] women'). This meaning is apparent because it is not the main purpose of the verse. This same verse, however, provides another two clear meanings, which constitute the principal theme of the verse – namely the limitation of four wives and prohibition against more than one wife if there is a fear that they will not be treated justly. Therefore, these two meanings are *naṣṣ* because they are clear and they are the main purpose of the verse. The proofs for such a statement are as follows:

(1) The Qur'ān mentions the first number, then the next, then the next, and says: 'But if you fear that you shall not be able to deal justly [with them], then only one.' It is obvious that the question here is one of number because the Qur'ān states 'if you fear [...] then only one'.

(2) Ḥasan and Ḍaḥḥāk argued that this verse abrogated the norm that

existed at the time of *jāhiliyyah* and in early Islam, when men could marry any number of free women. It placed a limit of four.[18]

(3) The lawfulness of marriage was known before this verse was revealed. It was known from other verses and from the practice of the Prophet. However, the limitation on the number of wives was unknown, and one of *fiqh*'s rules was: 'Establishing [a new meaning] has preference over the confirmation [of an existing meaning].'[19]

(d) The Qur'ān states: 'O Prophet! When you divorce women, divorce them at their *ʿiddah* [prescribed periods], and count [accurately] their *ʿiddah* [periods].'[20]

This verse carries an apparent instruction to Muslims not to divorce more than once. This legal ruling (*ḥukm*) is deduced from the apparent meaning of the text. It is *ẓāhir* because it is not the principal theme of the verse.

This verse, however, contains another clear meaning, which explains the legal time for having a divorce ('divorce them at their *ʿiddah* [prescribed periods], and count [accurately] their *ʿiddah* [periods]').[21] This meaning is the purpose of the verse and thus *naṣṣ*, because the reason for revelation (*sabab al-nuzūl*) increases the limpidity of the text. That additional meaning came from the Lawgiver and not from within the text itself.

Upon comparison *ẓāhir* and *naṣṣ* are clearly based on apparent meaning, although *naṣṣ* has an additional meaning which increases its limpidity. This additional meaning is the motive for revelation (*sabab al-nuzūl*). Hence *naṣṣ* was revealed for its meaning, and its indication represents the principal theme of the text.

The value of *naṣṣ*

Strict adherence to *naṣṣ* is a duty and obligation until a reliable proof indicates otherwise.[22]

NOTES

1. M.L. ʿA., *al-Muʿjam al-Wasīṭ*, II:296; Lane, *Arabic-English Lexicon*, II:2797–99; EI, VI:881; Baʿlabakī, *al-Mawrid*, p. 1173.

2. Dabbūsī, *al-Asrār fī al-Uṣūl wa al-Furūʿ fī Taqwīm Adillat al-Sharʿ*, I:260.

3. Nasafī, *Kashf al-Asrār*, I:206.

4. Bazdawī, *Uṣūl al-Bazdawī*, I:46.

5. Sarakhsī, *Uṣūl al-Sarakhsī*, I:164.

6. Nasafī, *Kashf al-Asrār*, I:206.

7. That is, the main purpose and the principal theme of the text.

8. Earlier Ḥanafī scholars did not stipulate this condition (Taftāzānī, *Sharḥ al-Talwīḥ ʿalā al-Tawḍīḥ*, I:124).

9. The possibility of *ta'wīl* in the case of *naṣṣ* is less likely because its indication represents the principal theme of the text. This is not the case with the *ẓāhir*. From the definition, however, we may see that *naṣṣ* is open to *ta'wīl* and *naskh*. For example, take the general indication of the verse: 'Forbidden to you [for food] are dead animals, blood.'(Qur'ān, V:3). This has been qualified by the verse 'Say [O Muḥammad]: For the one who wishes to eat it, I find nothing forbidden to eat in that which has been revealed to me, unless it is carrion or blood poured forth [after the slaughter]...' (Qur'ān, VI:145). This is because in the second verse blood is described as 'blood poured forth'. Furthermore, these two verses were both qualified by the tradition where the Prophet says that two types of dead carcasses, fish and locust, are permitted for consumption as well as two types of blood, liver and spleen (Tabrīzī, *Mishkāt al-Maṣābīḥ*, II:410 (no. 1567).

10. In *fiqh*, *naṣṣ* carried a wider meaning, and means definitive text or ruling of the Qur'ān or Sunnah. Hence, *naṣṣ* has two meanings: with respect to *ẓāhir*, *mufassar* and *mukḥam*; and in reference to every Qur'ānic verse and every *ḥadīth* of the Prophet. One may call the Qur'ān and *ḥadīth* *naṣṣ*, as *ẓāhir*, *naṣṣ* and *mufassar*, or say that this legal ruling is established by *naṣṣ*, not by analogy (*qiyās*)

11. Qur'ān, II:275.

12. Trading is lawful (*ḥalāl*) and the usury is prohibited (*ḥarām*). *Ḥalāl* and *ḥarām* are antonyms and therefore dissimilar.

13. Ibn Kathīr, *Tafsīr al-Qur'ān al-ʿAẓīm*, I:436–437.

14. Qur'ān, II:226.

15. One may note that there are some exceptions. Some divorcees are not included in this legal ruling and their waiting period is shorter. (Ibn Kathīr, *Tafsīr al-Qur'ān al-ʿAẓīm*, I:363).

16. Ibn Kathīr, *Tafsīr al-Qur'ān al-ʿAẓīm*, I:363–364.

17. Qur'ān, IV:3

18. Ṭabarī, *Jāmiʿ al-Bayān ʿan Ta'wīl Āy al-Qur'ān*, VII:532; Qurṭubī, *al-Jāmiʿ li Aḥkām al-Qur'ān*, V:12.

19. Isnawī, *al-Tamhīd*, p. 167; Suyūṭī, *al-Ashbāh wa al-Naẓā'ir*, p. 135; Ibn Nujaym, *al-Ashbāh wa al-Naẓā'ir*, p. 149.

20. Qur'ān, LXV:1.

21. The proof that this verse was revealed in order to explain when to legally divorce is the *ḥadīth* where the Prophet said to ʿUmar b. al-Khaṭṭāb, ' Order him [i.e., his son ʿAbdullāh b. ʿUmar, who had divorced his wife while she was menstruating] to take her back and stay with her until she is clean, and then to wait until her next period and she is clean again. Thereupon, if he wishes to stay with her, he may do so; if he wishes to divorce her, he may divorce her before consummation – And that is the prescribed period which God has fixed for women who are to be divorced.' (Bukhārī, *al-Jāmiʿ al-Ṣaḥīḥ*, VI:163 [68:1]).

22. Bazdawī, *Uṣūl al-Bazdawī*, I:48; Nasafī, *Kashf al-Asrār*, I:207.

CHAPTER 9

The Explained
(*al-Mufassar*)

The linguistic definition of *mufassar*

Mufassar refers to something explained, expounded, interpreted, disclosed. In the technical vocabulary of *uṣūl al-fiqh*, the term refers to a text in either the Qur'ān or the *ḥadīth* which is explained by a meaning included in the text or taken from other sources.[1]

The technical definition of *mufassar*

Bazdawī defined *mufassar* as '[a text] that is clearer than *naṣṣ* due to a meaning included in the text[2] or taken from other sources, so that is ambiguous [*mujmal*], but supplemented by a definite explanation [*bayān qaṭ'ī*][3] that closes the possibility of *ta'wīl*; or is taken to be *lafẓ 'āmm* [a general word] supplemented by certain explanations that precludes the possibility of *takhṣīṣ*'.[4] Sarakhsī defined *mufassar* as 'a name given to the unconcealed whose aim is revealed in a way[5] that leaves no possibility for *ta'wīl*'.[6] Nasafī offered the following definition: '*Mufassar* is [a text] that is clearer than *naṣṣ* in a way that leaves no possibility[7] for *ta'wīl* and *takhṣīṣ*.'[8]

From these definitions, the Ḥanafī school appears to consider as *mufassar* any expression whose meaning is so obvious and clear that it is spontaneously understood. That clear meaning and the legal ruling(s) deduced from this provision are the real purpose of the speech, as confirmed in other sources. These facts leave no room for interpretation beyond the obvious import and the specification of meaning (*takhṣīṣ*). There remains only the possibility of abrogation (*naskh*), which may have occurred in the lifetime of the Prophet. So compared to *ẓāhir* and *naṣṣ*, a *mufassar* is unmistakably clearer, because it is not open to the possibilities of *ta'wīl* and *takhṣīṣ*. *Mufassar* has two sources:

(a) the mood itself if it is not susceptible and open to *ta'wīl* and *takhṣīṣ*, as in the case of numbers,[9] and,

(b) the definitive explanation (*tafsīr qaṭʿī*) supplemented by the Lawgiver, in the same or in other texts, if that explanation removes ambiguity from the provision, by clarifying His intentions completely, so that the provision precludes *ta'wīl* and *takhṣīṣ*.

Examples of *mufassar*

(a) The Qur'ān states: 'God's command regarding your children's [inheritance]; to the male, a portion equal to that of two females; if [there are] only daughters, two or more, their share is two thirds of the inheritance; if only one, her share is half. For the parents, a sixth of the inheritance to each if the deceased left a child; if no children, and the parents are the only heirs, the mother has a third.'[10] This verse and others prescribe specific shares for legal heirs. They have fixed proportions which are *mufassar* in nature, because their values are unchangeable. Therefore, there is no possibility for an interpretation beyond the obvious meaning, and every legal heir is entitled to his or her precise share of inheritance.

(b) About the punishment for slander, the Qur'ān says: 'And those who accuse chaste women and fail to produce four witnesses [to support their allegations], flog them with eighty stripes.'[11]; and about the sentence for fornication[12]: 'The woman and the man guilty of illicit sexual relations, flog each of them a hundred stripes.'[13]

Both 'eighty' (*thamānīn*) and 'hundred' (*mi'ah*) are numbers, and numbers do not assume greater or lesser value than what is stated. Therefore, numbers are always counted as *mufassar*. The first verse clearly means that the slanderers should be flogged with eighty stripes; the second verse clearly means that adulterers should be flogged with a hundred stripes. These definitive (*qaṭʿī*) meanings are not open to *ta'wīl* or *takhṣīṣ*.

(c) Words with general meanings (*alfāẓ al-ʿumūm*) that are followed by an explanation which precludes specification and interpretation beyond the obvious import are *mufassar*. The Qur'ān states: 'So the angels prostrated themselves, all of them together.'[14] 'The angels' is a general term (*lafẓ ʿāmm*) which is susceptible and open to specification. It can mean the majority of the angels, not all of them. The possibility of specification, however, is excluded by the term 'all of them' (*kulluhum*).

At the same time, 'all of them' is susceptible to different interpretations. It might mean that the angels prostrated themselves in groups and at different times, but these meanings are excluded by the word 'together' (*ajmaʿīn*).[15] The words which carry general meanings are *mufassar* when they are followed by an explanation which excludes *takhṣīṣ* and *ta'wīl*.

(d) The ambivalent mood (*ṣighah mujmalah*) becomes *mufassar* when followed by a definitive explanation from the Lawgiver[16] which removes ambiguity from that mood and closes the possibility of *ta'wīl*.

The Qur'ān states: 'Truly man was created anxious; discontented when evil touches him and niggardly when good touches him. Except for worshippers who remain constant in their worship.'[17] Aḥmad b. Yaḥya was asked what 'anxious' (*halaᶜ*) in this verse means and he answered: 'It is explained by God and there is no explanation that is clearer than His. When evil touches him, a human being becomes fretful. When he gains something good, he is stingy and tries to keep everything for himself.'[18] So 'discontented' when evil touches him' explains 'anxious' (*halūᶜan*).

There are plenty of verses which are ambivalent: 'And be steadfast in prayer [*ṣalāh*] and give alms [*zakāh*].'[19]; 'Pilgrimage [*ḥajj*] to the House is a duty men owe to God.'[20]; 'O you who believe! Fasting [*ṣiyām*] is prescribed for you.'[21]

The words *ṣalāh*, *zakāh*, *ḥajj*, *ṣiyām* are ambivalent. Upon closer examination of the authoritative texts, we find that the Lawgiver used these words for special meanings, which are sometimes almost entirely different from their literal and original meanings. So far, the terms referred to had been clear before becoming ambiguous, since they later came to indicate more than one meaning. Consequently, the verses in which they appear are ambiguous. The Prophet, however, explained their meanings in his own words and deeds, providing both verbal and practical instructions. He prayed (performed *ṣalāh* with his Companions) and later said: 'Pray as you see me pray.'[22] He performed the pilgrimage and said: 'Take from me your rituals [holy rites].'[23] And he wrote about *zakāh*[24] and explained the rules for *ṣiyām*.[25] With these definitive explanations, ambivalent provisions (*mujmalah*) were explained (*mufassarah*).

Accordingly, every *mujmal* in the Qur'ān becomes *mufassar* when followed by a definitive explanation (*bayān qaṭᶜī*) in either the Qur'ān itself or the *Sunnah*.[26]

The value of *mufassar*

Adherence to *mufassar* is obligatory[27] until another reliable proof abrogates it.[28] *Mufassar* is not open to interpretation beyond the obvious sense of the text. It could only have been abrogated during the lifetime of the Prophet. Therefore, upon the demise of the Prophet *mufassar* became equivalent to *muḥkam*.

NOTES

1. M.L.ʿA, *al-Muʿjam al-Wasīṭ*, II:688; Lane, *Arabic-English Lexicon*, II:2397; Baʿlabakī, *al-Mawrid*, p. 1083.

2. Such as when a word or text is self-explanatory. This would be when the mood itself is not open to *ta'wīl* or *takhṣīṣ*, e.g., numbers (because their meanings are unchangeable). The text may contain an explanation as in the verse: 'Truly, man was created anxious; discontented when evil touches him' (Qur'ān, LXX:19–20). The second part of this verse explains the meaning of 'anxious'. Such explanations may appear in the same text, as in this verse, or in another text.

3. This excludes what is not definite (*qaṭʿī*) in meaning or conveyance. Accordingly, the *mujmal* cannot scale up to become *mufassar* by the support of a solitary tradition (*khabar al-wāḥid*)

4. Bukhārī, *Kashf al-Asrār*, I:49.

5. This should no doubt be related to its meaning. The meaning has to be definite.

6. Sarakhsī, *Uṣūl al-Sarakhsī*, I:165.

7. This possibility may be excluded by an explanation from the Qur'ān itself, the Prophet, or a word which carries a single meaning, like numbers.

8. Nasafī, *Kashf al-Asrār*, I:208.

9. Specific words which are constant in their literal and original meaning are intrinsically *mufassar*.

10. Qur'ān, IV:11.

11. Qur'ān, XXIV:4

12. For those who were never legally married.

13. Qur'ān, XXIV:2

14. Qur'ān, XXXVIII:73.

15. Someone could say that this verse is equally an example of *muḥkam*, because it is informative (*khabar*), and *khabar* is not open to abrogation. The answer to this is that *mufassar* is only one part of 'the angels all of them together', while 'prostrated' is the *khabar* and therefore cannot be abrogated.

16. The Lawgiver in Islam is God and His Messenger, who, according to Muslim belief, does not speak from himself but transmits from God.

17. Qur'ān, LXX:19–23.

18. Bukhārī, *Kashf al-Asrār*, I:50.

19. Qur'ān, II:43

20. Qur'ān, III:97

21. Qur'ān, II:183

22. Bukhārī, *al-Jāmiʿ al-Ṣaḥīḥ*, I:155 (10:18)

23. Nawawī, *Sharḥ Ṣaḥīḥ Muslim*, IX:45; ʿAsqalānī, *Fatḥ al-Bārī*, III:264; Shawkānī, *Nayl al-Awṭār*, V:70; Bayhaqī, *al-Sunan al-Kubrā*, V:130.

24. Bukhārī, *al-Jāmiʿ al-Ṣaḥīḥ*, II:123–124 (24:35); Muslim, *Ṣaḥīḥ Muslim*, II:673.

25. Bukhārī, *al-Jāmiʿ al-Ṣaḥīḥ*, II:225–251 (30); Muslim, *Ṣaḥīḥ Muslim*, II:758–783.

26. One obligation of the Prophet was to explain the Qur'ān. This is clear from the verse: 'And We have also sent down unto you [O Muḥammad] the Reminder [the Qur'ān] that you may explain clearly to men what is sent down to them, and that they may give thought' (Qur'ān, XVI:44)

27. Bukhārī said: 'And there is no disagreement among the scholars in this case.' (*Bukhārī, Kashf al-Asrār*, I:50).

28. Abrogation was possible during the life of the Prophet. After his demise the entire Qur'ān became *muḥkam* in the sense that it was no longer open to abrogation.

CHAPTER 10

The Firm
(*al-Muḥkam*)

The linguistic definition of *muḥkam*

Muḥkam refers to perspicuous, exact, precise, accurate, firm; a verse of the Qur'ān whose meaning is secured from change, alteration, specification, and interpretation beyond the obvious import, and abrogation. 'In it are verses that are entirely clear (*muḥkamāt*), they are the foundations of the Book.'[1] In the technical vocabulary of *uṣūl al-fiqh*, the term refers to an entirely clear text, of either the Qur'ān or the *Sunnah*, which is not open to *ta'wīl* or *takhṣīṣ* or *naskh*.[2]

The technical definition *of muḥkam*[3]

Bazdawī defined *muḥkam* in the following terms: 'If the [*mufassar*] is strengthened, and its purpose is beyond doubt, then it is called *muḥkam*.[4]

Sarakhsī defined *muḥkam* in the following terms: 'What went beyond and exceeded[5] what we mentioned previously.'[6] Nasafī offers the following definition: '[It is an expression] the objective of which is beyond doubt and which excludes the possibility of abrogation [*naskh*] and change [*tabdīl*].'[7]

One may conclude from these definitions and from the following considerations that in the Ḥanafī *madhhab* a *muḥkam* expression has a meaning which hastens to one's mind, because it is beyond doubt. The ruling deduced from that expression represents the real purpose for the transmission of this provision in a form that leaves no possibility for interpretation beyond the obvious sense or for abrogation. This is applicable during both the life of the Prophet and even more so after his demise.

Categories of *muḥkam*

In view of the causes of *muḥkam* which rule out the possibility of abrogation, some scholars divided *muḥkam* into two categories:[8]

(a) *muḥkam* by itself

(b) *muḥkam* because of another factor.

If *naskh* is impossible because of the text's meaning itself, such a text is said to be intrinsically and by itself *muḥkam*.[9] This is especially true when the text is not open to a different meaning, like the verses about the existence of the Creator, His attributes, the beginning of the World, etc.

On the other hand, the impossibility of *naskh* could be due to the absence of an abrogating text. This category is called *muḥkam li ghayrih*[10] and encompasses *ẓāhir, naṣṣ, mufassar* and *muḥkam*.[11]

Examples of *muḥkam*

While on the topic of *muḥkam*, it is helpful to clarify the development that causes some texts to be *muḥkam* and to preclude all possible abrogation. This development occurs for the following reasons:

(1) Reasons internal to the text, where the impossibility of abrogation is indicated in the text itself. This may be classified as follows:

(a) Undisputed legal rulings based on undisputed authoritative text. This is illustrated by matters relating to *dīn*. These are foundations of the *dīn*[12] and as such are not open to any change in the belief in God, His oneness, His attributes[13], the belief in His angels, His books, His prophets[14], the Last Day,[15] etc.

(b) News and information about what happened in the past and what will happen in the future.[16]

(c) Legal rulings that represent a basis for unalterable ethical rules, on condition that these rules are acceptable to the ordinary and unfettered mind, and are unchangeable under different circumstances – e.g., justice,[17] filial duty,[18] fulfilment [of a covenant],[19] etc.

(2) External reasons, when the given meaning understood from the text represents a partial ruling (*ḥukm juz'ī*) and is followed by the declaration of continuity. This declaration precludes the possibility of abrogation as in the following examples from the Qur'ān and the *Sunnah*:

(a) 'And it is not [right] that you should annoy God's Messenger, or ever marry his wives after [his demise].'[20] One partial ruling given by this verse is the prohibition against marrying the Prophet's widows; the continuity is in His words 'ever [...] after him' (*abadan*), which at the end of the verse is a clear declaration of continuity. This makes it *muḥkam* and rules out any possibility of abrogation.

(b) 'And those who accuse honourable women but bring not four witnesses [to support their allegations], flog them eighty stripes and reject their evidence ever after.'[21] One partial ruling given by this verse is the order that the testimony of someone who accuses an honourable person without producing four witnesses to support his allegation, must be rejected, whereas the continuity which makes it *muḥkam* is in the expression 'ever after'. It explicitly means permanency, which precludes the possibility of abrogation.

(c) 'O people, I had permitted you to contract temporary marriage with women, but God has forbidden it [now] until the Day of Resurrection. So he who has any [women with this type of marriage contract] he should release her, and take nothing back.'[22] The partial ruling in this *ḥadīth* is the prohibition of temporary marriage (*mutʿah*), whereas the continuity is in the Prophet's words 'until the Day of Resurrection'. It clearly means that this *ḥukm* is eternal, because according to Islamic beliefs that day will not come before the end of this world. This continuity causes this ruling to be *muḥkam* because it precludes the possibility of abrogation.

(d) '*Jihād* is under way from the time when God sent me, until the last [members] of my *ummah* fight the Antichrist.'[23] The partial ruling in this *ḥadīth* is that the *jihād* had begun by the beginning of the Revelation, whereas the continuity is in the Prophet's words 'until the last [members] of my *ummah* fight Antichrist'. The Antichrist, according to Islamic belief, will appear shortly before the Last Day, so the ruling is valid forever. According to that which has been mentioned, *muḥkam* is not open to *taʾwīl*[24] and *takhṣīṣ*[25] because it is explained in sufficient detail so to preclude any ambiguity or possibility for interpretation beyond the obvious import. At the same time, *muḥkam* is open to abrogation[26] neither in the time of Revelation nor after the Prophet's demise.[27]

The value of *muḥkam*

Adherence to *muḥkam* should be strictly obligatory because there is no possibility of *taʾwīl*, *takhṣīṣ* or *naskh* since *muḥkam* is not open to these.[28]

NOTES

1. Qurʾān, III:7
2. M.L ʿA, *al-Muʿjam al-Wasīṭ*, I:190; Lane, *Arabic-English Lexicon*, I:618; Baʿlabaki, *al-Mawrid*, p. 993.
3. After quoting Bazdawī's definition, Bukhārī expressed his view, from what was previously mentioned, that for the text to be *muḥkam* it must be very limpid, clear in its meaning and not open to abrogation. These conditions are generally acceptable to Ḥanafī scholars in *uṣūl al-fiqh*. However, Bukhārī quoted many definitions from Ḥanafī scholars who do not stipulate that *muḥkam* is not open to abrogation. This indicates that Ḥanafīs do not accord the scope to *muḥkam*. (Bukhārī, *Kashf al-Asrār*, I:51).
4. Bukhārī, *Kashf al-Asrār*, I:51.
5. In its clarity and explicitness.
6. He means *mufassar*. Sarakhsī, *Uṣūl al-Sarakhsī*, I:165.

7. Nasafī, *Kashf al-Asrār*, I:209.

8. Bukhārī, *Kashf al-Asrār*, I:51.

9. Because the impossibility of *naskh* has come from within the text.

10. Because the impossibility of *naskh* is caused from outside the text.

11. Because all of them had become *muḥkam* in the sense that they may not be abrogated due to the absence of an abrogating text and because such a text may not appear after the Prophet's demise.

12. Ibn Abī al-ʿIzz, *Sharḥ al-ʿAqīdah al-Ṭaḥāwiyyah*, II:511–513.

13. 'God! There is no God but He, the Ever Living, the One who sustains and protects all that exists. Neither slumber nor sleep overtakes Him' (Qur'ān, II:255). 'There is nothing like unto Him and he is the All-Hearer, the All-Seer' (Qur'ān, XLII:11). 'Verily, God knows all things' (Qur'ān, XXIX:62).

14. 'The Messenger [Muḥammad] believes in what has been sent down to him from his Lord, and [so do] the believers. Each one believes in God, His angels, His books and His messengers. They say, We make no distinction between one or another of His messengers' (Qur'ān, II:285).

15. 'It is not *birr* [piety] that you turn your faces towards the east and the west [in prayer]; but *birr* is [the quality of] the one who believes in God, the Last Day, the angels, the Book, the Prophets.' (Qur'ān, II:177)

16. '*Alif, Lām, Mīm*. The Romans have been defeated in the nearer land (Syria, Iraq, Jordan and Palestine), and after the defeat the latter will be victorious – in three to nine years. (Qur'ān, XXX:1–4).

17. 'But say: "I believe in whatever God has sent down of the Book and I am commanded to do justice among you.' (Qur'ān, XLII:15). 'O you who believe! Be steadfast witnesses for God and let not hatred of others incriminate you or make you unjust. Be just: this is nearer to piety.' (Qur'ān, V:8).

18. ' And your Lord has decreed that you worship none but Him. And that you be dutiful to your parents. If one of them attain old age in your life, say not to them a word of disrespect, nor shout at them but address them in terms of honour' (Qur'ān, XVII:23).

19. 'Those who fulfil the Covenant of God and break not the *mīthāq* (bond, treaty, covenant)' (Qur'ān, XIII:20); 'And fulfil the covenant. Verily, the covenant will be questioned.' (Qur'ān, XVII:34).

20. Qur'ān, XXXIII:53.

21. Qur'ān, XXIV:4.

22. Muslim, *Ṣaḥīḥ Muslim*, II:1025 (no.1406).

23. Abū Dāwūd, *Sunan*, III:18 (no.2532).

24. When *muḥkam* has specific (*khāṣṣ*) meaning.

25. When *muḥkam* has a general (*ʿāmm*) meaning.

26. That is why God has called the *muḥkamāt* verses 'the Mother of Book' (*umm al-kitāb*). A *muḥkam* is like a mother relative to her child, just as Mecca has been called 'the mother of villages' (*umm al-qurā*), being the place of pilgrimage and as referred to on the Day of Resurrection

27. Sarakhsī, *Uṣūl al-Sarakhsī*, I:165; Mayhawī, *Sharḥ Nūr al-Anwār ʿalā al-Manār*, I:209–210; Bukhārī, *Kashf al-Asrār*, I:151.

28. Nasafī, *Kashf al-Asrār*, I:209.

CHAPTER 11

Conflict (*ta^cāruḍ*) between categories of *wāḍiḥ*

As we have seen, the categories of *wāḍiḥ* in the Ḥanafī school are not at the same level of clarity. The most limpid is *muḥkam*, followed by *mufassar*, *naṣṣ*, then *ẓāhir*. The disparity between these categories becomes apparent and significant in the event of a conflict[1] between them.[2] In conflict, the 'clearer' one has precedence.[3]

Conflict (*ta^cāruḍ*) between *ẓāhir* and *naṣṣ*

On its technical definition the general characteristics of *ẓāhir* are regarded as follows:

(1) Its meaning is duly apparent.

(2) The deduced legal ruling of *ẓāhir* is not the main objective for the presence of the text and does not represent its principal theme.

(3) The possibility of interpretation beyond the obvious sense, the restriction of meaning and abrogation (*naskh*) still exists.

On the other hand, the characteristics of *naṣṣ* are as follows:

(1) Its meaning is duly clear.

(2) The deduced legal ruling of *naṣṣ* is the main objective for the presence of the text and represents its main purpose.

(3) The possibility of interpretation beyond the obvious sense,[4] restriction of meaning and abrogation still exists.

From the above characteristics it is obvious that *naṣṣ* is one degree 'stronger' than *ẓāhir* because the ruling deduced from it is the main objective for the presence of the text, while in the case of *ẓāhir* the deduced ruling is not the principal theme of the text nor its main objective. Consequently, when a conflict appears between the two, *naṣṣ* will take precedence.

Here are some examples of such a conflict:

(a) The Qur'ān states: 'The mothers shall suckle their children for two whole years.'[5] Another verse states: 'And bearing him and weaning him is thirty months.'[6] The purpose for the revelation (*sabab al-nuzūl*)[7] of the verse is to explain the length of the suckling period. Therefore, it is *naṣṣ* because the meaning of the text, which is clear, is further explained by *sabab al-nuzūl*.

However, the second verse brings out clearly that the suckling period is thirty months. It is *ẓāhir* because it was not revealed to explain the suckling period, but to bring to light the mother's merits in respect of her child. The proof for the statement that the verse was revealed for this purpose is the beginning of the same verse: 'And We have enjoined on man to be dutiful and kind to his parents. His mother bears him with hardship, and she brings him forth with hardship and bearing him and weaning him is in thirty months.'[8]

Applying the principle that *naṣṣ* has priority over *ẓāhir* gives precedence to the first verse and its meaning. Accordingly, the legal ruling deduced from the verse is that mothers should suckle their children for two years[9] if they wish to complete the full term of suckling.[10]

(b) The Qur'ān states: 'All others are lawful, provided you seek [them in marriage] with *mahr* from your property, desiring chastity, not illicit sexual relations.'[11] This verse has apparent meaning which permits any number of women to be taken in marriage.[12] After mentioning women who are forbidden, it states clearly that 'all others are lawful.' Hence, according to the apparent meaning of this verse a man could, at the same time, marry more than four wives.

However, another verse states: 'And if you fear that you shall not be able to deal justly with the orphan-girls, then marry [other] women of your choice, two or three, or four.'[13] This verse limits the number to four. Therefore, there is an apparent conflict between the two verses. But since the second verse was revealed to explain the number, it is a *naṣṣ* and *naṣṣ* has precedence over *ẓāhir*.[14] Consequently, the legal ruling (permission to have a maximum of four women at the same time) deduced from the second verse is preferable and any violation of this limit is unlawful.

(c) The Prophet stated: 'There is no prayer for someone who did not recite *fātiḥat al-kitāb*.'[15] The apparent meaning of this *ḥadīth* states that prayer is not valid without *fātiḥat al-kitāb*, whether the prayer was performed in congregation or alone. This ruling is indicated by the denial in Prophet's words 'There is no prayer.'

In another *ḥadīth* the Prophet said: 'For him who prays in congregation who has an *imām*, the recitation of the *imām* is recitation for him.'[16] This means that he who prays in congregation need not recite *fātiḥat al-kitāb*. Accordingly, when the recitation in congregation is in question, this *ḥadīth* disagrees with the former one.

However, the latter *ḥadīth* is, in this particular question, more clear than the former, because the purpose of the statement of this *ḥadīth* was to explain this particular question. Therefore, the latter *ḥadīth* is *naṣṣ* (because its meaning is supported by the presence of the text – *sabab al-wurūd*) and has precedence over *ẓāhir*. Accordingly, someone who prays in the congregation is not obliged to recite *fātiḥat al-kitāb*.[17] The former *ḥadīth* is related to someone who prays alone, or its purpose is to deny some quality of the prayer itself.[18]

Conflict (*ta'āruḍ*) between *naṣṣ* and *mufassar*

From its technical definition we have concluded that *naṣṣ* has three general characteristics.[19] On the other hand, the characteristics of *mufassar* are that:

(1) Its meaning is duly clear.

(2) The deduced legal ruling of *mufassar* is the main objective for the presence of the text and it represents its principal theme.

(3) The possibilities of *takhṣīṣ* and *ta'wīl* do not exist in *mufassar*. *Mufassar* is open to abrogation only during the Prophet's lifetime.

In conclusion, *naṣṣ* and *mufassar* share the first two characteristics, but they differ on the third one. *Mufassar* is 'clearer' because it is not susceptible to *takhṣīṣ* and *ta'wīl*, while *naṣṣ* is open to them. Therefore, if a conflict should arise between the two, *mufassar* would be given precedence. Here are some examples of conflict:[20]

(a) The Prophet said: 'Then wash up yourself and make ablution for every prayer.'[21]

In another narration of this *ḥadīth* he stated: 'Then wash up yourself and make ablution for the time of every prayer.'[22] This narration recommends, for a woman whose menstruation is longer than usual, a new ablution for every prayer at all times, whether it is an obligatory regular prayer performed at its proper time, or an obligatory prayer performed afterwards, or a supererogatory prayer.[23] This narration is clear and its meaning is the principal theme of the text. Therefore it is regarded as a *naṣṣ* for that legal ruling.

The meaning of the latter narration is evidently limpid – one ablution is enough for the period of one prayer, because 'for the time' is stated explicitly. This narration is considered *mufassar* because the word 'time' is explicit and explanatory, and it represents the principal theme of the text. When brought together these two narrations apparently disagree. Because the former narration is *naṣṣ* and the latter is *mufassar*, the latter is given precedence. Therefore, for the *mustaḥāḍah* women one ablution for one prayer period is sufficient. During this period they may pray any number of obligatory and supererogatory prayers.[24]

Since *naṣṣ* is susceptible to interpretation beyond the obvious sense and the *naṣṣ* of the former tradition is opposed by a reliable proof which suggests a different meaning, the provision 'for every' (*li kull*) may be interpreted as 'for the time of every' by adding 'the time'.[25] Consequently, the *ḥadīth* may be interpreted as follows: 'make ablution for the time of every prayer.' In this interpretation the apparent conflict disappears. Accordingly, one ablution is sufficient for the time of every prayer, during which any number of *farḍ* or *nafl* prayers are performed.

(b) The statement 'I have married a woman for a month' refers to a temporary marriage, not a legal marriage. This is what one infers from the fact that the expression 'I have married' is *naṣṣ* clearly related to marriage and that *mutʿah* is a general possibility. However, 'for a month' is an explanation (*tafsīr*) which adds the meaning of *mutʿah* marriage. He could not have meant legal marriage, because legal marriage is not susceptible to the limited duration 'for a month'.

According to the rule that *mufassar* has precedence over *naṣṣ*, the legal ruling in this case is that a marriage that is temporary is an illegal marriage according to the majority of scholars.

Conflict (*taʿārūḍ*) between *mufassar* and *muḥkam*

From its technical definition we have concluded previously that *mufassar* has three characteristics.[26] On the other hand, the characteristics of *muḥkam* are that:

(1) Its meaning is clear.

(2) The deduced legal ruling of *muḥkam* is the main objective for the presence of the text and represents the principal theme of the text.

(3) *Muḥkam* is not open to *taʾwīl* and *takhṣīṣ*.

(4) The abrogation of *muḥkam* is possible neither during the lifetime of the Prophet nor after his demise.

It may be concluded that both the *muḥkam* and the *mufassar* are similar in the first three characteristics. However, they differ on the fourth characteristic. *Mufassar* is susceptible and open to abrogation during the lifetime of the Prophet in contrast to *muḥkam*, which is not open to *naskh* at all times. Therefore, when the two conflict, *muḥkam* has precedence, as in the following example:[27] On evidence and testimony the Qurʾān commands: 'And take for witness two just persons from among you.'[28] This text is *mufassar* because its meaning, is clear. It represents the principal theme of the text, and it is further explained by the attribute 'just' and the fact that the cause of giving evidence is to be accepted. According to the general meaning of this verse the testimony of someone who has been punished for falsely accusing a chaste woman is accepted if he has repented and his status has been reinstated.

In another verse about the person punished for having unjustly insulted and accused a chaste woman, the Qur'ān states: 'And those who accuse chaste women and produce not four witnesses, flog them eighty stripes and reject their testimony forever, they indeed are *fāsiqūn* [evil-living persons] – except those who repent thereafter and correct [themselves], for verily God is Oft-Forgiving, Most Merciful.'[29]

The latter verse is *muḥkam* due to the occurrence of the word 'forever', which carries the meaning of continuity and therefore precludes all possibility of abrogation. Accordingly, the testimony of someone who has been punished for accusing a chaste woman is not accepted even if he has repented. This meaning disagrees with the meaning of the former verse. Since *muḥkam* has precedence over *mufassar*, the testimony of someone who has been punished for slander is not accepted, even if he has repented afterwards and his status is reinstated.[30]

Giving *muḥkam* precedence over *mufassar* because (unlike *mufassar*, which may be abrogated during the lifetime of the Prophet) the former is open to *ta'wīl*, seems to me a weak proof. With the demise of the Prophet *mufassar* instantly becomes equivalent to *muḥkam*. This is the reason why Islamic scholars do not rely completely on this proof in their argumentation, and avail themselves of other proofs.[31]

Conflict (*taʿāruḍ*) between *naṣṣ* and *muḥkam*

When comparing the characteristics of *naṣṣ* and *muḥkam*[32] one may note that *muḥkam* is more powerful because, unlike *naṣṣ*, it is open neither to interpretation beyond the obvious import nor to specification of meaning or abrogation. Therefore, when they conflict, *muḥkam* takes precedence, as illustrated in the following example:

The Qur'ān states: 'And if you fear that you shall not be able to deal justly with the orphan-girls, then marry [other] women of your choice, two or three, or four.'[33] This verse is *naṣṣ* with respect to the permission for marrying four women at one time. This clear meaning, which represents the principal theme of this verse, makes it *naṣṣ*. The legal ruling deduced from this verse addresses the Prophet – his wives could remarry after his demise. However, in other verses the Qur'ān states: 'And it is not [right] for you to annoy God's Messenger, or ever to marry his wives after [his demise].[34]

This verse is *muḥkam* with respect to the prohibition of marrying any of the Prophet's wives after his demise. It is *muḥkam* because the word 'ever after' rules out the possibility of *ta'wīl* or *naskh*. Because *muḥkam* has superiority over *naṣṣ*, the latter ruling has effect, and marriage to any of the Prophet's widows was not allowed.

NOTES

1. There is unanimous agreement among Islamic scholars that the contradictions in authoritative texts (Qur'ān and the *ḥadīth*) are apparent because real contradiction is only when texts are at the same level, presented at the same time and so opposed to one another as to make reconciliation impossible. Needless to say, however, this kind of contradiction never occurs, although it may exist in the mind of the *mujtahid* due to a lack of knowledge of when the text was delivered, of an understanding of the same text, etc. The examples cited below support this. (Sarakhsī, *Uṣūl al-Sarakhsī*, II:12)

2. There is disparity between the two only in respect of clarity and ambiguity; there is no disparity in respect of certainty and uncertainty. All categories should be *qaṭʿī al-thubūt*, otherwise there would be no proper disagreement because the indefinite (*ẓannī*) cannot oppose the definite (*qaṭʿī*).

3. The method for recognising the 'clearer' meaning in order to favour one proof over the other is essential to this study.

4. In the case of *naṣṣ* it is less possible than in the case of *ẓāhir* because *naṣṣ* represents the principal theme of the text, as distinct from *ẓāhir*.

5. Qur'ān, II:233.

6. Qur'ān, XLVI:15

7. Ibn Kathīr, *Tafsīr al-Qur'ān al-ʿAẓīm*, I:380–381.

8. Nasafī, *Kashf al-Asrār*, I:211–212; Ibn Kathīr, *Tafsīr al-Qur'ān al-ʿAẓīm*, IV:200–201.

9. This is the opinion of Abū Yūsuf and Muḥammad, unlike Abū Ḥanīfah, who maintained that the prescribed suckling period is thirty months (Ṭaḥāwī, *Mukhtaṣar al-Ṭaḥāwī*, p. 220; Kāsānī, *Badāʾiʿ al-Ṣanāʾiʿ*, IV:6; Marghīnānī, *al-Hidāyah*, I:223; Ibn al-Humām, *Fatḥ al-Qadīr*, III:5–6).

10. The Qur'ān says about this 'for those [parents] who desire to complete the term of suckling'. (Qur'ān, II:233).

11. Qur'ān, IV:24.

12. The verse is not *naṣṣ* in this meaning despite the fact that it is clear and apparent – because it was not revealed for the purpose of explaining the particular meaning, but to list women who cannot be taken in marriage. Therefore, the verse is *naṣṣ* in this second meaning.

13. Qur'ān, IV:3.

14. At the same time, the former verse is *naṣṣ* in its stipulation about dowry, and the latter verse is *ẓāhir* for not stipulating the dowry (the dowry is not mentioned). Consequently, the dowry is *wājib* because *naṣṣ* has precedence over *ẓāhir*.

15. Bukhārī, *al-Jāmiʿ al-Ṣaḥīḥ*, I:184 (10:95); Muslim, *Ṣaḥīḥ Muslim*, I:295 (no. 394).

16. Ibn Mājah, *Sunan*, I:277 (no. 850). This tradition is weak.

17. This question is a matter of wide discussion between scholars. Our example is in line with the Ḥanafī school, which holds that someone who prays in the congregation need not recite *fātiḥat al-kitāb* (Ṭaḥāwī, *Mukhtaṣar al- Ṭaḥāwī*, p. 27; Marghīnānī, *al-Hidāyah*, I:55).

18. It means that the prayer without *fātiḥat al-kitāb* is incomplete.

19. See 'Conflict between *ẓāhir* and *naṣṣ*'.

20. Nasafī, *Kashf al-Asrār*, I:212; Mayhawī, *Sharḥ Nūr al-Anwār ʿalā al-Manār*, I:212–213.

21. Bukhārī, *al-Jāmiʿ al-Ṣaḥīḥ*, I:63 (4:63); Ibn Mājah, *Sunan*, I:204 (no.624); Tirmidhī, *al-Jāmiʿ al-Ṣaḥīḥ*, I:217–218 (no. 125).

22. Marghīnānī, *al-Hidāyah*, I:32; Zaylaʿī, *Naṣb al-Rāyah*, I:204. Zaylaʿī stated that this narration is very strange (*gharīb jiddan*).

23. The *fuqahāʾ* who maintained that a *mustaḥādah* woman has to make ablution for every prayer made an exception when *nafl* and *qaḍāʾ* prayers are in question. They stated that she

is permitted to pray with one ablution more than one *nafl* or *qaḍā'* prayer. They argue that these prayers are too numerous, causing hardship and diffculty. (Shīrāzī, *al-Muhadhdhab*, :I:46; Ibn Qudāmah, *al-Mughnī*, I:342).

24. This conclusion is in harmony with the Ḥanafī view. The rule that gives *mufassar* precedence over *naṣṣ* and the narration in which 'the time' was mentioned are not the main proofs of the Ḥanafīs. They needed other proofs because the latter narration (which is *mufassar*) is weak and, as Zaylaʿī stated, 'very strange' (*gharīb jiddan*) and does not stand up to the former narration, which is *ṣaḥīḥ* (Ṭaḥāwī, *Sharḥ Maʿānī al-Āthār*, I:46, *Mukhtaṣar al-Ṭaḥāwī*, p. 22; Kāsānī, *Badā'iʿ al-Ṣanā'iʿ*, I:44; Marghīnānī, *al-Hidāyah*, I:32–33; Zaylaʿī, *Naṣb al-Rāyah*, I:204). However, the majority of *fuqahā'* are of a different opinion. They prefer the former narration ('Make ablution for every prayer') because it was narrated in the *Ṣaḥīḥ*. This is not the case in the latter narration, 'Make ablution for the time of every prayer'. Zaylaʿī maintained that this is 'very strange' (*gharīb jiddan*) (Zaylaʿī, *Naṣb al-Rāyah*, I:204).

25. Because in Arabic one may say '*ātīk li-ṣalat al-ẓuhr*' – which means 'I will come to you at [the time] of the prayer of *ẓuhr*'. 'The time' is not explicitly mentioned, but everyone understands it from the context.

26. See 'Conflict between *naṣṣ* and *mufassar*'

27. Mayhawī, *Sharḥ Nūr al-Anwār ʿalā al-Manār*, I:213–214.

28. Qur'ān, LXV:2.

29. Qur'ān, XXIV:4–5.

30. This question has been widely debated by Ḥanafīs and Shāfiʿīs. My conclusion (based on the rule that *muḥkam* has precedence over *mufassar*) is that the testimony of the *qādhif* (someone who has been punished for falsely accusing a chaste woman) is unacceptable. This is consistent with the Ḥanafī school. Both schools provide other proofs in support of their opinion (see chapters on *qadhf* and testimony in their respective books).

31. Ibn Kathīr, *Tafsīr al-Qur'ān al-ʿAẓīm*, III:354–355; Qurṭubī, *al-Jāmiʿ li Aḥkām al-Qur'ān*, XII:180–181.

32. See 'Conflict between *ẓāhir* and *naṣṣ*' and 'Conflict between *mufassar* and *muḥkam*'.

33. Qur'ān IV:3.

34. Qur'ān, XXXIII:53.

Introduction to the Shāfiʿī Approach to Clear (*wāḍiḥ*) Words

Shāfiʿī scholars[1] have a different approach to clear (*wāḍiḥ*) words from that of the Ḥanafīs. They divided clear words into two categories only: the apparent (*ẓāhir*) and the explicit (*naṣṣ*).

The fact that the Ḥanafīs divided *wāḍiḥ* into four categories may suggest that their division is clearer and more precise. This will be obvious when we determine the scope of *wāḍiḥ* in the Shāfiʿī school and the deep disagreement among their scholars in its interpretation. First, the apparent (*ẓāhir*) will be discussed.

NOTES

1. Some contemporary scholars categorised *wāḍiḥ* in a way that is similar to, yet clearer than, that of the Shāfiʿīs as follows: 1) A plain and explicit text which indicates detailed and fixed meaning unlikely to give sense to the interpretation beyond the obvious sense (*taʾwīl*); 2) a text which is neither plain nor explicit. This is a text which provides a meaning, with possible further meanings.

Those scholars utilise *taʾwīl*, preferring one meaning over another; in this process *sabab al-nuzūl* or *sabab al-wurūd* has no value. (Bardīsī, *Uṣūl al-Fiqh*, p. 171).

The Apparent
(*al-Ẓāhir*)

The linguistic definition of *ẓāhir*

Ẓāhir refers to apparent, plain, manifest, evident; *al-shay' ẓahara ẓuhūran* means that something appeared and became evident after having been concealed; *ẓāhiran*, outwardly and apparently;[1] *fi'l-ẓāhir*, in appearance.[2]

The technical definition of *ẓāhir*

Shāfiʿī scholars gave *ẓāhir* various definitions: Baṣrī defined it as: 'That which needs no other in expressing its apparent meaning.' He quoted another definition: 'It shows its objective [intended] and non-objective meanings, but the objective [intended] meaning is more apparent.[3] Baḍrī preferred the first definition. He maintained that a provision, when its meaning becomes clear, instantly becomes apparent, whether or not it is susceptible and open to another meaning. The difference between *ẓāhir* and *naṣṣ* lies in the fact that the former does not require another meaning for its full meaning to be asserted. This is in contrast to *naṣṣ*. Shīrāzī held that *ẓāhir* is a word (*lafẓ*) that denotes two meanings of which *ẓāhir* is the more apparent.[4] Qarrāfī defined *ẓāhir* as 'an expression that alternates between two or more meanings, and in one of them the *ẓāhir* is more eminent.[5]

Literal meaning may offer alternatives, such as the case of a word with a shared meaning (*lafẓ mushtarak*), or when one word is given as a name to many subjects. The Qur'ān states: 'But pay the due thereof on the day of its harvest.'[6] This has an apparent meaning related to duty, but it is unclear in relation to the amount. In relation to the apparent meaning of the provision, all three – the meaning of the provision, the ruling deduced from that provision and the provision itself – are called *ẓāhir*.

Ghazālī maintained that *ẓāhir* is a provision which is open to interpretation beyond the obvious sense (*ta'wīl*). He stated that according to the approach of Shāfiʿī, who did not distinguish between *ẓāhir* and *naṣṣ*, *ẓāhir* gives a meaning which is more likely to be understood, but the understanding is indefinite.[7] Elsewhere,[8] he stated that an expression may have either a specified and fixed meaning which precludes another meaning (called *mubayyan* or *naṣṣ*), or it may have two or more meanings. In the latter case, if none has precedence over the other, the expression is called *mujmal*; but if one meaning takes precedence that meaning is called *ẓāhir*.

Āmidī criticised Ghazālī's definition of *ẓāhir*, holding instead that it signifies its meaning according to the original (literal) or customary meaning, while supposing other less expected meanings.[9] Ījī maintained that: '*Ẓāhir* is what signifies an indefinite meaning.'[10] Taftāzānī defined *ẓāhir* as: 'What signifies its meaning clearly.'[11] Like Ījī, Anṣārī maintained that *ẓāhir* is what signifies an indefinite meaning.[12]

According to the Shāfiʿī school, *ẓāhir* seems to be 'a provision which signifies an indefinite meaning, yet prefers other (meanings) which are non-preferable'. Therefore, when an expression has more than one meaning, it is called *ẓāhir* in relation to the apparent and preferable (*rājiḥ*) meaning, and *mu'awwal*[13] in relation to the non-preferable (*marjūḥ*) meaning.[14]

Examples of *ẓāhir*

During the presentation of the examples of *ẓāhir* we may mention the provisions which provide apparent meanings:

(a) The absolute imperative (jussive) mood (*muṭlaq ṣīghat al-amr*). The imperative mood is apparent in obligation and may be interpreted beyond its obvious sense as praiseworthiness and permissiveness, as in the following verse: 'O you who believe! When you contract a debt for a fixed period, write it down [...] But take witnesses whenever you make a commercial contract.'[15]

The imperative statements 'write it down' and 'take' apparently signify obligation. However, most scholars interpreted this beyond its obvious sense, using the concept of *ta'wīl*,[16] and maintained that the purpose of this kind of order is not an obligation but rather praiseworthy.[17] Accordingly, it is not obligatory for Muslims to write down all contracts, but praiseworthy to do so.

(b) The absolute prohibition (jussive) mood (*muṭlaq ṣīghat al-nahy*). The prohibition mood is apparent (*ẓāhir*) in *taḥrīm*. It may, however, be interpreted beyond its obvious import to mean blameworthy. Examples of this are the Prophet's prohibitions of prayers at certain places, such as graveyards, toilets, camel sheds, etc. The absolute prohibition mood is apparent in *taḥrīm*. It may be interpreted, however, as blameworthy, if this interpretation is supported by a reliable proof.[18]

(c) The general meaning mood (*ṣīghat al-ʿumūm*) provides an apparent meaning which includes everything to which it is applicable. The restriction and specification of its meaning would be regarded as *ta'wīl*. An example of this is what the Prophet said in the following *hadīth:* 'No fasting is valid for someone who did not intend it the night before.'[19] 'Fasting' is an indefinite noun in a negative context. Indefinite nouns in a negative context, according to Arabic linguistic rules, normally carry a general meaning. Hence, the word 'fasting' by its apparent meaning includes all meanings of fasting, be they compulsory, supererogatory, or the performance of vows to God. Therefore, the specification (*takhṣīṣ*) of this tradition implies fasting during Ramaḍān only.

(d) The apparent meaning may appear in nouns, verbs and prepositions – e.g. to, until, up to. The apparent meaning of this word signifies the extent (*ghāyah*). The apparent (*ẓāhir*) meaning is open to *ta'wīl*. If the term 'to, until' is interpreted as a joining or connection between two matters, that interpretation would be regarded as *ta'wīl*.[20]

The effect of *ẓāhir* on legal reasoning

As mentioned, when a provision generates more meanings, the most obvious and probable is the apparent. Such a provision, however, is open to other meanings and may be interpreted beyond its obvious meaning when this is supported by reliable proof. This openness to *ta'wīl* has an enormous effect on legal reasoning, as seen in the following example.[21]

The Qur'ān states: 'Finding no water, perform *tayammum* with *ṣaʿīd ṭayyib* and rub therewith your faces and hands.'[22] Shāfiʿī, a master of the Arabic language, stated that *ṣaʿīd* is earthy dust (*turāb, ghubār*), and that *ṣaʿīd* and dust are synonymous. In his opinion *tayammum* may be performed with something like soil dust (*ṣaʿīd*)[23] because this is what the verse indicates by its apparent meaning.

Imām Mālik claimed that *tayammum* may be performed with anything which rises up from the earth (*mā ṣaʿada ʿalā wajh al-arḍ*) – like pebbles, stone, sand, dust – because *ṣaʿīd*, according to him, means precisely this.[24] Therefore, he interpreted the same verse not according to its obvious import, but to an extended meaning of '*ṣaʿīd*' by using *ta'wīl*.

The value of *ẓāhir*

Adherence to *ẓāhir* should be obligatory, and its meaning should be applied and strictly followed[25] except in cases where the definitive (*qaṭʿī*) meaning is required. The apparent meaning may be abandoned only in cases where a reliable proof suggests otherwise. In such cases the proper interpretation beyond the obvious sense (*ta'wīl ṣaḥīḥ*) may be used and its meaning followed.[26]

NOTES

1. According to the terminology of *uṣūl al-fiqh* no parallel is drawn between *ẓāhir* and *bāṭin*. The parallel is always drawn between *khafī* and *ẓāhir*. The term *bāṭin* (essence, interior, intrinsic nature) is normally found in *ʿilm al-kalām*.

2. M.L.ʿA, *al-Muʿjam al-Wasīṭ*, II:578; Lane, *Arabic-English Lexicon*, II:1926–30; EI², I:1039, I:1099; Baʿlabakī, *al-Mawrid*, p. 736.

3. Baṣrī, *al-Muʿtamad*, I:320.

4. Shīrāzī, *al-Lummaʿ*, p. 48.

5. Qarrafī, *Sharḥ Tanqīḥ al-Fuṣūl*, p. 37. He followed Rāzī in this definition. (Rāzī, *al-Mahṣūl*, I:1:315).

6. Qur'ān, VI:141.

7. Ghazālī, *al-Mustaṣfā*, p. 196.

8. Ghazālī, *al-Mustaṣfā*, p. 187.

9. Āmidī, *al-Iḥkām fī Uṣūl al-Aḥkām*, III:48–49.

10. Indefinite indication can be result of: 1) the linguistic usage of the word *waḍʿ al-lughah*. For example the word *asad* (lion) is preferable (*rājiḥ*) when used in connection with the wild animal that we know and not as a reference to a strong man; 2) usage of words by the Lawgiver (*Sharʿ*), in meanings which are different from the word's original and literal meaning. An example of this is *ṣalāh* (prayer). Ṣalāh originally meant apology and supplication (i.e, *duʿā*), but it became a term preferably associated with the known ritual that Muslims have to practise five times a day; 3) by customary usage (*ʿurf al-istiʿmāl*), such as the word *ghā'iṭ* – which is used to mean excrement, while originally referring to a lower part of the earth (*al-makān al muṭma'inn min al-arḍ*) (Anṣārī, *Ghāyat al-Wuṣūl*, p. 83; Ījī, *Mukhtaṣar al-Muntahā*, II:168). According to this definition, *naṣṣ* signifies its definite meaning. Hence *naṣṣ* is the partner of *ẓāhir*.

11. Taftāzānī, *Ḥāshiyat al-Taftāzānī*, II:168. According to this definition, *ẓāhir* is part of *naṣṣ*.

12. Anṣārī, *Ghāyat al-Wuṣūl*, p. 83.

13. That is, interpreted beyond the obvious meaning of the text.

14. If non-preferable meaning was given precedence over the preferable meaning.

15. Qur'ān II:282.

16. *Ta'wīl* may be used only when supported by a reliable proof.

17. Ibn Kathīr, *Tafsīr al-Qur'ān al-ʿAẓīm*, I:446–450; Qurṭubī, *al-Jāmiʿ li Aḥkām al-Qur'ān*, III:382–383.

18. ʿAbdullāh ibn ʿUmar related that the Prophet forbade prayer in each of seven places: 'The dunghill, butchery, graveyard, middle of the road, bathroom, camel shed and on top of the Kaʿba'. (Tirmidhī, *al-Jāmiʿ al-Ṣaḥīḥ*, II:177–178 (no. 346); Ibn Mājah, *Sunan*, I:246 (no. 746). Shawkānī, *Nayl al-Auṭār*, II:142–143.)

19. Nasā'ī, *Sunan*, IV:196 (no. 2331); Abū Dāwūd, *Sunan*, II:329 (no. 2454) (Shawkānī, *Nayl al-Auṭār*, IV:207.)

20. Āmidī, *al-Iḥkām fī Uṣūl al-Aḥkām*, I:55; Isnawī, *al-Tamhīd*, pp. 221–224.

21. Tilmisānī, *Miftāḥ al-Wuṣūl*, p. 45.

22. Qur'ān, V:6.

23. Shāfiʿī, *al-Umm*, I:43

24. Ibn Rushd, *Bidāyat al-Mujtahid*, I:71; Dassūqī, *Ḥāshiyat al-Dassūqī*, I:175.

25. Although this rule applies, there is disagreement amongst *fuqahā'* where the narrator of a certain *ḥadīth* provides an explanation which is not in harmony with the apparent (*ẓāhir*) meaning of the *ḥadīth*. Some say the apparent meaning should be followed, while others give precedence to the explanation of the narrator. (Baṣrī, *al-Mu'tamad*, II:670; Āmidī, *al-Iḥkām fī Uṣūl al-Aḥkām*, II:342).

26. Ibn Qudāmah, *Rawḍat al-Nāẓir*, II:29–30.

CHAPTER 13

The Explicit
(*al-Naṣṣ*)

The linguistic definition of *naṣṣ*

Naṣṣ refers to explicit, declared, manifest. The meaning of the root is 'to raise', especially 'to elevate the object so that is visible to all'; *al-naṣṣ*: the original written text. In the technical vocabulary of *uṣūl al-fiqh*, the term refers to either Qur'ān or a *ḥadīth* text.[1]

The technical definition of *naṣṣ*

Upon closer examination, the Shāfiʿīs' understanding (*mutakallimūn*) of *wāḍiḥ* shows it is obvious that they are less clear on this question than the Ḥanafīs. Their conception of *wāḍiḥ* would seem confused unless we accept the fact that the term '*naṣṣ*' and its conception had a natural evolution.

Shāfiʿī, the founder of the *mutakallimūn* school in *uṣūl al-fiqh*, did not himself draw any distinction between *ẓāhir* and *naṣṣ*. He used the one to refer to the other,[2] looking upon them as two names for the same concept. This may have been because he took into account the linguistic meaning. From a linguistic point of view, he is absolutely correct.[3] He defined *naṣṣ* as an utterance the intended legal ruling of which is known independently, or by the assistance of any other indicator.[4]

In his *Risālah* Shāfiʿī described *naṣṣ* as that which has definite and indefinite meaning. He said: 'The sum-total of what God has declared to His creatures in His Book, by which He invited them to worship Him in accordance with His prior decision, includes various categories. One of these is what He has declared to His creatures by '*naṣṣ*' [in the Qur'ān], such as the aggregate of duties [*jumal farā'iḍ*][5] owed to Him: That they shall perform the prayer, pay the alms tax, perform the pilgrimage and observe the fast. And that He has forbidden disgraceful acts – both visible and hidden– and in the textual [prohibition of] adultery, [the drinking of] wine, eating [the flesh of] dead things and of blood and pork; and He has made clear to them how to perform the duty of [the major] ablution and other matters stated precisely in the *naṣṣ* [of the Qur'ān].'[6]

Words like *ṣalāt*, *zakāt*, termed here as *naṣṣ*, have no definitive meaning because they are ambiguous (*mujmal*) and as such they need further explanation.[7] Their modus was made clear at a later stage by the Prophet both verbally and practically. He explained the number of prayers to be performed each day and the amount of *zakāh* and their time of fulfilment and so forth.

Shāfiʿī uses the term *naṣṣ* to refer to rulings to which either the Qur'ān or a *ḥadīth* refers.[8] Later, the majority of *mutakallimūn*[9] distinguished between *ẓāhir* and *naṣṣ*, but they disagreed in their approach to it, although the majority of them place *ẓāhir* and *naṣṣ* in opposition to *mujmal*. They also sometimes speak about *naṣṣ* as *mubayyan* or as a category of *mubayyan*.

ʿAbd al-Jabbār defined *naṣṣ* as: 'Speech whose meaning is understood.' From the three stipulated conditions, it is obvious that Baṣrī means by *naṣṣ* a provision which is not open to any other meaning.[10] Shīrāzī maintains that *naṣṣ* is every expression which provides a ruling by its plain and explicit meaning, in a way which leads to no other possibility.[11] The following verses are examples: 'Muḥammad is the Messenger of God'[12]; 'Approach not the unlawful sexual act'[13] and 'Kill not one whose life God has made sacred, except for a just cause [according to Islamic law].'[14]

Ghazālī[15] mentioned that scholars have three different approaches in their understanding and definitions of *naṣṣ*:[16]

(1) The Shāfiʿīs approach of identification and equivalence between *ẓāhir* and *naṣṣ* and calling *ẓāhir naṣṣ*.[17]

(2) The approach that takes *naṣṣ* as a provision which is not open to a potentially different meaning, such as numbers. As an example the number five is a *naṣṣ* because its meaning is unchangeable. Also the word horse can only mean that kind of animal. It can mean neither donkey nor camel. We may thus conclude that the provision of meanings which preclude other meanings, indicates *naṣṣ*.

(3) The approach that takes *naṣṣ* as a provision which may not lead to a different meaning even if supported by a proof. If the provision leads to another meaning, but that meaning is not supported by a proof, the provision could still be called *naṣṣ*.

Ghazālī holds that *naṣṣ* denotes all three meanings. However, he prefers the second approach, which maintained that *naṣṣ* is a provision (a meaning) that is not open to interpretation beyond the obvious import, for example, 'And approach not the illicit sexual act';[18] and 'Kill no one whose life God has made sacred, except for a just cause [according to Islamic law].'[19] Ghazālī preferred the second approach not because the other approaches are unacceptable in the *Sharīʿah* or in the language, but because the second is more widespread amongst the scholars. Furthermore the second approach is less likely to lead to confusion between *naṣṣ* and *ẓāhir*.

The majority of Shāfiʿīs have followed Ghazālī in the opinion that *naṣṣ* is a provision which is not open to *ta'wīl*. Ibn Qudāmah defined *naṣṣ* as: 'The meaning taken only from the provision which is not susceptible to any other possibility',[20] as in the verse 'making ten days in all'.[21] 'Ten days' is *naṣṣ* because its meaning is unchangeable and not open to *ta'wīl*.

This is his opinion, although he maintains that *ẓāhir* may be called *naṣṣ* because *naṣṣ* means *ẓuhūr* in Arabic.

Qarrāfī offers three different definitions of *naṣṣ*:[22]

(1) *Naṣṣ* is what provides definitive meaning and is not open to another definite meaning, as in the case of numbers.

(2) *Naṣṣ* is what provides definite meaning although it might denote another meaning. The example of this is the plural (*ṣiyagh al-jumūʿ*) which indicates the smallest definite amount of plural,[23] and may include more than that, such as the word *ikhwah* (brothers) in the following, verse: 'if the deceased left brothers or [sisters], the mother has a sixth.'[24] The word 'brothers' is in the dual sense, but it could indicate any number larger than two.

(3) *Naṣṣ* is what provides meaning through any means. Most of the *fuqahā'* used *naṣṣ* in this sense.

Of these definitions Ghazālī mentioned only the first – that *naṣṣ* is a provision which provides definite meaning and as such is not open to other meanings. Qarrāfī, too, preferred this definition like him. Some *kalām* scholars like Bayḍāwī,[25] Ijī[26] and Anṣārī,[27] maintained that *naṣṣ* is: 'What provides a definite meaning.' Shawkānī defined *naṣṣ* as: 'What leaves no room for interpretation beyond the obvious sense (*ta'wīl*).[28] ʿĪd defined *naṣṣ* as whatever connotes one meaning, and no more. He mentioned as well that *fuqahā'* use this term for expressions that strongly exhibit certain meanings.[29]

From these various definitions one may conclude that the Shāfiʿīs differ in their conceptions of *naṣṣ*. It seems to me, however, that the conception which regards *naṣṣ* as a provision which is not open to *ta'wīl* is preferable.

Naṣṣ in the Qur'ān and *ḥadīth*[30]

When definitions of *naṣṣ* are compared the deep divergence between the Ḥanafī and the *mutakallimūn* approaches to *naṣṣ* becomes evident. One may also note that the *mutakallimūn* themselves are in deep disagreement over this matter. This divergence led, among other things, to a disagreement about the *naṣṣ* which figure in the Qur'ān and *ḥadīth*. Some scholars maintained that the occurrence of *naṣṣ* in the Qur'ān and *ḥadīth* is very rare. Only a limited number of examples of *naṣṣ* can be identified, such as the following verse and tradition which provides a clear and explicit meaning.

The Qur'ān states: 'Say [O Muḥammad]: He is Allāh, [the] One'[31] and 'Muḥammad is the Messenger of God.'[32] The Prophet said, 'O Unays go to this woman. If she admits adultery stone her.'[33] Other scholars, however, maintain that there are more instances of *naṣṣ*. They argue that internal (textual) and external evidence raises the text to the level of *naṣṣ*. The former scholars do not take this argument into consideration.

The value of *naṣṣ*

Adherence to *naṣṣ* is obligatory and its meaning must be applied. This is because, according to the majority of the Shāfiʿī school, *naṣṣ* yields a definite meaning which is not open to *taʾwīl*. Yet, even if the meaning is indefinite, it should be applied until a reliable proof indicates otherwise. This is due to the consensus of scholars that an indefinite meaning must be applied until a reliable proof suggests otherwise. A meaning may be avoided only if abrogation (*naskh*) is ascertained.

NOTES

1. M.L.ʿA, *al-Muʿjam al-Wasīṭ*, II:926; Lane, *Arabic-English Lexicon*, II:2797–99; *EI*, VI:881; Baʿlabakī, *al-Mawrid*, p. 1173.

2. Ghazālī, *al-Mustaṣfā*, p. 196.

3. See the linguistic meaning of *ẓāhir* and *naṣṣ* in Lane's *Arabic-English Lexicon*, II:1926 and II:2797.

4. Baṣrī, *al-Muʿtamad*, I:319; Ghazālī, *al-Mustaṣfā*, p. 196.

5. Qur'ānic verses related to duties like prayer, alms tax and so forth are *mujmal* and, accordingly, have no definite meaning, although Shāfiʿī called them *naṣṣ*.

6. Shāfiʿī, *al-Risālah*, pp.67–68. Also, Baṣrī, *al-Muʿtamad*, I:319.

7. One may say that God has commanded the obligatory prayer by *naṣṣ* even if His command 'And offer prayer.' is *mujmal*. The answer is that it is not *mujmal* in relation to obligation, but in relation to form, time and other matters.

8. Shāfiʿī, *al-Risālah*, p. 81.

9. Baṣrī, *al-Muʿtamad*, I:319; Ghazālī, *al-Mustaṣfā*, pp. 187,196; Rāzī, *al-Maḥṣūl*, I:1:316; Shawkānī, *Irshād al-Fuḥūl*, p. 156.

10. Baṣrī, *al-Muʿtamad*, I:319.

11. Shīrāzī, *al-Lummaʿ*, p. 48.

12. Qur'ān, XLVIII:29.

13. Qur'ān, XVII:32.

14. Qur'ān, VI:151.

15. Ghazālī stated that provisions are divided into two categories: *mujmal* and *mubayyan*. The provision whose meaning is determined, definite and as such not open to other interpretations, is called *mubayyan* or *naṣṣ*. The provision which has two or more indefinite meanings, none of which can have precedence over the others, is called *mujmal*. If the

provision has more than one meaning, but one meaning is apparent and has precedence, that provision is called *ẓāhir* (Ghazālī, *al-Mustaṣfā*, p. 187).

16. Ghazālī, *al-Mustaṣfā*, p. 196.

17. Ghazālī regards this opinion as correct, because it is applicable to the language and there is no objection in *Sharīʿah* (Ghazālī, *al-Mustaṣfā*, p. 196).

18. Qurʾān, XVII:32.

19. Qurʾān, VI:151.

20. Ibn Qudāmah, *Rawḍat al-Nāẓir*, II:27–28.

21. Qurʾān, II:196.

22. Qarrāfī, *Sharḥ Tanqīḥ al-Fuṣūl*, pp. 36–37.

23. Although two is dual, the majority of scholars see it as a plural based on the *ḥadīth*: 'Two and more than that are a core.' (Rāzī, *Maḥṣūl*, I:2:605).

24. Qurʾān, IV:11.

25. Ibn al-Ḥājib, *Sharḥ al-ʿAḍud maʿa Mukhtaṣar al-Muntahā*, II:168.

26. Aṣfahānī, *Sharḥ al-Minhāj*, I:444.

27. Anṣārī, *Ghāyat al-Wuṣūl*, p. 83.

28. Shawkānī, *Irshād al-Fuḥūl*, p. 156.

29. The difference between Ḥanafī and *kalām fuqahāʾ* regarding this matter would be interesting to study, because there is no doubt that their jurists use the word *naṣṣ* in a way that carries different connotations. Subkī, *al-Ibhāj*, I:360.

30. Qarrāfī, *Sharḥ Tanqīḥ al-Fuṣūl*, pp. 36; Ibn al-Ḥājib, *Sharḥ al-ʿAḍud maʿa Mukhtaṣar al-Muntahā*, II:168; Anṣārī, *Ghāyat al-Wuṣūl*, p. 83; Shawkānī, *Irshād al-Fuḥūl*, p. 156.

31. Qurʾān, CXII:1

32. Qurʾān, XLVIII:29.

33. Bukhārī, *al-Jāmiʿ al-Ṣaḥīḥ*, VIII:24–25 (no. 86:30).

CHAPTER 14

Comparison between
Ḥanafī and *Shāfiʿī*

In the Shāfiʿī *madhhab*, *ẓāhir* is an expression with an indefinite meaning. This meaning may be based on the essential literal meaning of the word,[1] or on customary use of the word.[2] When the word keeps its preferred meaning, it is termed *ẓāhir*; when it takes on a non-preferred meaning it is *mu'awwal* or interpreted. If no meaning can take preference, it is *mujmal*.[3] One may conclude that *ẓāhir* in the Shāfiʿī *madhhab* represents only one of the Ḥanafī categories of *naṣṣ*, because the schools accept that different explanations are possible.

According to the majority of Shāfiʿīs, *naṣṣ* yields definite meaning – like numbers and nouns. Therefore, it is like *mufassar* in the Ḥanafī *madhhab*. *Mufassar*, in its technical meaning, is not widely known in the Shāfiʿī *madhhab*, who impute a different meaning to *mufassar* from that of the Ḥanafī *madhhab*. Shāfiʿī used it as the opposite of *mujmal*,[4] while Rāzī used *mufassar* to refer to two categories of provisions:

(1) The clear (*wāḍiḥ*), which is a provision that needs no further explanation.

(2) An expression which, in order to be understood, needs further explanation than that which has already been provided.[5]

Muḥkam in the Shāfiʿī *madhhab* gives a clear meaning either in a definite or an indefinite way. One may observe that *naṣṣ* and *ẓāhir* in the Ḥanafī *madhhab* are both called *muḥkam* while the Shāfiʿī *madhhab* does not distinguish between the two. It is obvious from the definition given by Ijī that *muḥkam* yields a clear meaning in both *naṣṣ* and *ẓāhir*.[6]

In my opinion the Ḥanafī division of *wāḍiḥ* is more accurate and precise for the following reasons:

(1) It is clearer in both definition and categorisation. A degree of clarity is more easily attainable by reference to the detailed definitions provided by the Ḥanafīs.

(2) Their division includes more meanings acquired through the different proofs.

NOTES

1. Such as the general word (ʿāmm), which provides a general meaning.
2. Such as the word ṣalāh (prayer).
3. Rāzī, *al-Maḥṣūl*, I:1:316.
4. Shāfiʿī, *al-Umm*, 7:180.
5. Rāzī, *al-Maḥṣūl*, I:3:227–228.
6. Badshāh, *Taysīr al-Taḥrīr*, I:144; Aṣfahānī, *Sharḥ al-Minhāj*, I:185.

Introduction to the Ḥanafī Approach to Unclear (*mubham*) Words

Mubham means an obscure, dubious, vague or unclear word; speech or language that is dubious, vague and not clearly expressed or understood.[1] The technical definition of *mubham* is based on its literal meaning. It is a provision with a dubious meaning and an objective obscured by the provision itself, or due to an external incident. Both the meaning and the objective of the *mubham* are attainable as a result of research. These provisions do not convey by themselves clear meanings, and in order to be understood additional explanations are needed.

As mentioned before, an authoritative text which a *mujtahid* is unable to understand is termed *mubham*. The indication of a legal ruling in the case of *mubham* is concealed. This is due either to the provision itself or to an incidental reason. On this basis Taftāzānī[2] divided *mubham* into two groups. In the first group the obscurity is due to the expression itself and includes *mushkil*, *mujmal* and *mutashābih*. Obscurity in the second group is due to an incidental reason and includes *khafī* only.

The obscurity of the first group can be removed by legal reasoning (*ijtihād*). If legal reasoning is sufficient for this task, what was unclear (*mubham*) is called *mushkil*. If the legal reasoning is insufficient, but support from an authoritative text is needed, the obscurity is called *mujmal*. If neither the legal reasoning nor the authoritative text is sufficient, it is termed *mutashābih*.

Because Islamic scholars have provided explanations for the most authoritative texts, one may conclude that obscurity can be removed mostly by legal reasoning (*ijtihād*). Sometimes, however, it can be removed only by an explanation from the Lawgiver. Without such an explanation the expression will be *mutashābih*.[3]

It might be added here that the obscurity in *mubham* is not always at the same level. This is why Ḥanafī scholars divided unclear legal texts (*mubham*) into four categories: *khafī*, *mushkil*, *mujmal*, and *mutashābih*. The most obscure is *mutashābih*, followed by *mujmal*, *mushkil* and *khafī*. We will now explore these categories, their degrees of vagueness or obscurity, and their effect on legal reasoning and the deduction of legal rulings from authoritative texts. To make such an exploration valid, we need to focus on the interpretation found in the process of juridical deduction (*istinbāṭ al-aḥkām*). The first category is *khafī*.

NOTES

1. Lane, *Arabic-English Lexicon*, I:268–269; Baʿlabakī, *al-Mawrid*, p. 948.

2. Taftāzānī, *Sharḥ al-Talwīḥ ʿalā al-Tawḍīḥ*, I:126.

3. The Qurʾān states that some of the verses are *mutashābih*: 'It is He who sent to you [Muḥammad] the Book. In it are verses that are entirely clear – they are the foundations of the Book [and these are the verses of *aḥkām* (commandments), *farāʾiḍ* (obligatory duties) and *ḥudūd* (laws for the punishment of thieves, adulterers, etc.)] – and others that are not entirely clear (*mutashābihāt*)' (Qurʾān III:7).

CHAPTER 15

The Hidden
(*al-Khafī*)

The linguistic definition of *khafī*

Khafī refers to hidden, covert, latent, unperceived or barely perceived, unknown, invisible.[1]

The technical definition *of khafī*

Ḥanafī scholars proffer different yet similar definitions of *khafī*. Dabbūsi defined it as: 'An expression whose meaning is obscured not by the language itself but because of an external factor. This would cause the meaning to be less understandable, unless analysed.[2] Bazdawī defined *khafī* as: 'An expression whose meaning is dubious not due to the language mood but due to an external factor. That meaning can only be grasped if analysed.'[3] Nasafī maintained that *khafī* is: 'An expression whose meaning is obscured due to an external matter rather than the language mood itself. That meaning could be grasped as a result of research only.[4]

From these definitions one may conclude that *khafī* in the Ḥanafī *madhhab* has a basic apparent meaning (*ẓāhir*), but that apparent meaning is disrupted by an external factor which causes obscurity and vagueness when we extend the apparent meaning to its implied applications. Therefore *khafī* is an expression with an apparent judgement applicable to more than one case; but where one case is clear, and the others are obscure. The obscurity and vagueness in these applications may be eliminated only through exercising *ijtihād* by referring to authoritative texts, and taking into consideration the aims and objectives of the Sharī'ah.

Examples of *khafī*

The Qur'ān states: 'Cut off the hand of the thief, male or female, as a recompense for that which they commit, an exemplary punishment from God.

And God is All-Powerful, All-Wise.'[5] This verse speaks about the thief (*sāriq*) and his punishment. According to the Islamic jurists (*fuqahā'*),[6] the word *sāriq* has an apparent meaning when applied to a person who secretly takes from others personal goods which are kept in their normal keeping place. The word *sāriq* is apparent with respect to the thief who is known by that name, but it is obscured in the case of the thief who is known by other names, such as pickpocket, grave robber, etc. Therefore, it is obscure whether or not 'thief' includes pickpocket, grave robber and so on, and whether such a person should be punished like a thief (*sāriq*) by the cutting off of his right hand.[7]

The meaning of theft is well known. The basic elements of theft, however, are present in many other illegal activities. People may seize the possessions of others (*māl al-ghayr*) illegitimately in various ways. These people are called by names other than thief, and their misdeeds may not count as theft. Should they then receive the same verdict as the thief, or should the verdict be different?

One example which may be cited here is that of the pickpocket (*ṭarrār*).[8] The pickpocket has the characteristics of a thief – he seizes the possessions of others illegitimately. However, he is not called a thief. His actions may have further characteristics which we would not find in a theft, because a pickpocket takes the possessions of others by surprise, unexpectedly, by using skill and trickery, when the owner is fully awake and thinks himself to be fully protecting his possessions. These further attributes are what makes the pickpocket a 'pickpocket'. Similarly, the grave robber (*nabbāsh*)[9] secretly takes valuables from graves. Should he receive the same verdict as the thief mentioned in the verse?

There is also the question of the person who borrows something from someone and then denies that he has borrowed it. Should he face the punishment prescribed for the thief?

The same situation applies to 'killer' in the *hadīth*: ' The killer shall not inherit.'[10] Does that word include unintentional killing, killing caused by negligence, killing by a mad person, lawful killing, justifiable killing, etc.? On the varieties of ways in which a person is killed, this tradition is hidden and obscured.[11]

Therefore, the ambiguity in these authoritative texts in relation to their possible applications (pickpocket, grave robber, etc.) arises from the fact that these applications have different names and attributes from those mentioned in the texts.[12] The basic linguistic rule is that every name is given to a particular subject and that certain attributes indicate differences. These subjects have different names and attributes and because of that the results have to be different. Therefore, we do not know whether they were given different names from that of thief, killer, etc., because the magnitude of the theft or killing is greater or smaller in their cases.

The only way to remove this vagueness is by exercising *ijtihād* to ascertain whether or not these deeds include the characteristics of theft, killing, etc. This has an important bearing on the verdict attached to that action, and on whether it should be classified as a theft or not. If in the deed all the elements stipulated by Sharīʿah are found, the person should receive the same verdict; if not the verdict should be different.[13]

By comparing the pickpocket with the thief, Ḥanafī jurists found that all elements of theft are present in the action of the first. A distinct name is given to the pickpocket, because the meaning of theft (skill and proficiency in stealing, danger, crime, offence) is more evident in the deed of the pickpocket than in theft itself. The pickpocket takes from others goods which are kept in well-protected places, while the owners are awake and careful in guarding their possessions but careless for a moment. So he steals with skill and cleverness, by acting just when the owner is not on his guard. When the character of the theft becomes apparent to us, the ambiguity is removed and we become sure that the pickpocket is in fact a thief, but not in an ordinary manner. He steals at the moment when the owner is careless, asleep or absent. The opinion of the Ḥanafī jurists was therefore unanimous that he should be classified as a thief and receive the same verdict.[14]

The majority of Ḥanafī jurists[15] maintain that the grave robber should not receive the punishment fixed by law (*ḥadd*) but by non-fixed punishment (*taʿzīr*). They hold that the meaning which explain the rulings (*manāṭ al-ḥukm*) on theft are not fulfilled in the case of grave robbers.[16] A dead person cannot be seen guarding his belongings in the grave, nor does he have the intention to do so. His ownership of his belongings is legally incomplete. Theft implies that the stolen item(s) were kept in an adequately safe place; whereas the description grave robber (*nabbāsh*) implies that the stolen goods were not preserved in an adequately safe place. Because of these doubts, the ruling for the grave robber cannot be the same as that for the thief by reference to the alluded meaning (*ishārat al-naṣṣ*).[17]

The value of *khafī*

Muslims should believe that the intended meaning of *khafī* is correct even if that meaning is obscure. They should make every effort to discover the intended meaning until the obscurity is removed.[18] *Khafī* should not be extended to dubious and obscure application before further research and proper *ijtihād*. When it is confirmed that the meaning of a word applies where it had been obscure, the ruling may be extended to that application. In his legal reasoning the *mujtahid* should depend on the aims and objectives of Islamic law and the authoritative texts relevant to the subject matter.

NOTES

1. Lane, *Arabic-English Lexicon*, I:776–7; Ba'labakī, *al-Mawrid*, p. 157.

2. Dabbūsī, *al-Asrār fī al-Uṣūl wa al-Furū' fī Taqwīm Adillat al-Shar'*, I:263.

3. It would be clearer to say '*bi'āriḍ min ghayr al-ṣīghah*'. The same applies to other definitions. In my translation of these definitions I have taken this into account. Bazdawī (*Uṣūl al-Bazdawī*, I:52).

4. Nasafī, *Kashf al-Asrār*, I:214.

5. Qur'ān, V:38.

6. Marghīnānī, *al-Hidāyah*, II:118; Ibn Rushd, *Bidāyat al-Mujtahid*, II:445; Ibn Qudāmah, *al-Mughnī*, VIII:240.

7. When the theft fulfils all its conditions and stipulations.

8. *Ṭarr* is taking goods from someone who is in a wakeful state, and who consciously protects and guards his goods, but is in a state of ignorance (Kawrānī, *Sharḥ Mukhtaṣar al-Manār*, p. 54).

9. *Nabsh* is taking clothes from dead persons in their graves, after their burial (Kawrānī, *Sharḥ Mukhtaṣar al-Manār*, p. 54).

10. Dārimī, *Sunan*, II:385.

11. This obscurity led to disagreement. Mālikīs maintain that killing by error, for example, is not included in this tradition, while Ḥanafīs include it in order to safeguard lives (Badrān, *Uṣūl al-Fiqh al-Islāmī*, p. 411).

12. Islamic scholars disagree on whether or not analogy (*qiyās*) may be used when the language is in question, so that we can call a subject by the name of another subject in cases where one subject has the characteristics of the other (Isnawī, *al-Tamhīd*, pp. 468–469).

13 The elements of theft stipulated by the Sharī'ah are: a) the possession is taken away secretly; b) it is taken away with criminal intent; c) the stolen item is legally owned by the person from whom it is stolen; d) the stolen item had been taken from the possession of its real owner; e) the stolen item should already have come into the possession of the thief; f) the stolen item should reach the value of *niṣāb*. If these elements are found in any kind of action they would make for theft; if any is missing they would not and *ḥadd* could not be applied.

14 Nasafī, *Kashf al-Asrār*, I:215; Sarakhsī, *Uṣūl al-Sarakhsī*, I:167; Bukhārī, *al-Tawḍīḥ fī Ḥall Ghawāmiḍ al-Tanqīḥ*, I:126; Kawrānī, *Sharḥ Mukhtaṣar al-Manār*, p. 54. Abū Ḥanīfah said that if the pickpocket stole from inside the pocket, *ḥadd* should be applied; but if he stole from outside, *ḥadd* should be avoided. His disciple Abū Yūsuf maintained that *ḥadd* applies in both cases. The latter opinion was preferred by Ṭaḥāwī (Ṭaḥāwī, *Mukhtaṣar al-Ṭaḥāwī*, p. 271). Ḥanafī jurists disagree on whether or not this ruling is deducible from the explicit meaning of the text (*'ibārat al-naṣṣ*) or from the alluded meaning (*ishārat al-naṣṣ*) . The majority maintained that this ruling is derived from *ishārat al-naṣṣ* because the ruling relating to theft is extended to include the pickpocket. (Nasafī, *Kashf al-Asrār*, I:216; Sarakhsī, *Uṣūl al-Sarakhsī*, I:167; Bādshāh, *Taysīr al-Taḥrīr*, I:157). It is important to note that the punishment fixed by law (*ḥadd*) cannot be established by analogy (*qiyās*), because the *ḥudūd* are averted by doubts and *qiyās* contains some doubt.

15. Ṭaḥāwī, *Mukhtaṣar al-Ṭaḥāwī*, p. 273; Marghīnānī, *al-Hidāyah*, II:121.

16. a) Ownership – a dead person has no legal right to own and his heir may inherit only what the deceased does not need, and he needs clothes; b) possession – a person cannot manage it; c) value – a valuable thing is what people desire and seek; the clothes in the grave are disliked and avoided; d) an adequately protected place; graves are not so.

17. Especially regarding punishments fixed by law (*ḥudūd*). These are averted by doubt. Nasafī, *Kasf al-Asrār*, I:215; Sarakhsī, *Uṣūl al-Sarakhsī*, I:167; Bukhārī, *al-Tawḍīḥ fī Ḥall*

Ghawāmiḍ al-Tanqīḥ, I:126; Kawrānī, *Sharḥ Mukhtaṣar al-Manār*, p. 54. See also the explanation of Qur'ān XVII:23.

18. Sarakhsī, *Uṣūl al-Sarakhsī*, I:168.

CHAPTER 16

The Problematic
(*al-Mushkil*)

The linguistic definition of *mushkil*

Mushkil refers to problematic, complex, hard to solve, difficult, intricate, equivocal.[1]

The technical definition of *mushkil*

Ḥanafī scholars have offered various definitions for *mushkil*. Dabbūsī defined it as an expression that 'has a meaning which is ambiguous to understand for the listener. The ambiguity is caused by the subtlety of that meaning or the metaphor, not by the deceptive action of the originator'.[2] Nasafī defined it as an expression that 'involves various equal meanings'.[3] Sarakhsī maintained that *mushkil* is a name for an expression whose intended meaning cannot be identified because it has a mixed meaning. It may be identified only by a proof that can highlight it among other meanings.[4]

Based on these definitions a comprehensive definition for *mushkil* may be formulated to the effect that *mushkil* is a self-obscured expression. Its obscurity is due to its variety of meanings. The intended meaning of *mushkil* can not be identified without external evidence to distinguish it from others. This can be done through further reflection. The *mushkil*[5] is the opposite of *naṣṣ*. By referring to the scale detailing the categories of the *muḥkam*, it can be seen to be one degree above *khafī*, just as the *naṣṣ* is one degree clearer than *ẓāhir*. *Mushkil* is more ambiguous than *khafī*, because the obscurity in *mushkil* is in the provision itself, which is inherently ambiguous. In *khafī* the obscurity is due to an external factor occurring when the basic apparent meaning is clear. The obscurity in the same provision is greater than that caused by an external matter.

Therefore, the effort needed to understand the *mushkil* is greater than that needed for *khafī*, because with *khafī* the *mujtahid* will examine the external matter for more or fewer meanings than the apparent meaning of the provision. In the case of *mushkil*, a *mujtahid* will consider the provision itself and its various meanings, which cannot be understood without proper research and consideration involving the external evidence and proofs. Hence, in the case of the *mushkil* ordinary research is insufficient; further scrutiny and careful examination are required in order to distinguish between closely related meanings which are indicated by the same provision. An example of a *mushkil* meaning is that of a person who leaves his country and mixes with people who are similar to him. Before finding him, one must find his place and then appraise everyone in order to distinguish him from the rest.

The origins of ambiguity in *mushkil*

The obscurity in *mushkil* is in the provision itself. The intended meaning of the provision is obscured due to one of the following reasons:

(a) Homonym[6] – When a word is originally coined to serve more than one meaning. The speaker normally means one of these meanings, while the listener does not know which one this is. The confusion may be due to the fact that the intended meaning is mixed with others, leading to obscurity. The listener will then be in need of legal reasoning (*ijtihād*) to discover the intended meaning and distinguish it from others implied by the word. This is the case with all homonyms when the expression does not contain a proof pointing to the intended meaning. In such situations a proper exercise of *ijtihād* is required to distinguish the intended meaning from that which is not intended by using all relevant external evidences that suggest the intended meaning.

(b) Rhetoric metaphor – When the metaphoric meaning of a word is used frequently, causing the word to be commonplace in its metaphoric meaning, as distinct from the original meaning of the word.

The intended meaning and other meanings may be distinguished through deep reflection and scrutiny by relying on outside proofs and evidences. As a result of this process, the preferable meaning emerges and becomes clear. At this point *mushkil* is similar to *khafī*, but it is above it because there is the need for further thought on the mood and its forms and categories.

Examples of *mushkil*

The Qur'ān states: 'If you are in state of ritual impurity (*janābah*),[7] purify yourselves (*fa-ṭṭahharū*).'[8] This verse is *mushkil* in relation to some parts of the body, like nostrils and the mouth cavity.[9] The reason for this is that exterior parts of the skin have to be washed and the internal parts do not. Both the nostrils and the mouth cavity are considered similar to the internal parts of the human body in a real (*ḥaqīqī*)[10] and legal (*ḥukmī*)[11] meaning. Because of this consideration there is no need to wash either the mouth or the nostrils during the *ṭahārah kubrā*. These parts are considered similar also to the external parts of the body.[12] Because of this consideration[13] the requirement to wash them during *ṭahārah kubrā* is based accordingly on the rule that all external parts have to be washed.

In the case of *janābah* there is the problem of whether or not the mouth and nose are similar to the internal or external parts of the body, since they have been found to be similar to both. According to *ijtihād* they were joined to the exterior in the case of *janābah* because the command related to purification is emphatically as *fa-ṭṭahhirū* (purify yourself).[14] Contrary to this, in the case of ablution (*wuḍū'*), the nostrils and the mouth cavity are joined to the inner parts of the human body. Therefore, one need not wash them. This is also supported by the following arguments:

(1) No language emphasis exists for the face, since only the word 'wash' is used (*fa-ghsilū wujūhakum*).

(2) In *wuḍū'* the *wājib* is washing the face (*wajh*)[15] and there is no visible surface in the case of the nostrils and the mouth cavity.

(3) In *janābah*, however, the *wājib* is washing the body. The body is a name given to both the exterior and inner parts, but what is difficult or hard to wash is excluded due to the impossibility of doing so (*taʿadhdhur*). For example, if the exterior part of the body is injured, it is excluded from washing; wiping the wound is sufficient.

(4) Since ablution is more frequent than washing the entire body, ablution becomes more eligible for convenience and exemption.

The Qur'ān states: 'So go to your tilth when or how you will.'[16] The word *annā*, mentioned in the Qur'ān twenty eight times, is a homonym (*lafẓ mushtarak*).[17] It is a *mushkil* when it forms part of an expression, because it could mean different things. For example, in the verse: 'He said: "O Mary! From were have you received this?"'[18] Here *annā* is used to mean 'from were'. *Annā* is also used to mean 'how', as in the verse: 'He said: "O my Lord! How can I have a son when I am very old, and my wife is barren?"'[19] Since *annā* is a homonym, there are different interpretations of the first verse:[20]

(1) Some maintain that *annā* means 'how' (*kayfa*). Therefore, the verse means: 'in any position you want'. This meaning was cited by many interpreters of the Qur'ān like Ibn ʿAbbās, according to whom the verse means: 'He approaches her however he likes, in any manner, as long as it is not from the rear, or during her menstrual period.'

Similar views have been recorded from ʿIkrimah, Mujāhid, Ibn Kaʿb and others.

(2) Some, like Ḍaḥḥāk, maintain that *annā* means 'when', i.e., at any time of day or night.

(3) Some maintain that *annā* means where (*ayna*), so the first verse means 'in any place you want, the vagina or the rear'. According to this interpretation, having sex with one's wife from the rear is allowed.

(4) Some hold that it means 'how' – i.e., go to your tilth and you may ejaculate however you like, in the vagina or out of it. This opinion is ascribed to Ibn ʿAbbās and Saʿīd ibn Musayyab.

In the first verse, however, *annā* is translated as 'when or how'[21] and interpreted thus by commentators of the Qurʾān. They said that the verse means: 'have sexual relations with your wives in any manner, in any position, and at any time, as long, as it is through the vagina and not the rear.'[22] This is the opinion of the majority of Islamic jurists as well.[23]

The ambiguity in *annā* is removed by careful examination of internal and external evidence and the reason for the revelation of the particular verse (*sabab al-nuzūl*). Some aspects of the internal and external evidence prove that *annā* in the first verse means 'how' and 'when', and not 'where'.

(1) Women are called 'tilth': 'Your wives are a tilth for you.' – i.e., they are the place for your husbandry (cultivation). Mentioning the place of cultivation proves that approaching one's wife through other bodily regions is forbidden. The permissible region is also indicated by the verse: 'And when they have purified themselves, then go into them as God has ordained for you.'[24]

Women are compared with arable land because the sperm is placed in their wombs just as crops are planted in arable land. 'Seed' can be planted only in a woman's uterus (because it is a fertile place), not the rear. This argument is supported by the fact that the main purpose for sexual intercourse in Islam is to produce children and not merely to satisfy sexual desire.[25]

(2) The second proof that *annā* means 'when' and 'how', not 'where', is based on the Islamic principle of prohibiting harmful and annoying actions. If having sex with one's wife during her menstrual period is prohibited[26] because it causes harm and annoyance (i.e., this is the ʿillat al-ḥukm), then it seems all the more fitting that the sexual act from the rear should be forbidden, because the issues relating to harm, lack of cleanliness and irritation are more pronounced.[27]

Ibn al-ʿArabī said: 'I asked al-Imām al-Qāḍī al-Ṭūsī this question and he answered: "The sexual act from the rear with the wife is forbidden under any circumstances. God has forbidden vaginal penetration during the period of menstruation because of the temporary dirtiness that accompanies it. Therefore it is all the more fitting that the sexual act from the rear be forbidden because of the inevitable dirtiness."[28]

(3) This verse was revealed in response to some people's claim that if a person has sexual intercourse with his wife, approaching her from the back

to the vagina, the child conceived would be cross-eyed. According to its *sabab al-nuzūl* this verse was revealed to deny that claim.[29] Therefore, the meaning of the verse '*annā shi'tum*' would be: have sexual relations with your wives in any manner by which this goal is achievable, and it is achievable if it is through the vagina (place for tilth) and not through the rear (place of feces).

The final conclusion is that *annā* generalises ways, not places.

The Qur'ān states: 'And divorced women shall wait [as regards their marriage] for three menstrual periods (*thalāthata qurū'in*).'[30] *Qur'* is a homonym which means both cleanliness and menstruation. Some scholars exercised *ijtihād* and concluded that, in this verse, it means cleanliness. Others have said that it means menstruation.[34]

In its description of the cups of Paradise the Qur'ān says: 'And amongst them will be passed round vessels of silver and cups of glass, bright as glass but made of silver.'[31] The meaning of *qawārira min fiḍḍatin* is *mushkil*, because the cup (*qarūrah*) is normally made from glass, not silver (*fiḍḍah*). Upon closer examination, however, we find that silver has two specifications: the first is negative in that it does not show what is inside; the other is positive and praiseworthy because it shines. Glass has the opposite specifications. From this usage we know that the cups described have the clarity and softness of glass, combined with the beauty and shine of silver. This is called rhetoric metaphor (*istʿārah badīʿah*). This use of this rhetoric metaphor means that we need further examination in order to comprehend factual meaning.[32]

The Qur'ān states: 'And divorced women shall wait [as regards their marriage] for three menstrual periods [*thalāthata qurū'in*].'[33] The word *qur'* is a homonym which means both the clean period between two menstruations (*ṭuhr*) and menstruation (*ḥayḍ*). Whichever of these distinct meanings is adopted, the legal ruling will differ accordingly. Some scholars exercised *ijtihād* and concluded that, in this verse, it means *ṭuhr*, while others maintained that it means *ḥayḍ*.

If someone makes a will to the effect that property should be given to his *mawālī*, it will need further explanation. If the testator dies before explaining whom he meant by his will, the will be invalid[35] because *mawlā* (pl. *mawālī*) is a homonym and includes both the one who frees (the master) and the one freed (his freed slave). The will becomes invalid because the beneficiary is unknown due to the fact that one meaning does not have precedence over the other and the implementation of the general meaning of the expression is impossible.[36]

The value of *mushkil*

Muslims should believe that the intended meaning of *mushkil* is the truth, even if that meaning is obscure. They should make an effort to understand until the intended meaning is discovered and obscurity removed. This takes place through analysis, scrutiny, careful examination and the use of methods leading to the intended meaning, which is then implemented when it becomes clear and distinct from other meanings.[37]

NOTES

1. M.L. ʿA, *al-Muʿjam al-Wasīṭ*, I:491; Lane, *Arabic-English Lexicon*, II:1588; Baʿlabakī, *al-Mawrid*, p. 1049

2. Dabbūsī, *al-Asrār fī Uṣūl wa al-Furūʿ fī Taqwīm Adillat al-Sharʿ*, I:264

3. That is, an equivocal expression in its meanings. Nasafī, *Kashf al-Asrār*, I:216.

4. Sarakhsī, *Uṣūl al-Sarakhsī*, I:168.

5. *Mushkil* and *mujmal* are very close to each other. This has caused some confusion for those scholars who maintained that they are the same. This opinion is incorrect. Sarakhsī, *Uṣūl al-Sarakhsī*, I:168.

6. Any homonym is at the same time *mushkil* and there is no objection for one thing to be called by two different names for different aspects. However, *mushkil* is more general because it may have other causes than the homonym. Ibn Amīr al-Ḥājj, *al-Taqrīr wa al-Taḥbīr*, I:159.

7. Ceremonial impurity (*janābah*) is normally associated with sexual discharge.

8. Qurʾān, V:6.

9. Some scholars mentioned this example for *khafī*, saying that *taṭahhur* is known in both a literal and a Sharīʿah sense, and from that perspective is similar to *ṭarrār* (pickpocket) and *nabbāsh* (grave robber). This assertion is inaccurate because the meaning or *taṭahhur* is unknown without research and scrutiny. It is known that *taṭahhur* means 'washing up the whole body', but does the 'whole body' imply mouth and nostrils? Taftāzānī, *Sharḥ al-Talwīḥ ʿalā al-Tawḍīḥ*, I:126–127.

10. Because they are covered by the skin.

11. On the basis of the ruling that swallowing saliva does not invalidate fasting.

12. On the basis of the ruling that fasting will not be invalidated if food touched them (by entering the mouth).

13. This consideration and the previous one are based on the Sunnah of the Prophet.

14. Before research and scrutiny we do not know if this exaggeration is related to quality or quantity. For example, Mālik maintained that it is related to quality. Because of that, he maintained that rubbing is *wājib* during bathing. Ḥanafī jurists maintained that it is related to quantity. Because of that they said that the mouth should be washed. Dassūqī, *Ḥāshiyat al-Dassūqī ʿalā al-Sharḥ al-Kabīr*, I:126; Marghīnānī, *al-Hidāyah*, I:16).

15. *Wajh* (the face) in Arabic literally means visible surface when the name is applied to the exterior part of the body.

16. Qurʾān, II:223.

17. Bādshāh quoted Riḍā as saying that *annā* could have three different meanings: where, how and when. (Bādshāh, *Taysīr al-Taḥrīr*, I:158–159.)

18. Qurʾān, III:37.

19. Qur'ān, III:40.

20. Ṭabarī, *Jāmiʿ al-Bayān ʿan Taʾwīl Āy al-Qurʾān*, IV:398–416; Ibn Kathīr, *Tafsīr al-Qurʾān al-ʿAẓīm*, I:351–358

21. See translations of the Qurʾān by Hilālī and Khān and by the Presidency of Islamic Research, IFTA, Call and Guidance.

22. Qurṭubī, *al-Jāmiʿ li Aḥkām al-Qurʾān*, III:91–94; Ibn Kathīr, *Tafsīr al-Qurʾān al-ʿAẓīm*, I:351–358.

23. Ibn al-ʿArabī, *Aḥkām al-Qurʾān*, I:174; Qurṭubī, *al-Jāmiʿ li Aḥkām al-Qurʾān*, III:91–94.

24. Qurʾān, II:222.

25. Therefore the sexual act from the rear with one's wife is forbidden, but this prohibition is indefinite (*ẓannī*). Therefore, someone who denies it is not considered a *kāfir*. This act is compared by analogy with sexual relations during a woman's period. The reason (*ʿillah*) for the latter's interdiction is the harm it may cause.

26. The Qurʾān states: 'They ask you concerning menstruation. Say: That is an *adhā* [i.e., it is harmful for the husband to have sexual intercourse with his wife while she is having her menses], therefore keep away from women during menses and go not unto them until they are purified [from menses and have taken a bath].' Qurʾān, II:222.

27. This conclusion is derived from the text by using the principle termed *dalalāt al-naṣṣ* or *qiyās awlā*.

28. Ibn al-ʿArabī, *Aḥkām al-Qurʾān*, I:174.

29. Ibn Kathīr, *Tafsīr al-Qurʾān al-ʿAẓīm*, I: 351.

30. Qurʾān, II:228.

31. Qurʾān, LXXVI:15–16.

32. Bukhārī mentioned many other examples of *mushkil*. Bukhārī, *Kashf al-Asrār*, I:52–53.

33. Qurʾān, II:228.

34. Ibn Kathīr, *Tafsīr al-Qurʾān al-ʿAẓīm*, II:89

35. This opinion is narrated from Abū Ḥanīfah (*ẓāhir al-riwāyah*). Ibn Amīr al-Ḥājj, *Taqrīr wa al-Taḥbīr*, I:159.

36. Bukhārī mentioned many other examples of *mushkil*. Bukhārī, *Kashf al-Asrār*, I:52–53.

37. Nasafī, *Kashf al-Asrār*, I:216; Sarakhsī, *Uṣūl al-Sarakhsī*, I:168.

CHAPTER 17

The Concise
(*al-Mujmal*)

The linguistic definition of *mujmal*

Mujmal refers to summarised, outlined, abridged, condensed, epitomised, concise, brief, short; a word, phrase, or speech which includes or implies a number of unexplained things requiring elaboration.[1]

The technical definition of *mujmal*

Ḥanafī scholars suggest various definitions for *mujmal*. Dabbūsī defined it as an expression 'whose meaning cannot essentially be understood due to unfamiliar language or metaphorical semantics.'[2] Bazdawī defined *mujmal* as an expression which 'carries various concise meanings, and the intended meaning becomes so ambiguous that it cannot be comprehended from the same expression but is rather arrived at by referring to the explanation, research and thinking.'[3] Nasafī offered an identical definition to that of Bazdawī's, but excluded the word *ta'ammul* [thinking or contemplation].[4] Sarakhsī maintained that *mujmal* is a word whose purpose cannot be understood without an explanation from the speaker, due to metaphorical semantics or its unusual syntax.[5]

From these definitions one may conclude that *mujmal* in the Ḥanafī *madhhab* is an expression the intended meaning of which is intrinsically hidden and unclear. Consequently, it is difficult to understand without an explanation from the originator, whether the ambiguity is due to the special meaning intended by the Lawgiver, or due to homonymous meanings, or the unusual usage of the word. The only way to remove this ambiguity is by referring back to the explanation of the Lawgiver, i.e., to the authoritative texts.

Comparison between *mujmal* and *mushkil*

By way of comparison, ambiguity occurs in the used expression. It is not caused by an external matter, as in the case of *khafī*. The explanation required in the case of *mujmal* can only be provided by the speaker. In the case of *mushkil* the explanation is attainable through analysis. Consequently, the *mujmal* is more ambiguous than *mushkil*, and may be contrasted with *mufassar*, which is a category of *wāḍih*.

Categories of *mujmal*

In respect of causes, *mujmal* may be divided into three categories:

(1) that which occurs through the use of the word in a particular legal context, not in its apparent literal meaning, in this manner conveying a technical or juridical concept intended by the Lawgiver, known as *naql sharʿī*;

(2) that which is caused by a competition of equal meanings (homonyms) with no possibility of preference to any one among them, and without any indication of which one might be the correct one; and

(3) that which is caused by the oddity of a totally unfamiliar word.

Examples of *mujmal*

The most common category of *mujmal* is the first one (*naql sharʿī*). At this juncture we have to point out that many Arabic words took on a new shades of meaning under the influence of Islam, because the Lawgiver used them for purposes other than the original ones. Words like prayer (*ṣalāh*), alms tax (*zakāh*) had certain literal meanings which were later enhanced and reproduced. This process of reproduction led to ambiguities that cannot easily be dispelled by research or reflection alone. The key to the meaning of *mujmal* is the prerogative of the Lawgiver. As such, these ambiguities cannot be removed without recourse to the Lawgiver's explanation.

In Islamic law, the *Sunnah* is seen as the main source for resolving ambiguity. Its predominating role in interpretation is attributable to the large Islamic legal corpus. The Qur'ān is no doubt primordial in its textual authority. However, the material used in interpretation is more voluminous in the *Sunnah* than in the Qur'ān.

The value of the *Sunnah* in this is clearly reflected in the writings of all Islamic legal scholars, whose principal support is the verse: 'And We have also sent down unto you [O Muhammad] the reminder [the Qur'ān], that you may explain clearly to men what is sent down to them, and what they may give thought to.'[6]

Shāfiʿī clearly highlighted the role of the *Sunnah* in his *Risālah*. In his view, there are obligations that the Almighty established in His Book, which He made clear by the tongue of the Prophet. The following examples provided by Shāfiʿī are in fact a classical model for a process of interpretation that can be found in many books of the *fiqh* – the daily number of prayers, *zakāh*.[7] When a *mujmal* is explained it becomes *mufassar*,[8] as in the following examples:

(a) Prayer is a duty upon every responsible Muslim. This ruling is derived from Qurʾānic verses. In one of them, repeated in the Qurʾān more then eighty times, prayer is demanded: 'And offer prayers'.[9] The verse: 'Verily, the prayer is enjoined on the believers at fixed hours'[10] is even stronger in enjoining this ritual upon the Muslims. However, one may ask what is meant by the word 'prayer' (*ṣalāh*). *Ṣalāh* in Arabic denotes call, invocation, supplication (*duʿāʾ*).[11] Muslims, however, designated this name to the special prayer required by their new faith of Islam. Prayers are defined by Islamic jurists as: 'Special acts and sayings [utterances] opened by *takbīr* [*Allāhu Akbar*] and concluded [ended] by *taslīm* [*assalām ʿalaykum*].'[12] Therefore, the word *ṣalāh* developed a new meaning (*maʿnā sharʿī*)[13] because the Lawgiver used it for a purpose other than the original one. Ibn al-Athīr defined *ṣalāh* by considering its new meaning and the known ritual which linguistically refers to supplication.[14]

The ambiguity in the word *ṣalāh* is largely caused by this new legal meaning occurring in the Qurʾān. The Qurʾān states: 'And offer prayers perfectly.' However, no verse explains the details – i.e., the forms, parts, number of prayers, or their times, number of obeisances and prostrations, its conditions, stipulations, duties, etc. Instead, the Qurʾān contains general statements about the times,[15] the manner and way of performing prayers.[16]

The verses referred to here are ambiguous because of their concise meanings. Consequently, they are in need of explanation, as provided by the *Sunnah*. The Prophet gave verbal and practical elaboration to those concise verses of the Qurʾān which were in need of an explanation. In the case of *ṣalāh* the *Sunnah* clarified the number of prayers, their level of obligation, their time, number of obeisances, prostrations and conditions. The Prophet was keen to explain everything related to the prayer. He once prayed on the *mimbar* and stated afterwards: 'Indeed, I have done this that you may copy me and learn my prayer.'[17] In another *ḥadīth* he said: 'Pray as you see me pray.'[18] With the *Sunnah*, the ambiguity of the previous verses disappeared.

(b) In dealing with *zakāh* the Qurʾān states: 'And give obligatory charity [*zakāh*].'[19] The word *zakāh* literally means growth and increase.[20] It sometimes means purification (*taṭhīr*), as in the verse: 'Take alms [*ṣadaqah*] from their wealth in order to purify them.'[21] When Islam appeared, the word *zakāh* was given a new dimension, to a certain extent connected with its literal meaning. Islamic jurists defined *zakāh* as: 'Paying out a fixed amount of wealth, which once reached, determines the minimum value [*niṣāb*] to be given to certain categories of people, which receive textual mention by the Lawgiver.'[22] The new meaning also indicated the amount paid. Therefore, it is a homonym which indicates both the paid amount and the act of paying.

The Islamic scholars held that *zakāh* in Islamic law had two meanings:

(a) Growth: the payment of *zakāh* causes wealth to grow through God's blessing on the donors. As the Prophet stated, 'Charity does not decrease one's wealth';[23] because *zakāh* is paid on goods which grow in value; because the rewards of the Hereafter are multiplied. The Qur'ān states: 'God deprives usurious gains of all blessings, whereas He blesses charitable deeds manifold.'[24] The Prophet said: 'God receives charity by His right hand, and then causes it to grow for each of you. Just as you raise a horse, colt, foal, or young weaned camel, so the morsel [of charity] becomes as large as the Mount of Uḥud.'[25]

(b) Purification: because it purifies a person from miserliness, or because it purifies a person from sins.

From numerous Qur'ānic verses it may be concluded that God has commanded the *zakāh*. That commandment, however, was general.[26] The Qur'ān explained which groups of people were to receive *zakāh*,[27] and gave strong warning to those who fail to pay it.[28]

Despite the clear order and warning in respect of *zakāh* in the Qur'ān, the meaning remained unclear and ambiguous. This resulted from the fact that the Qur'ān does not give the details of *zakāh*, i.e., who should pay *zakāh*, the amount to be paid and the time for the payment. As discussed above, the ambiguity in these verses was removed by the *Sunnah*. The Prophet explained these questions in detail. On the authority of Sālim and his father, Zuhrī reported the following tradition: 'The Messenger of God, upon whom be peace, had the rules of *ṣadaqah* written down but could not send them to his governors. After the Messenger's demise, Abū Bakr dispatched them and applied them, a practice which the caliph 'Umar also followed and wanted others to follow, as indicated in his will.'[29] Many similar traditions are quoted from the Prophet on this matter,[30] such as the following *ḥadīh* from 'Alī, who reported that the Prophet said: 'There is nothing upon you in gold, until it reaches twenty *dinars*. Thus, if you have twenty *dinars* at the end of the year, then half a *dinar* may be levied [as *zakāh*]. Any additional amount will be calculated in this manner. There is no *zakāh* on property until it has been owned for one year.'[31] Shāfiʿī mentioned some of the *mujmal* verses, commenting that they were clarified by the tongue of God's Apostle. These relate to the required number of prayers, their times and the modes of their performance; the amount of *zakāh* and the times of payment; the performance of the major (*ḥajj*) and minor (*ʿumrah*) pilgrimages and when these duties are required.[32]

Therefore, many verses related to the commandment of God are *mujmal*. This includes verses about worship, dealings (business), crime, war and peace, international relations, etc. Where these verses are not explained by the Qurʾān itself, they are explained by the *Sunnah* – none are left unexplained.[33] This is why the *mujtahid* must refer to the *Sunnah* when exercising *ijtihād*.[34]

The second category of *mujmal* is that which is caused by a competition of equal meanings (homonyms), with a lack of any external or textual evidence upon which any precedence could be given to one of them. This category does not appear to exist in authoritative texts any more, because the Prophet is seen to have fulfilled his duty and explained whatever needed explanation.[35] The Qurʾān says: 'And We have also sent down unto you [O Muḥammad] the reminder and the advice [the Qurʾān], that you may explain clearly to men what is sent down to them, and that they may give thought.'[36] This category is manifested in our speech, when words which carry more than one meaning are used, like the Arabic word *ṣārim*, which means morning and evening, and like the word *nāhil*, by which Arabs called a person sated with water and the one who is thirsty.[37]

The third category of *mujmal* is that caused by an unusual and unfamiliar word, one which is inherently vague.[38] The Qurʾān states: 'Truly man was created, very impatient [*halūʿan*]; he is discontented when evil touches him and niggardly when good touches him.'[39] The word '*halūʿ* can mean greed and stinginess, or anxiety and impatience. This word is intrinsically odd; its meaning is unintelligible without some explanation. Because of this the Qurʾān provided the explanation: 'discontented when evil touches him and niggardly when good touches him.' Therefore, '*halūʿ* is a person who shows extreme impatience and anxiety when something bad happens to him, and shows extreme miserliness when he receives something good. Aḥmad ibn Yaḥya was asked what '*halaʿ* was and answered 'God explained it, and no explanation can be clearer than that. It is a human being who, touched by evil, becomes frightened; and who, on gaining something good, becomes miserly and tries to keep everything to himself.'[40]

The value of *mujmal*

Ḥanafī scholars consider *mujmal* to mean that which is inapplicable unless explained by the *mujmil*, i.e. the one who uttered it, the originator. They say, as well, that the intended meaning of the Lawgiver is a truth even if we do not know it.[41] Muslims are required to search for the explanation from the relevant sources.

NOTES

1. M.L. ʿA, *al-Muʿjam al-Wasīṭ*, I:136; Lane, *Arabic-English Lexicon*, I:461; Baʿlabakī, *al-Mawrid*, p. 981.

2. Dabbūsī, *al-Asrār fī al-Uṣūl wa al-Furūʿ fī Taqwīm Adillat al-Sharʿ*, I:265.

3. Bukhārī, *Kashf al-Asrār*, I:54.

4. Nasafī, *Kashf al-Asrār*, I:218

5. Sarakhsī, *Uṣūl al-Sarakhsī*, I:168

6. Qur'ān, XVI:44.

7. Shāfiʿī, *al-Risālah*, p. 68.

8. If the explanation, however, is insufficient, it may become *mushkil*, the ambiguity of which may be removed by proper *ijtihād*.

9. Qur'ān, II:43.

10. Qur'ān, IV:103.

11. M.L.ʿA, *al-Muʿjam al-Wasīṭ*, I:522; Ibn Qudāmah, *al-Mughnī*, I:369.

12. Qalʿajī, *Muʿjam Lughat al-Fuqahā'*, p. 275.

13. Which, in fact, still has some relation to its original literal meaning.

14. Ibn al-Athīr, *al-Nihāyah fī Gharīb al-Ḥadīth*, I:273.

15. 'Offer prayers [*aqim al-ṣalāh*] from sunset until the darkness of the night, and recite the Qur'ān in the early dawn. Verily, the recitation of the Qur'ān in the early dawn is ever witnessed' (Qur'ān, XVII:78). 'And offer perfect prayers at the two ends of the day and at the approaches of the night. Verily, the good deeds remove the evil deeds [i.e., small sins]' (Qur'ān, XI:114). 'Guard strictly the prayers, especially the middle prayer' (Qur'ān, II:238).

16. 'O you who believe! Bow down and prostrate yourselves.' (Qur'ān, XXII:77).

17. Abū Dāwūd, *Sunan*, I:283–284 (no. 1080). Albānī stated that this tradition is narrated by Bukhārī, Muslim Ibn Ḥanbal, Nasā'ī and Ibn Mājah (Albānī, *Irwā' al-Ghalīl*, II:332).

18. Bukhārī, *al-Jāmiʿ al-Ṣaḥīḥ*, I:155 (10:18).

19. Qur'ān, II:43.

20. M.L.ʿA, *al-Muʿjam al-Wasīṭ*, I:396.

21. Qur'ān, IX:103.

22. Qalʿajī, *Muʿjam Lughat al-Fuqahā'*, p. 275.

23. Muslim, *Ṣaḥīḥ Muslim*, IV:2001 (no. 2588).

24. Qur'ān, II:276.

25. Tirmidhī, *al-Jāmiʿ al-Ṣaḥīḥ*, III:28 (no. 662).

26. 'And give *zakāh* [obligatory charity]' (Qur'ān, II:43); 'Eat of their fruit when they bring fruit, but pay the due thereof on the day of its harvest' (Qur'ān, VI:141).

27. 'Ṣadaqāt are only for the *fuqarā'* [the poor who do not beg] and the *masākīn* [the poor who beg]; those employed to collect the [funds]; those whose hearts are to be reconciled; to free the captives; for those in debt; for God's cause; and for the wayfarer – a duty imposed by God. And God is All-Knowing, All-Wise' (Qur'ān, IX:60).

28. 'And those who hoard up [*yaknizūn*] gold and silver and spend it not in the way of God, announce unto them a painful torment' (Qur'ān, IX:34). 'And woe to the *mushrikūn*. Those who give not the *zakāh*, and are unbelievers in the Hereafter' (Qur'ān, XLI:6–7).

29. Sābiq, *Fiqh al-Sunnah*, chapter about *zakāt al-ibil*.

30. See chapters on *zakāh* in any collection of the Prophet's traditions.

31. Abū Dāwūd, *Sunan*, II:99–100 (no. 1572); Tirmidhī, *al-Jāmiʿ al-Ṣaḥīḥ*, III:25–26 (no. 631).

32. Shāfiʿī, *al-Risālah*, p. 75.

33. If the explanation is fully detailed, the text becomes an interpreted text (*mufassar*) which needs neither further clarification nor *ijtihād*. But if the explanation is insufficient, the text becomes problematic (*mushkil*), and further research and *ijtihād* are needed.

34. Shāṭibī, *al-Muwāfaqāt*, III:218.

35. That the Prophet's duty was to explain whatever needed explanation is reflected in the Islamic emphasis on the *Sunnah*. This has led to the compilation of a large number of traditions of which the accuracy is certain. Despite this, not all the *Sunnah* reached every scholar. Consequently, this kind of *mujmal* may have existed in relation to those who had no access to some of the Prophet's traditions. This can be called temporary *mujmal*. One may argue that the explanation sometimes is insufficient, and that further scrutiny and *ijtihād* is needed (as in the case of *mushkil*). Despite this, the statement that the *Sunnah* explains what needs explanation remains valid. Even when the explanation is insufficient, the homonym is not such that the *mujtahid* cannot give preference to one of its meanings.

36. Qur'ān, XVI:44.

37. Fayrūzabādī, *al-Qāmūs al-Muḥīṭ*, IV:139; Bukhārī, *Kashf al-Asrār*, I:43.

38. The ambiguous mood (*ṣīghah mujmalah*) becomes *mufassar* when it is followed by sufficient and certain explanation from the Lawgiver which removes ambiguity from that mood and closes any possibility of *ta'wīl*. As stated earlier, 'Lawgiver' in Islam refers to God and His Messenger. According to the Qur'ān the Messenger does not speak from himself but transmits whatever God tells him.

39. Qur'ān, LXX:19–21.

40. Bukhārī, *Kashf al-Asrār*, I:50; Ibn Kathīr, *Tafsīr al-Qur'ān al-ʿAẓīm*, IV:542.

41. Sarakhsī, *Uṣūl al-Sarakhsī*, I:168; Nasafī, *Kashf al-Asrār*, I:219.

CHAPTER 18

The Intricate
(*al-Mutashābih*)

The linguistic definition of *mutashābih*

Mutashābih refers to similar, alike, akin, analogous, parallel, comparable, identical, intricate. *Mutashābihāt* in the Qur'ān refers to the verses that are ambiguous – i.e. open to different interpretations; or unintelligible verses, as openings of some chapters.[1]

The technical definition of *mutashābih*

The most ambiguous category of *mubham* in the Ḥanafī *madhhab* is *mutashābih*. Sarakhsī describes *mutashābih* as 'the name for [an expression] for which there is no hope of understanding the meaning.[2] Bazdawī,[3] Nasafī,[4] and other Ḥanafī scholars[5] provided identical or similar definitions to that of Sarakhsī. In their view, *mutashābih* is an expression which does not disclose its meaning on its own, and there is no textual or external evidence that can help disclose it. That meaning remains a total mystery for us. The Lawgiver alone knows it.

Mutashābih and the science of ʿilm al-kalām

Mutashābih in this sense does not exist in the authoritative texts of Islamic law.[6] This is why no appropriate example of *mutashābih* can be traced in any references of *uṣūl al-fiqh*. The only examples of *mutashābih* to be found[7] are not related to *fiqh*. Instead they pertain to the field of *tawḥīd* and ʿilm al-kalām. Some examples of *mutashābih* in ʿilm al-kalām are individual (abbreviated) letters (*muqaṭṭaʿāt*)[8] found at the beginning of some Qur'ānic chapters and in some verses which refer to God and ascribe certain attributes to Him.[9]

The notion that only God knows the actual meaning *of mutashābih* is clear from these two examples. To say that these letters have a certain meaning is only a hypothesis. The individual letters in the Qur'ān mean nothing on their own; their mystery has not been unravelled for us by God. Only He knows their real meaning and knows best what He referred to by them. Abū Bakr al-Ṣiddīq said: 'God has placed His mystery in every book, and His mystery in the Qur'ān are these letters.'[10]

Similarly, some verses indicate an apparent similarity between God and His creatures. These are the anthropomorphic verses, which, if taken literally, would seem to ascribe human attributes or acts to God. Consequently, it is imperative that the apparent literal meaning should not be taken as the real meaning of the verses since the Qur'ān clearly denies such similarity: 'There is nothing like unto Him, and He is the All-Hearing, the All-Seeing.'[11] At the same time, God did not explain what He meant by 'His arm', 'His face', etc. Therefore, their precise meaning cannot be known.

The opinion of the first generations of Muslims (*salaf*) is that God alone knows what the verses mean. They maintain that the Muslims should accept their incapacity to understand their meanings. Therefore, they should not try to interpret them in any sense. The next generation have been more inclined to explanation and interpretation beyond the obvious or apparent meaning of *mutashābih* (*ta'wīl*). They held that the apparent meaning of these verses is unknowable; thus they must be interpreted beyond their obvious sense. Consequently, they draw suitable metaphorical meanings. For example they interpreted, 'the hand' as His might, 'the eye' as His comprehension and protection, etc.[12] These interpretations were rejected by later scholars, who regarded them as neither satisfactory, nor certain, safe, or essential.

The reason for this disparity is disagreement regarding the verse which speaks of the *mutashābihāt* verses: 'It is He who has sent down to you the Book. In it are verses that are entirely clear (*muḥkamāt*), the foundations of the Book; and others which are not entirely clear (*mutashābihāt*). As for those whose hearts contain deviation, they follow that which is not entirely clear thereof, seeking *fitnah* and seeking its hidden meanings, but none knows its hidden meanings save God. And those who are firmly grounded in knowledge say: 'We believe in it; it is all from our Lord.''[13] This verse maybe punctuated in two ways – with a full stop placed after the word 'God', or after the word 'knowledge'.

Those who accepted the first postulation maintained that the interpretation of unclear verses is known only to God. They placed the full stop after the word 'God'; whereas those who placed the full stop after the word 'knowledge'[14] maintained that those who are firmly grounded in knowledge also know the meaning of unclear verses. The more reliable opinion is that the unclear verses are known by God alone,[15] and the full stop would be correctly placed after the word 'God'. The efforts of some interpreters to explain the *mutashiābihāt* are little more than guesses that do not rest on scientific proof, since the meanings of these verses are known only by the author of the text.[16]

According to Islamic law, no person may interpret the Qur'ān according to personal opinion in the absence of a reliable proof. The Prophet said, 'He who speaks his own view of the Qur'ān is wrong even if what he says is right.'[17] The method of Qur'ānic interpretation of the first generations (the *ṣaḥābah* and the *tābi'ūn*) and those who followed was always accompanied by proofs, while those who rejected this method arbitrarily interpreted the Qur'ān without producing the necessary evidence. The Qur'ān confirms this: 'Those whose hearts deviate [from the truth] follow that which is not entirely clear thereof, seeking *fitnah* and seeking its hidden meanings.' Moreover, 'And those who are firmly grounded in knowledge say: 'We believe in it, the whole of it [including the clear and unclear verses] is from our Lord.'

Examples *of mutashābih*

Scholars of *uṣūl al-fiqh* mention many examples of *mutashābih*. However, these examples are unrelated to *fiqh*. Since no *mutashābih* verse serves as an authoritative text, we may conclude that *mutashābih* lies beyond the scope of the science of *uṣūl al-fiqh*.

The value of *mutashābih*

The scholars of *uṣūl al-fiqh* mention a disagreement on the possibility of understanding the unclear verses. However, because they mention no example pertaining to *fiqh*, but only those relating to other disciplines, *mutashābih* is not a question for scholars of *uṣūl al-fiqh* but for those of *tawḥīd* and *'ilm al-kalām*.

Comparison between categories of *mubham*

The *mutashābih* is ambiguous. Its meaning cannot be known in this world, and Muslims are not obliged to search for it because God arrogated knowledge of it for Himself. Muslims are obliged only to believe that His words are the truth.

Mujmal may be understood if the speaker offers an explanation. Therefore, Muslims are obliged to search for such an explanation. *Mushkil* may be understood by research, reason and scrutiny. *Khafī* can be understood by research only.

NOTES

1. *al-Muʿjam al-Wasīṭ*, I: 471; Lane, *Arabic-English Lexicon*, II:1499–1501; Baʿlabakī, *al-Mawrid*, p. 958; *EI²*, I:275 and I:409.

2. Sarakhsī, *Uṣūl al-Sarakhsī*, I:169.

3. Bukhārī, *Kashf al-Asrār*, I:55.

4. Nasafī, *Kashf al-Asrār*, I:221.

5. Bādshāh, *Taysīr al-Taḥrīr*, I:160.

6. Shaʿbān said, 'Investigation and scrutiny lead us to believe that *mutashābih* in this sense does not exist in either the Qurʾān or the Sunnah to explain practical legal injunctions' (Shaʿbān, *Uṣūl al-Fiqh al-Islāmī*, p. 297). This opinion is widespread among past and modern scholars of *uṣūl al-fiqh*.

7. Ḥanafī scholars probably mentioned *mutashābih* only in order to contrast the *wāḍiḥ* and the *mubham*.

8. Like *alif-lām-mīm*, the *ṭā-hā*, *yā-sīn* and many other combinations that occur on twenty-nine occasions in the Qurʾān.

9. 'The Hand of God is over their hands' (Qurʾān XLVIII:10). 'And construct the ship under Our eyes and with Our inspiration (Qurʾān, XI:37). 'There is no secret counsel of three, but He is their fourth, nor five but He is the sixth [with His Knowledge], nor less than this or more, but He is with them [with His Knowledge] wheresoever they may be.' (Qurʾān, LVIII:7).

10. Nasfī, *Kashf al-Asrār*, I:223. Some scholars tried unsuccessfully to explain these letters, because their explanations were speculative, not based on reliable proofs.

11. Qurʾān, XLII:11.

12. The disagreement between *salaf* and *khalaf* is discussed in great detail in *uṣūl al-fiqh* (in the chapter about *mubham*), *tawḥīd*, *ʿilm al-kalām* (discussing the attributes of God) and *tafsīr*.

13. Qurʾān, III:7.

14. According to them the verse is punctuated as follows, 'but none knows its hidden meanings save God and those who are firmly grounded in knowledge'.

15. Some scholars, like Kamali, gave preference to the opinion that *mutashābih* is what is open to conjecture and doubt. This opinion would lead to great confusion, because all the categories of *mubham* (*khafī*, *mushkil*, *mujmal*) are open to doubt (Kamali, *Principles of Islamic Jurisprudence*, p. 103).

16. Ibn Kathīr, *Tafsīr al-Qurʾān al-ʿAẓīm*, I:460–464.

17. Tirmidhī, *al-Jāmiʿ al-Ṣaḥīḥ*, V:183 (no. 2950); Abū Dāwūd, *Sunan*, III:320 (no. 3652).

Introduction to the Shāfiʿī Approach to Unclear (*mubham*) Words

As we saw earlier *mubham* in the Ḥanafī *madhhab* is of four types. Shāfiʿī scholars of *kalām* classify *mubham* into two types: *mujmal* and *mutashābih*. These encompass all the Ḥanafī categories of *mubham*. However, Shāfiʿīs disagree among themselves regarding this classification. Many of them see *mutashābih* as a category of *mujmal*, while others consider it a part of *mujmal*. This makes the Shāfiʿī approach to *mubham* less clear than that of the Ḥanafīs. Let us first explore *mujmal* from the perspective of the Shāfiʿī point of view.

CHAPTER 19

The Concise
(*al-Mujmal*)

The linguistic definition of *mujmal*

Mujmal refers to summarised, outlined, abridged, condensed, epitomised, concise, brief, short; a word, phrase, or speech which includes or implies a number of unexplained things requiring further explanation.[1]

The technical definition *of mujmal*

Shāfiʿī scholars (*mutakallimūn*) suggest various definitions for *mujmal*.[2] They describe it as an expression which cannot be understood from its words but needs to be explained by another expression.[3] Ghazālī offered the following definition: 'It is an expression which alternates between two or more meanings, none of which have precedence over the others.[4] Rāzī divided *mujmal* into three types. The first corresponds to that of Ghazālī. His definition is not focused on the subject. He defined its character and the method for understanding it as follows: '*Mujmal* occurs when an expression accepts many possible meanings, none of which is preferred over the others.[5] Aṣfahānī defined *mujmal* as 'an expression which gives equal value to the several meanings that the expression might imply.' He mentioned another, shorter definition similar to that of Ibn Ḥājib[6]: 'It is an expression the indication of which is not clear.'[7] All these definitions agree that *mujmal* is an expression which does exhibit a clear meaning. A *mujmal* expression has a meaning, but that meaning is not entirely clear and needs something else to clarify it.

Existence of *mujmal* in authoritative texts[8]

Regarding the disagreement among Shāfiʿīs on this question, Shawkānī maintained that the majority agreed that *mujmal* is found in both the Qurʾān and the Sunnah. The only exception was Dāwūd al-Ẓāhirī. Those who maintain that 'no ambiguous text has been left by the Prophet' see no *mujmal* in the Qur'ān. Juwaynī held that no *mujmal* existed in any texts having to do with commandments and obligations. A *mujmal* command would be an order impossible to fulfil,[9] which is unacceptable in Islamic law. In other authoritative texts (unrelated to commands) *mujmal* may still be found. Māwardī stated that a *mujmal* expression may convey a command even before it is explained. He cited the example of the Prophet, who sent his companion Muʿādh ibn Jabal to Yemen to instruct the people of Yemen that God had commanded alms to be collected from their wealthy people and distributed among their poor. This happened before alms-giving had been explained in detail. There were two reasons: to prepare people to accept it when it was detailed and because God made certain injunctions clear and others hidden so that people could be rewarded for their efforts to discover the hidden meanings.

That most Shāfiʿī scholars have provided examples of *mujmal* confirms that they recognise it in their *madhhab*. Upon analysis, it appears that most of them make no distinction between *mujmal* and *mutashābih*, or they confuse them.

Examples of *mujmal*

Shāfiʿīs[10] maintain that *mujmal* may be in the form of both expressions and deeds.[11] They mention many examples *of mujmal* and its causes. From the variety and multiplicity of their examples it appears that no scholar has collected all cases and examples in one document. It is also interesting to observe that those scholars disagree about whether many examples are *mujmal* or not.[12]

1. Examples of *mujmal* in expressions:[13]

(a) When a homonym appears. The homonym contains different meanings[14] (which sometimes can be opposite). It generates ambiguity and needs additional material (in the form of internal or external evidence or an additional explanation) in order to be fully understood. The homonym may also be a constructed expression (*lafẓ murakkab*) as in the verse: 'And if you divorce them before touching them, and you have appointed unto them the *mahr*, then pay half of that; unless they agree to forgo it, or he, in whose hands is the marriage tie.'[15] The constructed word or *lafẓ murakkab* ('in whose hands is the marriage tie') may mean either the husband and the *walī*. Therefore, to be understood this construction needs further explanation.

(b) When a word does not have a specified personal meaning (*mutawāṭi'*). The Qur'ān states: 'Eat of their fruit when they bring fruit, but pay what is due thereof on the day of its harvest.'[16] The word '*ḥaqqah*' (what is due thereof) does not have a specific meaning and needs further explanation.

(c) The Prophet said: 'I have been commanded to fight against the people until they testify that there is no god but God, offer prayers perfectly and give *zakāt*. If they perform all this, then spare their lives and properties except in the right cause.'[17] The words 'people' (*nās*), and 'the right cause' (*ḥaqq*) in this *ḥadīth* are of unknown type and amount. Therefore, they are *mujmal* and need additional explanation.

(d) When an expression has a specific meaning which is applicable to many examples. When such a word is indefinite (non-specified), but only one of its meanings is intended by the originator, the meaning becomes *mujmal*. This may be explained by the following example from the Qur'ān: 'And [remember] when Moses said to his people: "Verily, God commands you to slaughter a cow."'[18] He commanded them to slaughter one unspecified cow. Because this expression can be ambiguous, the Israelites claimed not to know which cow ought to be slaughtered and asked Moses: 'Call upon your Lord for us, that He may make plain to us what it is!'[19]

(e) When an expression has a specified meaning followed by an unknown exception that needs further clarification. The Qur'ān states: 'Lawful to you [for food] are all the cattle except that which will be announced to you.'[20] 'That which will be announced to you' was not clear when the verse was revealed, and the meaning of this verse remained concise (*mujmal*) until the promised announcement was made.

(f) When a word is given a new meaning (different from its original literal meaning)[21] by the Lawgiver – e.g., the words: *ṣalāh*, *zakāh*, *ḥajj*, etc. Therefore, when these words appear in an authoritative text they will be treated as *mujmal*, in need of further explanation.

Sometimes *mujmal* is caused by different possibilities of punctuation, an example of which is the Qur'ānic verse discussed earlier: 'But none but God knows its hidden meanings. And those who are firmly grounded in knowledge say: "We believe in it; the whole of it [clear and unclear verses] is from our Lord."'[22]

2. Examples of *mujmal* amongst the Prophet's deeds:[23]

(a) When the Prophet's deed indicates two equal meanings – e.g., the tradition that he combined two prayers in a trip.[24] This tradition is concise (*mujmal*) because it is susceptible to more than one interpretation – i.e., a short or a long trip. In this and in similar situations, one may not choose one meaning and reject the other without proof.

(b) When the Prophet passes judgement on a case applicable to one or more situations. In one *ḥadīth*, a person broke his fast and the Prophet commanded him to offer penance. This is *mujmal* because we do not know whether he broke his fasting by engaging in sexual relations, by eating or by something else. To apply one of the meanings without proof would be inappropriate.

The value of *mujmal*

Shīrāzī has been quoted as saying that there is no *mujmal* unless it is explained, and it is incorrect to use its apparent meaning as an argument. From this view and Māwardī's[25] position, we can conclude that the method of understanding *mujmal* should be based on careful thinking and scrutiny before the meaning is attained. The meaning identified should be supported by additional explanation and customary usage, or any other kind of internal or external evidence. Therefore, an effort is required to discover the intended meaning. This search has to continue until the objective is reached.

NOTES

1. *al-Muʿjam al-Wasīṭ*, I:136; Lane, *Arabic-English Lexicon*, I:461; Baʿlabakī, *al-Mawrid*, p. 981.

2. Shawkānī, *Irshād al-Fuḥūl*, p. 147.

3. Shīrāzī, *al-Lummaʿ*, p. 49.

4. Ghazālī, *al-Mustaṣfā*, p. 187. A similar definition was provided by Qarrāfī in his book *Sharḥ Tanqīḥ al-Fuṣūl*, pp. 275–277. He did not mention the last part 'while none of them has precedence over the others'.

5. Rāzī, *al-Maḥṣūl*, I:3:233–234. In his book *al-Iḥkām fī Uṣūl al-Aḥkām* (III:10), Āmidī employed several definitions. He preferred the one similar to Rāzī's.

6. Ibn al-Ḥājib, *Mukhtaṣar al-Muntahā maʿa Sharḥ al-ʿAḍud*, II:158.

7. Aṣfahānī, *Sharḥ al-Minhāj*, I:436–437.

8. Shawkānī, *Irshād al-Fuḥūl*, p. 148.

9. Because the order is unknown.

10. Shīrāzī, *al-Lummaʿ*, pp. 49–52; Āmidī, *al-Iḥkām fī Uṣūl al-Aḥkām*, III:9–24; Aṣfahānī, *Sharḥ al-Minhāj*, I:437–443.

11. The *mujmal* of deeds may be found only in the Sunnah, but as an expression it can be found in both the Qur'ān and the Sunnah.

12. Baṣrī, *al-Muʿtamad*, I:317, I:324–337; Shīrāzī, *al-Lummaʿ*, pp. 50–52; Ghazālī, *al-Mustaṣfā*, pp. 187–191; Rāzī, *al-Maḥṣūl*, I:3:241–258; Āmidī, *al-Iḥkām fī Uṣūl al-Aḥkām*, III:12–24; Qarrāfī, *Sharḥ Tanqīḥ al-Fuṣūl*, pp. 275–277; Aṣfahānī, *Sharḥ al-Minhāj*, I:440–443; Shawkānī, *Irshād al-Fuḥūl*, pp. 149–151.

13. These examples are found in both the Qur'ān and the Sunnah.

14. This applies to the opinion that a homonym cannot include all its meanings.

15. Qur'ān, II:237.

16. Qur'ān, VI:141.

17. Muslim, *Ṣaḥīḥ Muslim*, I:51–52 (no. 22).

18. Qur'ān, II:67.

19. Qur'ān, II: 68.

20. Qur'ān, V:1.
21. It is called *naql sharʿī*.
22. Qur'ān, III:7.
23. This *mujmal* is found in the Sunnah only.
24. Muslim, *Ṣaḥīḥ Muslim*, I:488–489 (no.703).
25. Shawkānī in *Irshād al-Fuḥūl*, p. 148.

CHAPTER 20

The Intricate
(*al-Mutashābih*)

The linguistic definition of *mutashābih*

Mutashābih refers to similar, alike, akin, analogous, parallel, comparable, identical. The *mutashābihāt* of the Qur'ān are the verses that are equivocal, or ambiguous – i.e. susceptible of different interpretations, or unintelligible verses as in the commencements of many chapters.[1]

The technical definition of *mutashābih*

While exploring *mujmal* one gets the impression that most Shāfi'ī *mutakallimūn* do not differentiate between *mujmal* and *mutashābih* This is also the conclusion of some contemporary scholars, who maintain that, with regard to clarity and ambiguity, non-Ḥanafīs[2] classify expressions as either *mujmal* or *mutashābih*. In the Ḥanafī *madhhab*[3] these two types of expressions in reality consist of four categories. Shīrāzī observed that Shāfi'īs attach four special features to *mutashābih:*

(1) *Mutashābih* and *mujmal* are one – i.e., that *mutashābih* has the same definition as *mujmal*. This effectively joins the two categories.

(2) *Mutashābih* is the meaning that only God knows and has not been disclosed to any of His creatures.

(3) *Mutashābih* includes the narratives, maxims, parables, wisdom, and the lawful and unlawful.

(4) *Mutashābih* includes the individual letters at the beginning of some chapters.[4] Shīrāzī agreed that *mutashābih* and *mujmal* are the same, clarifying his opinion with the following statement: 'The former is correct because the essence of *mutashābih* is whatever has indefinite and mixed meanings.'[5]

Ibn Ḥazm does not acknowledge *mutashābih* in the commandments (*awāmir* and *nawāhī*). Anyone who makes such a claim is ignorant. According to him, the only category of ambiguity (*mubham*) is *mujmal*.[6] *Mutashābih* is found in verses unrelated to the Divine commandments – as when God swears by some of His creatures, and the individual letters found at the beginning of some chapters.[7]

Examples of *mutashābih*

Because the majority of Shāfiʿīs do not differentiate between *mujmal* and *mutashābih*, the latter may be illustrated by the same examples as those of *mujmal*. According to Ibn Ḥazm, there are no examples of *mutashābih* because it does not exist in the commandments.

The value of *mutashābih*

As we have seen, the majority of Shāfiʿīs do not distinguish between *mujmal* and *mutashābih*. Consequently, *mutashābih* takes the same ruling as *mujmal*. Accordingly, in authoritative texts Islamic scholars are duty-bound to research *mutashābih* thoroughly, using any possible evidence for the meanings intended. When these meanings are identified, they have to be implemented. No meaning of *mutashābih* is applicable unless one meaning has precedence over others by way of proof (an explanatory, customary, or any other internal or external evidence). According to Ibn Ḥazm, however, there is no *mutashābih* in Islamic law (*fiqh*); therefore, it is not a matter for the science of *uṣūl al-fiqh*, but rather other sciences like *tawḥīd* and *ʿilm al-kalām*.

Conclusion

In the Shāfiʿī *madhhab*, *mujmal* includes all categories of *mubham* that are found in the Ḥanafī *madhhab* except for *mutashābih* which carries a wider meaning in Shāfiʿī *madhhab*. This is because every *mujmal* in the Ḥanafī *madhhab* is *mujmal* in the Shāfiʿī *madhhab* and not the opposite. Yet we have to bear in mind that the majority of Shāfiʿīs do not differentiate between *mujmal* and *mutashābih*, and that they regard *mujmal* as a category of *mutashābih*.

The difference in terminology between the Ḥanafī and Shāfiʿī *madhhabs* indicates that the explanation of *mujmal* in the Shāfiʿī *madhhab* is not restricted to the Author; it may be reached through textual or external evidence and legal reasoning (*ijtihād*). In fact, one category of *mujmal*, as in the Ḥanafī *madhhab*, can be explained only by the Author.

Most scholars consider *mutashābih* and *mujmal* the same. Those who distinguish them do not acknowledge *mutashābih* in the commandments and therefore do not regard it as pertinent to *uṣūl al-fiqh*. All scholars agree that every ambiguous authoritative text which contains commandments is clarified elsewhere, either by the Qur'ān or the *Sunnah*. The Ḥanafī approach to *mubham* seems to be more accurate and more precise, if we exclude their exaggeration in the case of *mutashābih*.

The less obscure category of *mubham* is *khafī*. In *khafī*, the apparent meaning has been disrupted by an external factor which can easily be eliminated by exercising *ijtihād*. Then comes *mushkil*, a self-obscured expression the intended meaning of which cannot be identified without external evidence, research and proper *ijtihād*. Then comes *mujmal*, an expression which is hidden in itself and the intended meaning of which cannot be understood without an explanation from the Author. These three categories cover all obscure authoritative texts pertinent to *fiqh*.

The Ḥanafī division allows for the accurate verification of obscure authoritative texts, which leads to better understanding and precision in the derivation of legal injunctions from these texts. Anything that can help remove the obscurity of a text must be considered, in accordance with the level of obscurity and ambiguity. This Ḥanafī approach identifies the obscure texts, the level of obscurity and the ways to interpret them, with a view to removing their obscurity, reaching the intended meaning and deriving the legal rulings contained in the authoritative texts.

NOTES

1. *al-Muʿjam al-Wasīṭ*, I: 471; Lane, *Arabic-English Lexicon*, II:1499–1501; Baʿlabakī, *al-Mawrid*, p. 958; *EI²*, I:275 and I:409.

2. In the science of *uṣūl al-fiqh*, generally speaking, there are only two *madhhabs* – the Ḥanafī and the Shāfiʿī. The scholars frequently refer to the Shāfiʿī school (which in the science of *uṣūl al-fiqh* is classed alongside the Mālikī and Ḥanbalī schools, but excepts the Ḥanafīs) as one of *kalām*.

3. For example, Shaʿbān, *Uṣūl al-Fiqh al-Islāmī*, p. 298.

4. Although the last two appear to be examples, Shīrāzī still includes them among the definitions (*taʿrīfāt*).

5. Shīrāzī, *al-Lummaʿ*, p. 52.

6. Ibn Ḥazm, *al-Iḥkām fī Uṣūl al-Aḥkām*, I:42.

7. Ibn Ḥazm, *al-Iḥkām fī Uṣūl al-Aḥkām*, I:42, IV:123.

Generality and Specificity of Words

Introduction

In every language, words carry general as well as specific meanings. The general meaning, however, is more frequent. These words remain generic until they are specified or restricted.

The Arabic language, the language of the authoritative texts of Islamic law, is not an exception. Indeed, most Arabic words are general in their roots, i.e., they include many pertinent things. This is especially true of the Qur'ān and the *Sunnah*.[1] Expressions in these two sources are abridged and condensed. Sometimes, however, certain subjects are excluded from the general meaning of a particular word, making this meaning specific to some of its subjects. And some indications may be given that the general meaning is not intended by the Lawgiver.

These facts may impede the *mujtahid*'s task of understanding the authoritative legal texts. The Prophet's companions (*ṣaḥābah*) were able to differentiate, without difficulty, between the general and the specific. Moreover, they had the advantage of asking the Prophet directly for explanations. The next generation of Muslims (*tābi'ūn*), amongst whom were many whose mother tongue was not Arabic, had no such opportunity, and they had difficulty differentiating between the general and the specific. This led to differences in their understanding of authoritative texts which implied general rules and meanings. The understanding of texts and the deduction of legal rulings from them required an accurate knowledge of the general and its variant forms, shapes, kinds, words and indications of rulings, and the degree of its inclusion of subjects to which it is linguistically applicable.

Legal reasoning in Islamic law seems impossible without the ability to differentiate between the general (*'āmm*) and the specific (*khāṣṣ*) meaning. This prompted Islamic scholars to identify certain linguistic patterns which could help both ordinary Muslims and *mujtahids* to differentiate between general and specific meanings contained in the legal texts. While general and specific meanings are distinguishable conceptually, they do not always appear in the grammatical forms of words. Islamic scholars have identified the linguistic patterns of words which help differentiate the general from the specific.[2] In determining the scope of a general provision both Arabic linguistic rules and common usage are considered.[3] In the event of a conflict between linguistic meaning and common usage, the latter has priority. We will examine the general meaning, the specific and its effects on ʿāmm in cases of conflict.

NOTES

1. There is unanimous agreement among the Companions of the Prophet that the words of the Qur'ān and Sunnah are generic, unless a reliable proof warrants a limitation of the general indication to the specific (Badrān, *Uṣūl al-Fiqh al-Islāmī*. p. 375).

2. It appears that Islamic scholars have successfully developed ways of distinguishing general from specific meanings. This is all the more significant when we recall that they did this a thousand years ago.

3. Words may be used generically, but the intention of the Lawgiver is not generic and might even be specific. Accordingly, the scope of the general provision is determined by reference to the intention of the Lawgiver and the context of the provision. However, unless a proof suggests its specification or restriction, it is regarded as general.

CHAPTER 21

The General Meaning
(al-ʿĀmm)

The linguistic definition of ʿāmm

ʿĀmm refers to general, common, universal.[1]

The technical definition of ʿāmm

Bayḍāwī defined *ʿāmm* as 'a word that includes [in its meaning] everything to which it is applicable to in one setting'.[2] Rāzī similarly defines it 'the word that includes that to which it is applicable in one setting'.[3] According to Anṣārī *ʿāmm* is 'a word that includes what it is applicable to without any specification'.[4]

Based on these definitions we may put forward the following definition: *ʿāmm* is 'a word coined to indicate a single meaning[5] which includes everything[6] to which it is applicable, by way of comprehension and inclusion, without any specification or limitation'. Therefore, it is a word that has a single meaning applied to an unlimited number of subjects without specification, as in the word 'thief' (*al-sāriq*) in the following verse: 'Cut off the hand of the thief, male or female.'[7] The word 'thief' is coined for one meaning related to theft and it includes everyone to whom the meaning of theft is applicable without specification or limitation.

Types of ʿāmm[8]

Islamic scholars came to the conclusion that the general meaning may be divided into three types:

(1) What is known with certainty in respect of the general meaning intended by the Lawgiver. This is the general meaning accompanied by evidence that excludes all possibility of specification of meaning. This *ʿāmm* is absolutely general, and is exemplified by the following verse: 'And there

is not a living creature on the earth but whose sustenance depends on God.'[9] In this verse the prefix 'there is not a living creature' (*mā min dābbatin*)[10] is an expression which, according to Islamic teaching, confirms the object of divine law, which is unchangeable and therefore cannot expect any kind of specification.[11] Accordingly, *mā min dābbatin* applies, without exception, to everything it could possibly be applicable to, and no particular is excluded.

(2) The general meaning which a specified indication undoubtedly intends. This is the type accompanied by an evidence (from the Qur'ān, the *Sunnah*, or human understanding) but where the general meaning is not intended by the Lawgiver. This general meaning is meant to imply the specific meaning, and to include those of its subjects to which it may be applied. The following verses are clear examples of these indications: 'It is not for the townsfolk of Medina and those wandering Arabs to stay behind, [as] the Messenger of God [goes forth] and to prefer their lives to his.'[12] The indications of this verse imply that everyone in the town of Medina, and all the Bedouins, are included in its meaning. This verse, however, did not mean the old, the disabled, children, lunatics and those incapable of bearing hardship. It certainly meant those able to bear the burden of fighting. By reason, these categories of people who could not bear it are excluded.

Another verse further illustrates the general declaration which is intended to be entirely particular: 'Those unto whom the people said, "Verily, the people have gathered against you, therefore fear them." But it increased their faith, and they said, "God is Sufficient for us, He is the best disposer of affairs."'[13] The people (*al-nās*) in Arabic applies to three or more[14] persons and may include all of humanity. The general declaration 'the people' is intended to be entirely particular because we know by certainty that all people did not gather against them.

(3) The unlimited general meaning is unaccompanied by any evidence which denies the specification of general indication.[15] This indication is provided by texts which are generally unlimited and unaccompanied by linguistic, rational or customary evidence. This kind provides the general indication and continues to do so until a reliable proof suggests otherwise, as in the following verse: 'Women who are divorced shall wait, and keep away for three [monthly] courses.'[16] This verse is apparently generic in its effect and includes all divorced women, without specification. It is considered generic until a reliable proof specifies it.

Implementation of the *ʿāmm*[17]

Islamic scholars may be divided on this matter into three groups.[18]

(1) The majority of Islamic scholars maintain that the apparent meaning of 'general' should be applied. This includes everything to which it is

applicable, and the general meaning should be applied until a reliable proof suggests otherwise.

(2) Ashʿarīs and some Shāfiʿīs (*mutakallimūn*) maintain that the implementation of general words is suspended until a proof emerges to confirm the general or specific indication. The scholars who follow this opinion are called Wāqifiyyah. Sarakhsī claims that this group emerged in the fourth century AH.[19]

(3) Balkhī and Jubbāʾī maintain that the general should be applied in its most specific sense. This can be the only sense if it is a generic type (*jins*) and if it is in the plural form. Some scholars have debated this, but the question is related to Islamic belief (*ʿaqīdah*) rather than to commandment rulings (*aḥkām taklīfiyyah*) because the examples cited are all about *ʿaqīdah*. There is no mention of instances where authoritative texts are suspended on this basis. Moreover, those who disagree with the majority of scholars are not supported by any reliable proof from the language or from authoritative texts.[20] From an Islamic point of view their opinion is unacceptable because it leads to disagreement with the Prophet and his Companions and to putting aside most authoritative texts. There is no narrative indicating that the Prophet or any of his Companions put aside any authoritative text because it was generic.

In view of these facts I will not discuss this disagreement in full detail, but mention some proofs provided by the majority of scholars:

(1) Language conveys meanings for purposes of communication. Every meaning must have its own name. Therefore, the general categories should have their own names and the names of their particular subjects if they are to be differentiated from each other.

(2) The Prophet and his Companions – i.e. those who were most knowledgeable about the language of the authoritative texts – implemented the general, except when it was specified by a reliable proof.[21] It is well known that they were looking for proofs by which to specify the general, and not proofs that the general includes everything to which it is applicable.[22] The latter idea was an axiom that needed no proof. This occurred during the time of the Prophet, and therefore could have been corrected by him if it demonstrated an incorrect methodology. The following are examples which clearly show the correctness of the former claim. The first example is related to the Prophet and the rest to his Companions:

(a) As one of the Prophet's Companions was praying, he was called by the Prophet. He did not respond immediately, but quickly finished his prayer and approached him. The Prophet asked what prevented him from responding when he was called. The Companion answered that he was praying. Then the Prophet told him: 'Did you not know what was revealed unto me 'O you who believe! Obey God and His Messenger when He calls you to that which quickens you."[23] The Prophet used the general meaning of the verse 'O you who believe' to include every believer and therefore this Companion.[24]

(b) Abū Bakr deprived the Prophet's daughter of her father's inheritance, despite the general indication of the verse: 'God charges you concerning [the inheritance for] your children: to the male the equivalent of the portion of two females.'[25] He argued that the Prophet said: 'We the Prophets do not bequeath. What we leave behind us is charity.'[26] The Companions understood that the general meaning of the verse included all children,[27] and a reliable proof[28] was required in order to specify its generic effect.

(c) When the verse: 'Those who believe and obscure not their belief by injustice.'[29] was revealed, the Companions found it hard to follow, and objected: 'Who amongst us has not done injustice to himself?' They understood this verse to include every wrongdoing and knew it was impossible to avoid every wrongdoing. The Prophet afterwards explained to them that the verse did not include every wrongdoing to which it was applicable. It referred only to the greatest wrongdoing, i.e. *shirk* (worshipping someone or something beside God or associating something or someone with Him).

The opinions of most scholars are based on the following grounds:

(1) Their approach safeguarded the nature of the Arabic language, which all agree tends to be basically general – its words retain generality unless specified.

(2) They follow the way of the Prophet, his Companions and the scholars of the first generations in interpreting the texts. Because they were closer to the language of the authoritative texts, they understood it better than later generations.

(3) The general meaning (*ʿāmm*) among Arabs, before and after the Prophet's lifetime, clearly supports the opinion that Arabic is basically general; as we know, the authoritative texts are in pure Arabic.

(4) By accepting the opinion of the majority, authoritative texts will not be set aside. This is a safe way for a Muslim, because Islam regards putting aside an authoritative text without a reliable reason a major sin, which brings about the excommunication of the perpetrator. The second opinion requiring that the implementation of the general be suspended is, according to Islamic scholars, extremely dangerous, since it denies the authority of many authoritative texts.

(5) The third opinion – that the general should be applied in its most specified meaning – runs contrary to the nature of Arabic and therefore opposes the Qur'ān and *Sunnah*.

(6) The general indication includes in itself the specific – which is a more cautious and guarded opinion.

Examples of *ʿāmm*

As mentioned previously, Islamic scholars identified certain linguistic patterns which helped distinguish between the general (*ʿāmm*) and the specific (*khāṣṣ*) meanings of words. Based on their meditation on this matter, it seems that *ʿāmm* is a grammatical term which takes several identifiable forms in Arabic. The following practical examples illustrate these patterns.

(1) The following are words which convey general meaning by their substance: '*kullun*'[30], '*jamīʿun*', '*kāffatun*', '*qāṭibatun*' and '*ʿāmmatun*'.[31] These words mean: all, entire, total, whole, everyone, entirely, completely, fully. When any of these accompany another word, that word includes everything to which it pertains, as in the following examples: 'Lo! We have created everything (*kulla shay'in*) in measure.'[32] 'Everything' is generic and includes everything created without exception. 'He it is who created for you all (*jamīʿan*) that is on the earth.'[33] This verse means that everything on earth has been created for the benefit of human beings. 'And We have not sent you except as a giver of glad tidings and a warner to all mankind (*kāffatan li al-nās*) but most men know not.'[34] 'All mankind' is generic and includes all humankind at all times.

(2) Conditional nouns (*asmāʾ al-sharṭ*) such as 'who', 'whoever' (*man*), 'wherever' (*aynamā*), and 'whatever' (*mā*). 'Whoever (*wa man*) kills a believer in error must set free a believing slave.'[35] This verse indicates that anyone who kills a believer by error is obliged to set free a believing slave in expiation for the offence. The following verses provide similar examples too. 'Whoever believes in God and the Last Day and does righteous good deeds shall have his reward with the Lord; for him there shall be no fear, no shall he grieve.'[36] 'Unto God belong the East and the West, but wherever you turn, there is God's countenance.'[37] 'Whatever good you do, [be sure] God knows it.'[38] The word 'whatever' (*mā*) acts in the verse as an interrogative noun. Therefore, it is generic and the verse means that every good deed of man is known to God.

(3) Interrogative nouns – who, whoever (*man*)[39] and when (*matā*) as in the following verses: 'Say: Have you any thought: If [all] your water were to disappear into the earth, who then would bring you gushing water?'[40] '...and were so shaken that even the Messenger and those who believed with him asked, When [will come] the help of God?'[41] 'So whoever witnesses the month he must fast that month.'[42] The interrogative noun 'who', 'whoever' (*man*) has a generic meaning. The last verse indicates that everyone who has reached maturity (*mukallaf*) is ordered to fast. The same general meaning is indicated by all these verses.

(4) Indefinite words (*nakirah*) when used to convey negation, prohibition and when proceeded by 'of' (*min*). When used to convey the negation,

nakirah is illustrated by the following tradition: 'No harm shall be inflicted or reciprocated.'[43] This tradition negates what is applicable, because it is general in its import – *lā-darara* and *lā-dirār* both being indefinite words used in negation. When used to convey prohibition *nakirah* is illustrated by the following command of the Qur'ān to the Prophet: 'And never [O Muḥammad] pray for one of them who dies, nor stand by his grave.'[44] The word 'one' (*aḥad*) is indefinite. It is used to convey prohibition. Therefore, it is generic in its effect. The indefinite word (*nakirah*) is preceded by *min* in three places:

(a) before the subject of a verbal sentence exemplified by the following verse: 'Unto whom no warner came before you';[45]

(b) before the object exemplified by the following verse: 'We sent no messenger but that he should be obeyed by God's leave';[46]

(c) before the start (*mubtada'*) of a nominal sentence in the following verse: 'And there is no god save God'. [47]

(5) Relative pronouns like *alladhīna* (those men who), *allātī* (those women who), *mā* (what) are exemplified by the following verses: 'Those who swallow usury cannot rise up save as one whom the devil has prostrated by [his] touch.'[48] The word *alladhīna* (those) includes everyone who deals in usury. 'As for those of your women who are guilty of lewdness, call four of you to witness against them.'[49] The word *allātī* (those women who), includes everyone guilty of lewdness. Therefore, the ruling is general as it applies to all women who can possibly be included in its scope. It remains general until the appearance of a reliable proof to specify it.[50]'Lawful unto you are all beyond what has been mentioned.'[51] The word *mā* (what), includes all women who were not mentioned in the previous verse.

(6) Singular or plural forms of a noun when preceded by the definite article (*al*) which is not used for a definition (*'ahd*)[52] but for inclusion and comprehension (*istighrāq*) and (*shumūl*)[53] or when it becomes definite by the genitive case as in the following examples from the Qur'ān: 'The adulterer and the adulteress, scourge each of them a hundred stripes.'[54] In this verse 'the adulterer and the adulteress' (*al-zāniyah wa al-zānī*) are both in the singular form.[55] Because they are preceded by the definite article which denotes *istighrāq* and *shumūl*, it is generic and includes all adulterers, male and female. The prescribed punishment pertains to all of them. 'Divorced women shall wait, keeping themselves apart for three [monthly] courses.'[56] The word *al-muṭallaqāt* (the divorced women) is a plural with the definite article (*al*), indicating inclusion (*istighrāq*). Therefore, it provides general meaning and includes all the women to whom it could apply.

The same rule applies when the singular or plural form of a noun is defined by the genitive. The Prophet stated about the sea that: 'its water is pure and its dead are permissible [for consumption].'[57] The words 'water' (*mā'*) and 'dead' (*mayyitah*) are singulars defined by the genitive construction 'its water' (*māʾuh*) and 'its dead' (*mayyitatuh*). Therefore, this tradition indicates that all sea water is pure for ablution and one is permitted to eat all the animals which live in it even if they were not slaughtered before their death.

The Qurʾān states: 'God commands you regarding your children's [inheritance].'[58] 'Take alms from their wealth in order to purify them and sanctify them with it.'[59] In these two verses the plural 'children' (*awlād*) and 'wealth' (*amwāl*) are definite through the governed noun (*muḍāf*) of a genitive construction (*iḍāfah*) – *awlādikum* and *amwālikum*. Therefore, it includes all children and wealth without any specification or limitation.

(7) The plural when it is defined by the genitive construction:[60] 'Forbidden unto you are your mothers.'[61] The word 'mothers' is plural, defined by the genitive construction *ummahātukum*. Therefore, it is generic and includes all mothers without any specification of the number.

(8) The indefinite noun when followed by a general adjective: 'A kind word with forgiveness is better than almsgiving followed by injury.'[62] The expression 'a kind word' (*qawlun maʿrūfun*) provides a general meaning and includes every polite word because 'word' (*qawlun*) has been followed by the general adjective 'polite' (*maʿrūf*).

The indication of *ʿāmm*[63]

When the indication of *ʿāmm* is in question, we have to differentiate between *ʿāmm* which has already been specified and that which has not been specified. In the former it has been agreed that the indication is indefinite (*ẓannī*), because any of its remaining subjects have been specified. Because the indication is indefinite (speculative), it can be further specified by reliable proof, which may be speculative – e.g., a solitary tradition (*khabar wāḥid*) and analogy (*qiyās*).

There is a disagreement between Islamic scholars regarding the general meaning which has not already been specified, i.e., whether its indication is definite or indefinite. The majority of scholars[64] maintain that the application of the general to all that it includes, when the general (*ʿāmm*) is already specified, is indefinite (*ẓannī*). They argue that every *ʿāmm* is supposed to be specified, except those accompanied by evidence which excludes such a possibility, as in the following verse: 'There is not a beast on earth but that God gives it sustenance.'[65] Their conclusion that there is no general that is not specified has become a maxim. They reached that conclusion by following the specifications of authoritative texts which originally implied the general meaning. Yet this conclusion casts suspicion over the general, i.e., whether it includes all its subjects or not, and whether the specific has already appeared before us or not. The possibility of this should necessarily cause indefiniteness because the definite meaning is incompatible with suspicion and open-endedness.

Most Ḥanafī scholars like Karkhī, Jaṣṣāṣ and Dabbūsī maintain that the application to all that it encompasses makes the general definite (*qaṭʿī*). They conclude this by studying different branches and particular issues in Ḥanafī law. They argue that Abū Ḥanīfah has clearly stated that the specific cannot eliminate the general. The specific, however, can be abrogated by the general, as in the case of the tradition about the permission to use the urine of animals that can be eaten.[66] This ruling was abrogated by general indications in other traditions which command Muslims to keep away from urine.[67]

These scholars further argue that the majority of scholars have agreed that the words originally provided the general meaning (i.e. to be generic in their effects). They must continue to provide that meaning until a reliable proof indicates otherwise. Possibilities which are not supported by proofs cannot affect the original indications of words. Therefore, consider the verse: 'Those who may die and leave behind wives, they [the wives] shall wait, keeping themselves apart four months and ten days.'[68] This includes all women whose husbands have died, whether they died before consummating the marriage or after. It continues to provide this indication until a reliable proof suggests otherwise.

Ḥanafīs rejected the proof provided by the majority that since it is possible to specify the general, it cannot be definite (*qaṭʿī*). They did not claim to reject every possibility, but insisted that the possibility should be based on a proof. The possibility that is not based on a reliable proof is not acceptable. Therefore, if the general is specified with respect to some of its subjects, the possibility of specifying its remaining subjects is based on proof. As such it is acceptable, and the indication of the general becomes indefinite (*ẓannī*). This position results from the Ḥanafī convention with respect to the article that accounts for specification (*mukhaṣṣiṣ*). Ḥanafīs maintain that the specification takes place only when the article which makes the specification is independent (*mustaqill*), joined and associated (*muqtarin*). Accordingly, the cases of specification of the general (*ʿāmm*) are very rare.[69] Therefore, what others consider specification of meaning is not so. In their opinion, the maxim 'There is no general which is not specified' is wrong. Moreover, stating that the general provides the indefinite indication may, according to Shāṭibī,[70] cancel general Qurʾānic expressions and the possibility of arguing by the Qurʾān at all. At the same time it violates the eloquence of the Qurʾān.

This consideration is rejected because specification does not take place without a reliable proof, and that process is governed by strict and precise rules. Therefore, it does not lead to a cancellation of Qurʾānic expressions. The specification of meaning (*takhṣīṣ*) does not affect the eloquence of the

Qur'ān so long as the apparent meaning is followed and the specification of meaning is based on a reliable proof. The fact remains that most general expressions in the Qur'ān (*ʿumūmāt al-Qur'ān*) have been made specific and yet the Qur'ān's eloquence has not been affected.

It seems that the majority opinion is stronger because the possibility for the specification of the general exists in most authoritative texts, whether we regard it as definite or indefinite. Furthermore, it must be borne in mind that in this matter indefiniteness has to do with how the general meaning encompasses its subjects, and the indication of the general, from its original meanings, is unquestionably definite.

The practical result of this disagreement[71] appears in cases of conflict between a general provision of the Qur'ān, or a *mutawātir ḥadīth*, and a speculative proof – like the *qiyās*, and a weak (*ḍaʿīf*) and solitary (*āḥād*) *ḥadīth* which, although definitive in meaning, is speculative in relation to its authenticity.

Ḥanafīs do not allow for such specification because the general provisions of the Qur'ān and *mutawātir ḥadīth* are definite in their authenticity and indication, and the definite (*qaṭʿī*) may not be specified by a speculative proof.

According to the rule, the speculative cannot stand in opposition to the definitive. In this case the general of the Qur'ān or a *mutawātir ḥadīth* is definite, whereas *qiyās*, and weak and solitary *ḥadīth* are all speculative. Ḥanafīs found support for their position in the opinions of some Companions of the Prophet such as Abū Bakr, ʿUmar and ʿĀ'ishah, and in the tradition where Fāṭimah bint Qays claimed that the Prophet granted her alimony and accommodation during the waiting period, although the divorce was irrevocable. ʿUmar objected to her claim by saying, 'How can we abandon the Book of our Lord because of the statement of a woman who perhaps memorised it or perhaps she forgot?' ʿUmar had in mind the verse of the Book, 'Lodge them where you dwell, according to your wealth, and harass them not, so as to straiten life for them.'[72] He refused to accept her *ḥadīth*.

The majority of scholars, however, allow for this kind of specification because the general, in their opinion, provides indefinite (i.e., speculative) indication. Therefore, this specification does not contradict the mentioned rule because the general of the Qur'ān and *mutawātir ḥadīth* are speculative. Accordingly, the general provisions of the Qur'ān and *mutawātir ḥadīth* can be specified by both definite and indefinite proofs. They supported their opinion by examples from the Companions who limited and specified many general meanings of the Qur'ān with solitary traditions. For example, they specified the general indication of the verse, 'Lawful unto you are all beyond those mentioned.'[73] This verse includes paternal and maternal aunts.

However, paternal and maternal aunts are excluded from it by the tradition where the Prophet forbade a man to be married at one and the same time to a woman and her paternal or maternal aunt.[74] They rejected the Ḥanafī proof. According to them, ʿUmar rejected that tradition only because he did not know whether or not it was ṣaḥīḥ. He did not reject it because he did not allow the Qurʾān to be limited and specified by a solitary tradition. This is upheld by the following facts: a) he used the word 'abandon' and did not use the word 'specify'; b) in an other narration ʿUmar justified his position by saying that it was 'the statement of a woman who perhaps memorised it or perhaps forgot'. Therefore, he had suspicions as to whether she had memorised the episode correctly or had forgotten. If he was certain that she had memorised it he would probably not have rejected it. Accordingly, he did not reject it because he did not allow the Qurʾān to be specified by a solitary tradition.

The Ḥanafīs rejected the arguments provided by the majority of scholars by saying that these traditions are famous (mashhūr), and mashhūr may specify the general provision of the Qurʾān. According to the Ḥanafīs, the mashhūr may specify the general provision[75] because mashhūr was solitary (āḥād) in the first generation, the beginning of the chain of transmitters, and became mutawātir afterwards. The following example illustrates the practical result of this conflict. The Qurʾān states: 'And eat nothing on which God's name has not been pronounced, for lo! it is an abomination.'[76] This verse is concerned with the slaughter of animals. It is general in its application and its general ruling includes all animals slaughtered without mentioning God's name.

In the following tradition, however, the Prophet's words provide a different implication: 'The believer slaughters in the name of God whether or not he pronounces the name of God.'[77] This tradition affirms that what the believer slaughters may be eaten even if the name of God had not been pronounced. It opposes the general indication of the verse. This tradition is, however, a solitary tradition.[78] Even if supported by another narration[79] it may not rise up to the level of mutawātir.

According to Shāfiʿī scholars, this tradition may specify the verse, because in their opinion the general is indefinite in its indication. Therefore, the verse which implies the ʿāmm meaning may be specified by a speculative proof (in this case, a solitary tradition). It results in the ruling that slaughter carried out by a Muslim is lawful even without pronunciation of the name of God. They interpreted the verse by saying that 'that on which Allāh's name has not been pronounced' refers to that which is slaughtered to the idols, since another verse affirms: 'and that which has been immolated to [the name of] anything but God'.[80] Moreover, they analogised 'that which is left deliberately' with 'that which is forgotten'. This analogy is rejected by Ḥanafīs – 'that which is forgotten' is not excluded from the general meaning of the verse, because the person who slaughters has pronounced the name of God,[81] as mentioned before.

Ḥanafīs, however, maintain that slaughter by a Muslim is unlawful for consumption without pronunciation of the name of God. They do not specify the verse by using the previous traditions because the general of the Qur'ān may not be specified by solitary traditions.[82] The practical result of this disagreement about the possibility that the general may be specified by analogy and solitary ḥadīth may be seen in the following example. The Prophet said: 'What was watered by the sky and springs or by its roots ten percent, and what was watered by sprinkling five percent.'[83] This tradition offers a general indication because of the word 'what' (mā) that is used. It does not specify and fix certain amounts as niṣāb. Therefore, it includes everything that grows from the earth, whether or not the produce has been cultivated on the land, and no matter what the amount of produce. Accordingly, alms should be given for the smallest amount of agricultural produce no less than for the greatest. In another ḥadīth, the Prophet stated that there are no alms on dates and grains until they reach five awsuq.[84] Therefore, the second text specified niṣāb to five awsuq. Accordingly, it specified the general indication of the former tradition and declared that alms are not obligatory for agricultural products if they are less than five awsuq.

These two traditions apparently disagree because the first, by its general meaning, includes what is less then five awsuq, while the second, which is specific, excludes it. Due to the difference in the indication of the general (ʿāmm), Islamic scholars disagreed about niṣāb in agricultural produce. Abū Ḥanīfah maintained that alms must be paid for any amount. Ḥanafīs argue that these two traditions apparently disagree on an amount less than the five awsuq, and one tradition cannot be preferred to the other. The general indication, however, accords with the general command of the Qur'ān on alms. Moreover, its application more easily fulfils the command. Meanwhile, the tradition with the general indication is more famous and deserving of precedence. Other scholars specified the former tradition by the latter. They maintained that no alms are to be paid until niṣāb (five awsuq) is reached. This conclusion is the result of the selection of the latter tradition over the former one.

From the previous examples, it is clear that differences about the indication of ʿāmm, whether definite or indefinite, resulted in differences about the niṣāb relating to agricultural produce.

The value of ʿāmm[85]

Legal adherence to ʿāmm is seen by Islamic law as obligatory (*wājib*) as is the implementation of its general meaning until a reliable proof suggests otherwise. It must continue to be generic unless there is a specifying clause which particularises its application. In cases where ʿāmm is partially specified, the part that remains unspecified retains its legal authority. The implementation of ʿāmm is unaffected by the disagreement about whether it provides definite or speculative indication,[86] because prevailing speculative indications must be implemented until a reliable proof suggests otherwise.[87]

NOTES

1. *al-Muʿjam al-Wasīṭ*, II: 629; EI², IV:1098; Baʿlabakī, *al-Mawrid*, p. 745.

2. Aṣfahānī, *Sharḥ al-Minhāj*, I:351.

3. Rāzī, *al-Maḥṣūl*, I:2:513.

4. Anṣārī, *Ghāyat al-Wuṣūl*, p. 69.

5. This condition differentiates the ʿāmm from the homonym (*mushtarak*), which has more than one meaning.

6. This condition, which implies that ʿāmm applies to an unlimited number of subjects, differentiates it from the specific (*khāṣṣ*).

7. Qurʾān, V:38

8. Shāfiʿī, *Risālah*, pp. 96–108; Shawkānī, *Irshād al-Fuḥūl*, pp. 140–141; Khallāf, *Uṣūl al-Fiqh*, p. 219; Bardīsī, *Uṣūl al-Fiqh*, p. 404.

9. Qurʾān, XI:6.

10. *Dābbah* is incorrectly rendered here, by some, as beast (see Pickthall's translation of this verse). It means, however, any moving living creature (*mā yadubbu ʿalā al-arḍ*), including man.

11. Shāfiʿī commented on this verse by citing from Qurʾān XI:8: 'Everything – heaven and earth, things with a living spirit, trees and the like – God has created them all. And God is responsible for the sustenance of every living creature and He knows its lodging place and its repository' (Shāfiʿī, *Risālah*, p. 96).

12. Qurʾān, IX:120.

13. Qurʾān, III:173.

14. The preponderant opinion in *uṣūl al-fiqh* is that the core may apply to two persons or more.

15. The distinction between the second and third types is in the fact that the second is accompanied by evidence suggesting that the specific meaning is intended, while the third is unaccompanied by any evidence suggesting either the general or specified meaning. This is clear from the examples provided for these two types.

16. Qurʾān, II:228.

17. Sarakhsī, *Uṣūl al-Sarakhsī*, I:132; Bukhārī, *Kashf al-Asrār*, I:298; Taftāzānī, *Sharḥ al-Talwīḥ ʿalā al-Tawḍīḥ*, I:138.

18. Bazdawī and Sarakhsī, however, divided them into two groups. They put the second and the third groups together and called them Wāqifiyyah.

19. Sarakhsī, *Uṣūl al-Sarakhsī*, I:132.

20. Ghazālī, *al-Mustaṣfā*, I:225–233; Ibn Ḥazm, *al-Iḥkām fī Uṣūl al-Aḥkām*, III:109–117; Ījī, *Mukhtaṣar al-Muntahā*, II:102; Shawkānī, *Irshād al-Fuḥūl*, p. 116.

21. It is recorded by the unanimous agreement (consensus) of the Companions that the meaning of numerous authoritative texts includes all that they are applied to. For example, the following verses and traditions: 'As for the thief, both male and female, cut off their hands' (Qur'ān, V:38); 'The adulterer and the adulteress, scourge ye each one of them a hundred stripes' (Qur'ān, XXIV:2); 'O you who believe! Squander not your wealth among yourselves in vanity' (Qur'ān, IV:29); 'There is no testament for an inheritor' (Zaylaʿī, *Naṣb al-Rāyah*, IV:403). This was the methodology of generations of scholars who came after the Prophet and his Companions, until the emergence of the Wāqifiyyah in the fourth century. The Wāqifiyyah violated the consensus of the Companions. This led Islamic scholars to reject their opinions. Their rejection was fundamentally based on the rule that consensus cannot be abrogated (Bazdawī, *Kashf al-Asrār*, I:303).

22. Bukhārī, *Kashf al-Asrār*, I:303.

23. Qur'ān, VIII:24

24. Ṭabarī, *Jāmiʿ al-Bayān ʿan Ta'wīl Āy al-Qur'ān*, XIII:466.

25. Qur'ān, IV:11.

26. Muslim, *Ṣaḥīḥ Muslim*, III:1379 (no. 1759).

27. This is indicated by the fact that they asked for their part of the inheritance.

28. A reliable proof used by Abū Bakr is the *ḥadīth* just mentioned.

29. Qur'ān, VI:82.

30. The generic meaning of *kull* is individual, single, solitary – i.e. it includes all pertinent subjects but in individual form, one after another. This word, moreover, is considered the most general (Shawkānī, *Irshād al-Fuḥūl*, p. 110).

31. The generic meaning of '*jamīʿ* ', '*kāffah*', '*qāṭibah*' and '*ʿāmmah*' is that of a group – i.e. it includes everything that pertains to a group. *Qāṭibah* and *ʿāmmah* are words by which scholars normally intend the general meaning. These two words, however, do not appear in the Qur'ān.

32. Qur'ān, LIV:49.

33. Qur'ān, II:29.

34. Qur'ān, XXXIV:28.

35. Qur'ān, IV:92.

36. Qur'ān, II:62.

37. Qur'ān, II:115.

38. Qur'ān, II:197.

39. 'Who [*man*] may be a conditional [*sharṭiyyah*], interrogative [*istifhāmiyyah*], relative pronoun [*ism mawṣūl*], and substantive [*mawṣūf*]. In the former two cases it is definitely the general meaning, while in the latter it is general and specific. The specific meaning may be illustrated by the following verses: 'Of them are some who listen to you' (Qur'ān, VI:25); 'Among them are those who look towards you' (Qur'ān, X:43). In these two verses, who (*man*) refers to some of the hypocrites, though not all of them. This is why translators have translated it as 'some who'.

40. Qur'ān, LXVII:30.

41. Qur'ān, II:214.

42. Qur'ān, II:185.

43. Ibn Mājah, *Sunan*, II:784 (no. 2340)

44. Qur'ān, IX:84

45. Qur'ān, XXVIII:46

46. Qur'ān, IV:64.

47. Qur'ān, III:62.

48. Qur'ān, II:275.

49. Qur'ān, IV:15.

50. This verse has been specified by another verse (Qur'ān, XXIV:6), which made an exception for the husband who is allowed to support his charge of adultery against his wife by taking four solemn oaths instead of four witnesses. His wife, however, may rebut such a charge by the same oaths.

51. Qur'ān, IV:24.

52. As in the sentence: 'The man has come' (jā'a al-rajul) if the person is known (ma'hūd) to them.

53. As in the following sentence: 'It is a strong obligation upon every person to be dutiful to his/her parents'.

54. Qur'ān, XXIV:2.

55. The definite article (al) in al-zāniyah and wa al-zānī may grammatically be a relative pronoun which means 'that woman who commits adultery' (allatī taznī) and 'that man who commits adultery '(alladhī yaznī). However, no matter how it is viewed, the phrase provides a general indication in both situations.

56. Qur'ān, II:228.

57. Tirmidhī, al-Jāmi' al-Ṣaḥīḥ, I:101 (no. 69); Abū Dāwūd, Sunan, I:21 (no.83); 'Asqalānī, Bulūgh al-Marām, p. 9.

58. Qur'ān, IV:11.

59. Qur'ān, IX:103

60. Scholars disagree about whether the indefinite plural is generic in effect. Most maintain that the indefinite plural is not generic. See the discussion about the verse 'If there were therein gods beside God' (XXI:22), in Qurṭubī, al-Jāmi' li Aḥkām al-Qur'ān, II:279.

61. Qur'ān, IV:23.

62. Qur'ān, II:263.

63. Sarakhsī, Uṣūl al-Sarakhsī, I:134; Bukhārī, Kashf al-Asrār, I:291; Shāṭibī, al-Muwāfaqāt, III:164–165; Ibn Qudāmah, Rawḍat al-Nāẓir, II:166; Taftāzānī, Sharḥ al-Talwīḥ 'alā al-Tawḍīḥ, I:39–40.

64. Sarakhsī, Uṣūl al-Sarakhsī, I:144; Bukhārī, Kashf al-Asrār, I:294; Taftāzānī, Sharḥ al-Talwīḥ 'alā al-Tawḍīḥ, I:39–40; Sha'bān, Uṣūl al-Fiqh al-Islāmī, p. 274.

65. Qur'ān, XI:6.

66. Bukhārī, Jāmi' al-Ṣaḥīḥ, VII:13 (76:6).

67. Ibn Mājah, Sunan, I:125 (nos. 347, 348, 349).

68. Qur'ān, II:234.

69. If the specifying proof were not joined (associated) (muqtarin), it would be abrogation and not specification according to the Ḥanafis.

70. Shāṭibī, al-Muwāfaqāt, III:165.

71. Bukhārī, Kashf al-Asrār, I:294; Ibn al-Ḥājib, Mukhtaṣar al-Muntahā', II:149–151; Āmidī, al-Iḥkām fī Uṣūl al-Aḥkām, II:525; Shawkānī, Irshād al-Fuḥūl, p. 158.

72. Qur'ān, LXV:6.

73. Qur'ān, IV:24.

74. Bukhārī, al-Jāmi' al-Ṣaḥīḥ, VI:28 (67–27).

75. Ibn Amīr al-Ḥājj, al-Taqrīr wa al-Taḥbīr, II:219.

76. Qur'ān, VI:121.

77. Bayhaqī, al-Sunan al-Kubrā, VII:240; Zayla'ī, Naṣb al-Rāyah, IV:182.

78. Zayla'ī stated that it is: 'Strange in this version' (gharīb bi hādha al-lafẓ) (Naṣb al-Rāyah, IV:182).

79. Like the following tradition: 'A carcass killed by a Muslim is ḥalāl whether or not the name of God was pronounced' (Zayla'ī, Naṣb al-Rāyah, IV:182).

80. Qur'ān, II:173.

81. By his belonging to Islam.

82. Marghīnānī, *al-Hidāyah*, IV:63. The Ḥanafīs excluded from these ruling those who forgot to say God's name, because He forgave forgetfulness, as when someone forgets and breaks his fast. His fast is correct and he may continue to fast. The tradition previously mentioned, some say, relates to those who forget, not to those who remember and fail to pronounce the name of God while slaughtering an animal. According to them, whoever forgets to pronounce does not leave pronunciation, because the Lawgiver has replaced the pronunciation by belonging to Islam; he is counted as having pronounced it.

83. Bukhārī, *al-Jāmiʿ al-Ṣaḥīḥ*, II:133 (24:55).

84. Muslim, *Ṣaḥīḥ Muslim*, II:673 (no. 979). *Awsuq* (sing. *wasq*): camel-load (=sixty $ṣāʿ$=165 litre)

85. Khallāf, *ʿIlm Uṣūl al-Fiqh*, p. 183.

86. Khuḍarī Bak preferred the opinion of the Ḥanafīs that the general provides definite indication until a reliable proof suggests otherwise (Khuḍarī Bak, *Uṣūl al-Fiqh*, p. 156).

87. Sarākhsī, *Uṣūl al-Sarākhsī*, I:132; Bukhārī, *Kashf al-Asrār*, I:291.

CHAPTER 22

The Specific
(*al-Khāṣṣ*)

The linguistic definition of *khāṣṣ*

Khāṣṣ refers to special, particular, specific, individual, distinctive.[1]

The technical definition of *khāṣṣ*

The early scholars of *uṣūl al-fiqh* preferred to define the effect of *khāṣṣ* (i.e., *takhṣīṣ*)[2] rather than *khāṣṣ* itself. Bearing in mind that *khāṣṣ* is opposite to *ʿāmm*, which includes an unlimited number of subjects, *khāṣṣ* may be defined as 'a word which applies to one subject[3] or more, but these subjects are specific in number like the numbers two, five, hundred, etc.'

From this definition, *khāṣṣ* may refer to one subject (personal names like Ḥasan, or Ḥusayn), or more, but these subjects should be specified in number; it does not include everything to which it is applicable, such as a house. In other words, it does not include an indefinite word (*nakirah*) used to convey the positive meaning. This is clear in the following verse: 'And from the outermost part of the city came a man running.'[4] In this verse the word 'a man' (*rajulun*) is indefinite and conveys positive meaning. Although it may include any man, it refers only to one person. These indefinite words will be specific as long as they apply to a single subject, or have a specified number thereof, and convey the positive meaning.[5] Otherwise they will be regarded as general (*ʿāmm*). When the general and the specified have the same subjects there is conflict.

Specification of the general meaning

As we saw, the majority of Islamic scholars maintain that the general is meant to include everything to which it is applicable. Therefore, a ruling deduced from the general provision relates to all subjects to which the word with generic implication is applicable. Sometimes, however, this general indication may be interrupted by a proof (which is specific and limited) that suggests that some subjects of the general are not intended, or are excluded. This specification of meaning is called *takhṣīṣ*.

NOTES

1. M.L.ʿA., *al-Muʿjam al-Wasīṭ*, I:237–238; EI², IV:1098; Baʿlabakī, *al-Mawrid*, p. 499.

2. This effect appears only when it disagrees with ʿāmm.

3. As in the case of the indefinite noun which provides the positive: 'I saw a man in the house.' Although the word 'a man' does not specify the person, and therefore may refer to anyone, it implies only one person.

4. Qurʾān, XXXVI:20.

5. It is very important to recognise the specific in the general. One reason for this is that the legal rulings which are conveyed in specific terms are definite. This means that these rulings are not subject to the interpretation beyond the obvious import, should they be implemented.

CHAPTER 23

The Specification of Meaning (*al-Takhṣīṣ*)[1]

The linguistic definition of *takhṣīṣ*

Takhṣīṣ refers to specification, particularisation, individualisation.[2]

The technical definition of *takhṣīṣ*

Because the Ḥanafīs have a slightly different approach to *takhṣīṣ*[3] from that of the Shāfiʿīs, their definition is also slightly different. First the Shāfiʿī definitions. Baṣrī defines *takhṣīṣ* as 'excluding some [meanings] included by the text due to the conflict between the two'.[4] Shīrāzī defines the specification of the general meaning as the explanation of what was not intended by the general word.[5] Ibn al-Ḥājib defines *takhṣīṣ* as 'the limitation of the general to some of its subjects'.[6] Similarly to Baṣrī, Bayḍāwī defined it as 'excluding some [meanings] from the scope of the word'.[7] According to these definitions, *takhṣīṣ* is the limitation of the general provision to some of its subjects.[8] According to Ḥanafīs, *takhṣīṣ* is limitation of the general provision to some of its subjects by an independent[9] and joined[10] proof.[11] Unlike other schools, therefore, they stipulate that the qualifying proof must be independent, chronologically parallel and joined to the general.

Takhṣīṣ is opposite to the basic status of words

The Arabic language normally assumes that a word maintains all the meanings to which it is applicable within its compass. This is because words are coined for a meaning, and a linguistic rule states 'that everything should remain unchanged.'[12] Accordingly, a word with a general provision continues to be generic. Moreover, given that the basic rule is not a generic indication of words, the understanding of authoritative texts and communication among people would be extremely difficult if not impossible, because we would not know whether a general or a specific meaning was intended by the locutor. There would be endless questioning about what was intended regarding these two possibilities.[13] Therefore, the restriction, specification and exclusion of some of the subjects from the general provision is opposite to the basic status of words. Specification, restriction and exclusion can be done, according to Ḥanafīs, by specification or partial abrogation.

Takhṣīṣ of the general provisions of authoritative texts is so frequent that it has given rise to the maxim: 'There is no general provision that is not specified.'[14] That *takhṣīṣ* is opposite to the basic status of words is important to know, because whenever there is a disagreement on applying specification, and there is no reliable proof, the basic rule is non-specification.

The difference between abrogation and specification

Islamic scholars who have studied the differences between abrogation and specification have arrived at the following conclusions.[15]

(1) The specification of meaning acts upon some subjects of the general provision, while abrogation acts upon all of them.

(2) Abrogation can affect any legal injunction, whether that injunction is related to one subject or many, while specification can take place only when a number of subjects are involved.

(3) Abrogation can occur after the abrogated text has already been implemented, while specification may not happen after what is specified has been implemented.[16]

(4) Abrogation cancels a ruling after it has been established, while specification explains the intention of the general proposition (i.e. that all subjects are not intended by the general, or that some of them are excluded).

(5) Specification explains 'what was intended' by the general, while abrogation explains that which was not intended by the abrogated.

(6) Abrogation occurs on account of the authoritative texts only, while specification occurs because of authoritative texts, reason, evidences and other proofs.

(7) The consensus (*ijmāʿ*) may be a proof for specification but not for abrogation.

(8) Specification may affect only the general meanings while abrogation may affect both general and specific meanings.

(9) There are several kinds of *naskh:* textual abrogation, injunction abrogation, or both, whereby *takhṣīṣ* applies only to the rulings.

Specifying proofs[17]

The majority of scholars disagree with the Ḥanafīs on the specifying proofs. The majority maintain that a general provision may be specified either by a dependent clause that occurs in the same text or by an independent locution that occurs in another text. They attach only one stipulation to the specifying clause, when it is independent of the general – that it appear before the general meaning is implemented.[18] If it appears after the general is implemented, it causes abrogation, not specification of meaning.

The specifying proofs according to Ḥanafīs[19]

Ḥanafīs defined *takhṣīṣ* as intending some subjects of the general meaning by an independent and chronologically joined proof. The proofs of specification are, according to them, divided into three kinds: a) reason, b) custom and habits[20] and c) an authoritative text which is independent and chronologically joined to the general.

Ḥanafīs put forward two conditions for the specifying proof that must be fulfilled in order to cause *takhṣīṣ*: that the proof which specifies the general be independent of the text that provides the general provision; that the proof which specifies the general be chronologically parallel (i.e., revealed at the same time) and attached to the general. The differences between the above conditions put forward by the majority and by the Ḥanafīs are related to dependency and chronology among the general provisions and specifying proofs (provisions). If the specifying proof is dependent – such as the attached exception (*istithnā' muttaṣil*), the condition (*sharṭ*), the attribute (*ṣifah*) and the extent of application (*ghāyah*) – it is called limitation (*qaṣr*) and not specification (*takhṣīṣ*). This is due to the stipulation put forward by the Ḥanafīs that in the case of specification there should be a kind of conflict. This is not the case in a situation when these proofs are in question.

When the chronological order is in question it might be parallel in origin, different, or unknown. According to Ḥanafīs, specifying proofs specify general provisions only when they are parallel or when this order is unknown.[21] If they are not parallel, the latter would cause partial[22] or complete abrogation (*naskh juz'ī* or *naskh kullī*),[23] not specification.[24] For examples to the Ḥanafī approach, we may take the Shāfiʿī examples of *takhṣīṣ* with respect to specifying proofs which are independent and chronological to the general.[25]

The specifying proofs according to Shāfiʿīs[26]

Shāfiʿīs have concluded that proofs which qualify the general provisions of authoritative texts may be divided into those that are dependent and independent.

The dependent and joined proofs

According to Shāfiʿīs, the dependent proof is a part of the text that contains the general provision. It cannot stand on its own and cannot be separated from the text in which it appears. Therefore it is dependent (*ghayr al-mustaqillah*) and joined (*muttaṣilah*). The most important dependent proofs of specification (*mukhaṣṣiṣāt*) are as follows:

(1) The attached exception (*istithnāʾ muttaṣil*)[27] effected by *illā* (except, save, but) or substitute *illā*, as in the verse: 'Be not averse to writing down [the contract] be it small or great, with [record of] the term thereof. This is more equitable in the sight of God and more certain for testimony, and the best way of avoiding doubt in your midst – save only in the case where you transfer actual merchandise among yourselves from hand to hand.'[28] The expression 'be it small or great' includes all contracts; but the exception 'save only in the case where you transfer actual merchandise among yourselves from hand to hand' excludes contracts where goods are transferred from hand to hand. Therefore, the general indication 'be it small or great' has been specified, and it includes only merchandise contracts where goods are not transferred from hand to hand, and these contracts have to be written down.[29]

The question arises, when an attached exception comes after a few joined sentences, whether it affects all of them or only the last one. This may be exemplified by the verse: 'And those who accuse chaste women, and produce not four witnesses, flog them eighty stripes, and reject their testimony forever; they indeed are evil-doers. Except those who repent thereafter and do righteous deeds. Verily, God is Oft-Forgiving, Most Merciful.'[30] The exception here follows three joined sentences. It may cause different juridical implications, depending on whether it affects all the sentences or only the last one. Islamic scholars have disagreed on this question.[31] The majority maintain that the exception affects all the sentences because this is apparent, and the opposite would need to be proved. Accordingly, if those who accuse unjustly repent, their status will be reinstated, their testimony will be accepted and they will not be considered disobedient afterwards. Abū Ḥanīfah, however, maintains that the exception affects the last sentence alone because this is the only certainty.[32] Accordingly, such people will not be considered disobedient afterwards, but their testimony will be rejected forever.

(2) The condition (*shart*)[33] may specify a general indication, if it is literally expressed and attached to that which is stipulated (*mashrūt*)[34] as in the following example: 'And unto you belongs half of what your wives leave, if they have no child.'[35] This verse prescribes the share of the husband in the estate of his deceased wife. In the first part – 'And unto you belongs half of what your wives leave' – the general indication implies that the husband should take a half in all circumstances. The second part 'if they have no child' however, posits the condition that his wife has no child. Therefore, this condition has specified the general provision which indicated that a husband should inherit half his wife's estate.

In another verse the Qur'ān states: 'And when you go forth in the land, it is no sin for you to curtail [your] worship.'[36] In this verse curtailing worship is made dependent on travelling. The article used for specification is *idhā* (when). If this condition were not made, prayer would be curtailed at all times, no matter whether someone was travelling or not.

(3) The attribute may specify the general provision, if it is literally expressed and attached to that which is described. Here, an attribute is considered an abstract characteristic, not just a grammatical adjective. Therefore, it includes the adjective, the circumstantial expression (*ḥāl*), adverbs of time and place (*ẓarf zamān* and *ẓarf makān*), specification (*tamyīz*), etc. The Qur'ān states: 'And those of you who are not able to afford to marry free, believing women, marry from the believing maids whom your right hands possess.'[37] In this verse maids is specified by an adjective to include only the believing ones and exclude all others.

In another verse the Qur'ān states:[38] 'And Pilgrimage to the House is a duty to God for mankind, for him who can find a way thither.'[39] The word mankind comprises all people, but those who cannot find means to make pilgrimage are excluded by the second part of the verse 'who can find a way thither', and this embodies an exception to 'mankind'.

In another verse the Qur'ān states: 'Forbidden unto you are [...] your step-daughters who are under your protection, [born] of your women unto whom you have gone.'[40] The first part embodies the general prohibition on step-daughters. This part, however, has been qualified by the description 'born of your women unto whom you have gone'. This description excludes all step-daughters of mothers with whom a step-father has not consummated the marriage.

(4) The extent of application (*ghāyah*) signified by articles (*ilā*, *ḥattā*, etc.) which limit the extent of application, may specify general provisions, as in the following Qur'ānic verses: 'They question you [Muḥammad] concerning menstruation. Say: It is an ailment, so let women alone at such times and go not unto them until they are cleansed.'[41] The part 'and go not unto them' provides a general provision indicating that it is not allowed to go to

them at all. The second part 'until they are cleansed' specifies the time until when the general provision is applicable. In another verse the Qur'ān states: 'O you who believe! When you rise up for prayer, wash your faces, and your hands up to the elbows.'[42] This verse first prescribes the washing of the hands: 'wash your faces, and your hands'. This ruling is general because it includes all of the hands and does not specify the area. The next part of the verse 'up to the elbows', however, specifies the area and thus specifies the general provision of the verse.

The independent proofs

Independent proofs that specify general provisions are not a part of the text which provides these provisions. There are three types:

(1) Reasoning (*ʿaql*). This is illustrated by the verse which prescribe *ḥajj* and the Ramaḍān fast: 'And *ḥajj* to the House is a duty that mankind owes to God.'[43] Clearly, this duty is prescribed to all of mankind since the word 'mankind' (*nās*) includes all human beings. In respect of reason, however, some people, like those who are not responsible (*mukallaf*) as infants and lunatics, are excluded from the scope of this obligation. On the fast the Qur'ān states: 'So whoever sights the month must fast that month.'[44] The word 'whoever' is generic and includes everyone. Therefore this verse apparently includes all believers.[45] Reason, however, excludes those who are not responsible (*mukallaf*). These conclusions have been confirmed by authoritative texts.[46] For example the Prophet said. 'Three persons are not morally responsible: a sleeping person before waking, a youth before sexual maturity (i.e. the legal age of maturity in Islamic law), and an insane person before he becomes lucid.'[47] In this tradition these persons are not *mukallaf* and therefore the obligations brought forward by Islamic law are not applicable to them.

(2) Oral traditions and customs[48] (*ʿurf qawlī*).[49] When the Lawgiver uses a word which provides a general provision (in Arabic) with a specified meaning (in *Sharīʿah*) – e.g. the word 'trade' in the verse: 'Whereas God has permitted trade and forbidden usury...'[50] The word trade (*bayʿ*) is generic in Arabic, and includes all kinds of exchange of goods and other items. Going by the practice of the Lawgiver, however, it implies only trading in goods. This custom therefore does not include every kind of exchange.[51]

Furthermore, the general provision may be specified by customary usage when a group of people use a general provision to indicate some of its subjects. Its meaning accords with people's custom. Consequently, when a particular word which appears generic is used, but according to custom includes only some of its subjects, it is treated according to its customary meaning. Therefore, a *mujtahid* has to consider the customs and habits of the 'linguistic' environment of the original authoritative texts in order to understand the intended meaning correctly. It is impossible to understand authoritative texts and derive rulings without having such knowledge. On this point, Shāṭibī said: 'It is essential for everyone who wants to study the Qur'ān and the *Sunnah* to know the Arabs' speech customs and practices at the time of Qur'ānic revelation, and the explanations of God's Prophet, because ignorance of these leads to ambiguities and complications, from which one cannot escape without this knowledge.'[52] 'This knowledge' is important for everyday law too. For example, if an Egyptian makes a will in pounds without specifying the currency, they will be considered Egyptian rather than British pounds, because by custom 'pound' means Egyptian currency, not British.

(3) The authoritative text. This may take either of two forms: a) joined to the general provision, that is, mentioned after it in the same text;[53] b) separated from it.[54]

(a) The Qur'ān states, 'Whereas God has permitted trade and forbidden usury.'[55] The word 'trade' is generic in the Arabic language and means exchanging goods for goods. Therefore, it may include trading with usury. Trade, however, was specified and that which contains usury was excluded by an independent text in another sentence: 'and forbidden usury'. This independent text is joined to the text which carries the general meaning. In another verse the Qur'ān states: 'So whoever of you sights the month he must fast that month, and whoever is ill or on a journey, the same number of other days.'[56] The first part of the verse is generic and means that any *mukallaf* who is sure that the month of Ramaḍān has begun should fast. However, the second part, which is independent and joined to the general provision in appearance, specifies it and excludes from the general meaning those who are ill or travelling.

(b) The Qur'ān states[57]: 'And divorced women shall wait [as regards their marriage] for three menstrual periods.'[58] This verse is a generic verse that includes all divorced women, whether the divorce took place before consummation of the marriage or afterwards. Another verse, however, specifies it by indicating that the woman with whom her husband did not consummate the marriage should not wait three menstrual periods. The Qur'ān states: 'O you who believe! When you marry believing women, and then divorce them before you have sexual relations with them, no *ʿiddah* [prescribed waiting period] have you to count in respect of them. So offer them a gift, and set them free in a comely manner.'[59] In the latter verse, therefore, an independent and separated text specifies the general provision of the former verse, and explains that the general provision of the former verse does not include women who are divorced before having sexual intercourse with their husbands. The former verse is specified by another verse: 'And for those who are pregnant their *ʿiddah* is until they deliver [their burdens]'.[60] Therefore, pregnant women are excluded from the general provision of that verse. Whether she is divorced or her husband has died, an expectant divorcee's *ʿiddah* is until the birth of her baby.

Another example may show us how the tradition of the Prophet may specify the general provision of the Qurʾān. The Qurʾān states: 'Forbidden to you [for food] are: the dead animals (*mayyitah*).'[61] The word *mayyitah* includes all animals which have not been properly slaughtered. The following tradition of the Prophet specifies this verse and excludes from it the dead animals which live in the sea. He said about the sea: 'Its water is pure [for ritual ablution] and its dead is permissible [as food].'[62]

Some scholars[63] have mentioned consensus (*ijmāʿ*), analogy (*qiyās*) and intuition (*ḥiss*) as independent proofs, although they should rather be classified under one of the previously mentioned proofs. Therefore, consensus, which is always based on an authoritative text, may be classified under the authoritative texts, or under reason, because consensus has to be based on an authoritative text, and reason must be used before consensus can be reached. The latter classification is less suitable. An example of this kind of specification is the tradition narrated by Abū Hurayrah where the Prophet forbade the deceptive contract (*bayʿ al-gharar*).[64] By consensus[65] speculation (*muḍārabah*) is excluded from the general indication of this tradition.

Analogy may be classified under the authoritative texts or under reason, because it is based on authoritative texts and is reached by the use of reason. The Qurʾān states: 'The woman and the man guilty of illegal sexual intercourse, flog each of them a hundred stripes.'[66] The word 'the woman' is generic. In another verse, however, girl-slaves are excluded from the general indication of the word 'the woman': 'And whoever of you has not the means wherewith to wed free, believing women, let him wed believing girls from among those [captives and slaves] whom your right hands possess [...] And after they have been taken in wedlock, if they engage in illicit sexual relations, their punishment is half that of a free [unmarried] woman.'[67] The general indication of 'the woman' is furthermore specified by analogy. Female slaves are also excluded by analogising them with the girl-slaves specified by the authoritative text.

Intuition (*ḥiss*) may be classified with reason. An example of this is the verse about Mecca: 'Have We not established a secure sanctuary [Mecca], to which are brought fruits of all kinds, a provision from Us, but most of them know not.'[68] The expression 'all kinds' provides a general provision. By the use of intuition we see that the previous verse is specified, because intuition suggests that the verse does not mean all kinds of fruit but many of them.

Conflict between ʿāmm and khāṣṣ

If both ʿāmm and khāṣṣ provide a ruling for the same subject, there will be conflict between the two. This view is however restricted to the Ḥanafīs, who regard both of them as definite. The same situation will not lead to a conflict according to the Shāfiʿīs, because in their opinion ʿāmm is indefinite and therefore cannot oppose khāṣṣ, which provides definite meaning.

Depending on the chronological order between ʿāmm and khāṣṣ, this conflict may produce different results. The chronological order may be parallel in origin, or it can be different, or unknown. If both of them are independent locutions, and both are parallel, or this order is unknown, specifying proofs would specify general provisions.[69] If they are not parallel, the latter would cause partial[70] or complete abrogation.

The status of ʿāmm when provoked by a specific cause[71]

An authoritative text containing a general provision may appear without being provoked by a special cause, as exemplified by the following verses: 'Successful indeed are the believers. Those who offer their prayers with humility. And those who turn away from vain talk.'[72] 'O you who believe! Fulfil [your] obligations.'[73]

The general provision, however, may be caused by special occasions known as asbāb al-nuzūl, such as the questions put to the Prophet regarding certain events. The question that may arise in the latter case is whether the cause of the general provision may specify and limit its applications. Some scholars maintain that the cause of a general provision may operate as a specifying factor. However, the great majority of scholars believe that it may not act in this way. According to them, if a ruling is conveyed in general terms, it should be applied in the same way, even if the cause behind that ruling is specific. The majority opinion is preferred because the Prophet and his Companions[74] applied, without any limitation and restriction, the general rulings engendered by specific occasions. If we recall that the great majority of authoritative texts are caused by specific occasions, it will be easier to understand the rule which the scholars of uṣūl al-fiqh have produced: 'What is important is the generality of the word, not the specificity of the cause.' Next are some examples of authoritative texts engendered by specific causes, but their general rulings remain generic and applicable in all similar cases. The Qurʾān states: 'Those among you who make their wives unlawful (ẓihār)[75], they [the wives] cannot be their mothers. Only those who gave birth to them can be their mothers. They merely utter an abomination and a falsehood. And God is Oft-Pardoning, Oft-Forgiving.'[76]

The occasion of the revelation of this verse, and therefore the ruling of *ẓihār*, relates to the Companions Khawlah bint Thaʿlabah and her husband Aws b. Ṣāmit. Khawlah went to the Prophet complaining about certain actions of her husband. The Prophet said to her that she was now forbidden to him. She said that she complained about her difficult situation to God. After this, the verses which explain the ruling of *ẓihār* were revealed.[77]

The Qurʾān states: 'As for those who accuse their wives, but have no witnesses except themselves, let the testimony of one of them be four testimonies [i.e. testifying four times], by God, that he is of those who speak the truth. And the fifth [testimony should be] the curse of God on him if he is one of those who tell a lie [against her].[78] These verses, known as the curse invocation verses (*liʿān*), were revealed after Saʿd b. ʿUbādah complained about the difficulty a person may have in proving, through four eyewitnesses, an act of adultery by their spouse.[79] The difficulty was, shortly afterwards, experienced by one of the Companions,[80] who found a man with his wife.[81] While the cause of the revelation is specific, the ruling remains general and applicable in any similar case.

Another example from the *Sunnah* is the previously mentioned *hadith*: 'Its water is pure [for ritual ablution] and its dead is permissible [as food].'[82] This *hadīth* provides a general provision caused by a specific occasion – a person said to the Prophet: 'We sail by sea and carry with us little water. If we make ablution with that water we will be thirsty. Can we make ablution with sea water?' Although the general ruling allowing for the purity of sea water for ritual ablution answered a specific case, its ruling remained general enough to make sea water good for ritual ablution and other uses. It also makes no difference whether or not the substance is liquid, the situation being one of necessity. No scholar is recorded[83] to have specified or restricted the general ruling because of its cause.

The value of *khāṣṣ*

The legal adherence to *khāṣṣ* in Islamic law is obligatory (*wājib*) and its meaning must be implemented. Islamic scholars generally agree that it provides definite meaning.

NOTES

1. On *takhṣīṣ* and its effect on legal reasoning when it disagrees with the status of words like *iḍmār*, *majāz*, *naql*, *ishtirāk* and *naskh*: Ramic, *Taʿāruḍ mā Yukhill bi al-Fahm wa Atharuh fī al-Aḥkām al-Fiqhiyyah*, pp. 36–66, 69–133.

2. Ibn Manẓūr, *Lisān al-ʿArab al-Muḥīṭ*, I:841–842; EI², IV:1098; Baʿlabakī, *al-Mawrid*, p. 294.

3. They placed some conditions for specifying proofs.

4. Baṣrī, *al-Muʿtamad*, I:252.

5. Shīrāzī, *al-Lumma*ʿ, p. 30.

6. Ijī, *Mukhtaṣar al-Muntahā*, I:129.

7. Aṣfahānī, *Sharḥ al-Minhāj*, I:361.

8. Anṣārī, *Ghāyat al-Wuṣūl*, p. 75; Fattūḥī, *Sharḥ Kawkab al-Munīr*, p. 387.

9. By this condition, attached exception (*istithnāʾ muttaṣil*), condition (*sharṭ*) and attribute (*ṣifah*) and extent of application (*ghāyah*) are all excluded because the specification needs a kind of conflict, and these proofs do not cause conflict because they explain what a general provision does not include in its meaning.

10. By this condition, abrogation (*naskh*) is excluded, because when a specifying proof appears after the general provision, it is abrogation, not specification. This is the main point of disagreement between the majority and the Ḥanafīs when the difference between specification and abrogation is in question.

11. Bukhārī, *Kashf al-Asrār*, I:37; Badshāh, *Taysīr al-Taḥrīr*, I:271; Mayhawī, *Sharḥ Nūr al-Anwār*, I:169.

12. Ibn Nujaym, *al-Ashbāh wa al-Naẓāʾir*, p. 57; Lubnānī, *Sharḥ al-Majallah*, p. 20.

13. A question may arise as to whether the general provision, after being specified, continues to provide a real meaning (*ḥaqīqah*) in its remaining subjects, or becomes *majāz*. After studying this question, I have come to the conclusion that it continues to provide a real meaning. Ramic, *Taʿāruḍ mā Yukhill bi al-Fahm wa Atharuh fī al-Aḥkām al-Fiqhiyyah*, pp. 38–39.

14. Nasafī, *Kashf al-Asrār*, I:161; Taftāzānī, *Sharḥ al-Talwīḥ ʿalā al-Tawḍīḥ*, I:40.

15. Baṣrī, *al-Muʿtamad*, I:251–252; Shawkānī, *Irshād al-Fuḥūl*, 125–126.

16. Because this would be regarded as abrogation, not specification.

17. Shaʿbān, *Uṣūl al-Fiqh*, pp. 270–273.

18. Therefore, according to the majority, specification is the limitation of the general provision to some subjects by dependent or independent proofs, chronological or not, which appear before the general provision is implemented.

19. Taftāzānī, *Sharḥ al-Talwīḥ ʿalā al-Tawḍīḥ*, I:42–43; Bukhārī, *Kashf al-Asrār*, I:306; Mayhawī, *Sharḥ Nūr al-Anwār*, I:169.

20. There is no doubt that accepting reason and custom as specification proofs, which can specify authoritative texts, gives the *Sharīʿah* the legal flexibility for the adjustment of its changeable laws (*mughayyirāt*) according to what is beneficial and good for the people. Therefore, the changeable laws of *Sharīʿah* may be developed according to the new and developing needs of people.

21. This is because they presume that they are parallel in such cases.

22. The majority of scholars regard this as specification and not abrogation.

23. Partial abrogation occurs when the specifying proof comes after general provision, while complete abrogation occurs when general provision comes after the specific provision.

24. The independent proofs 3b

25. The independent proofs 3a.

26. Shīrāzī, *al-Lumma*ʿ, pp.33–34; Aṣfahānī, *Sharḥ al-Minhāj*, I:381; Ijī, *Mukhtaṣar al-Muntahā*, II:131–155; Anṣārī, *Ghāyat al-Wuṣūl*, pp. 76–79; Shawkānī, *Irshād al-Fuḥūl*, pp.128–143.

27. Scholar have disagreed on whether or not the disconnectedness of the exception (*istithnāʾ munqaṭiʿ*) specifies the general indication. Sālim, *Tashīl al-Wuṣūl ilā Fahm ʿIlm al-Uṣūl*, p. 37.

28. Qurʾān, II:282.

29. On conditions for the correctness of exceptions, see Sālim, *Tashīl al-Wuṣūl ilā Fahm ʿIlm al-Uṣūl*, pp. 37–38.

30. Qur'ān, XXIV:4–5.

31. Ibn Kathīr, *Tafsīr al-Qur'ān al-ʿAẓīm*, III:354–355; Sālim, *Tashīl al-Wuṣūl ilā Fahm ʿIlm al-Uṣūl*, p. 38.

32. This question is very important for every day law. An example is when someone makes a will, saying: 'Give my property to the poor, the needy, those who are in debt, but except those who are immoral among them.' Does the exception affect all three groups or only the last one?

33. The condition referred to here is the linguistic condition by which one object is dependent on another. This condition has many articles – e.g. if (*in*) and when (*idhā*).

34. This is the only stipulation whereby the condition may cause specification.

35. Qur'ān, IV:12.

36. Qur'ān, IV:101.

37. Qur'ān, IV:25.

38. Some mentioned another dependent proof, based on the *badal al-baʿḍ min al-kull*. This verse is an example. (Ijī, *Mukhtaṣar al-Muntahā*, II:132; Qaṭṭān, *Mabāhith fī ʿUlūm al-Qur'ān*, p.227; Sālim, *Tashīl al-Wuṣūl ilā Fahm ʿIlm al-Uṣūl*, p. 40).

39. Qur'ān, III:97.

40. Qur'ān, IV:23.

41. Qur'ān, II:222.

42. Qur'ān, V:6.

43. Qur'ān, III:97.

44. Qur'ān, II:185.

45. It includes only believers because only they have been addressed in the beginning of the verse.

46. According to Islamic teaching there cannot be a conflict between sound reason and *Sharīʿah*.

47. Tirmidhī, *al-Jāmiʿ al-Ṣaḥīḥ*, IV:24 (no. 1423); Nasā'ī, *Sunan*, VI:156 (no. 3432).

48. Namely, at the time when a general provision appears. If customs and habits are temporary, they may not specify general provisions, except when based on the basic rules of Islamic law. (Jawziyyah, *Iʿlām al-Muwaqqiʿīn*, III:89).

49. There is a disagreement about whether or not practical customs and habits specify general provisions. Ḥanafīs and most Mālikīs maintain that they do specify general provisions (Ibn Amīr al-Ḥājj, *al-Taqrīr wa al-Taḥbīr*, I:282; Isnawī, *Nihāyat al-Sawl Sharḥ Minhāj al-Wuṣūl*, II:469).

50. Qur'ān, II:275.

51. This happens when the *Sharīʿah* employs a term that carries a different meaning from what it literally means in Arabic. In the science of *uṣūl al-fiqh* this is called *naql* (move, transfer).

52. Shāṭibī, *al-Muwāfaqāt*, III:151.

53 These examples are equally valid for Ḥanafīs.

54. In the Ḥanafī *madhhab* this would be partial or complete abrogation (*naskh juz'ī* or *naskh kullī*). It is noteworthy that the general provision of a verse may be specified by another verse, such as: 'And divorced women shall wait [as regards their marriage] for three menstrual periods' (Qur'ān, II:228). This verse is specified, and pregnant women are excluded by: 'And for those who are pregnant their *ʿiddah* [prescribed period] is until they deliver [their burdens]' (Qur'ān, LXV:4). The general provision from the Qur'ān is specified by the *ḥadīth* in the following examples. The Qur'ān states: 'Forbidden to you [for food] are dead animals' (Qur'ān, V:3). This verse is specified by the *ḥadīth* where the Prophet says, 'Two [kinds] of

dead things are lawful to us [for food] and two [things of] blood. The two dead are locusts and whales; the two [things of] blood are liver and spleen.' (Narrated by Aḥmad ibn Ḥanbal and Ibn Mājah. Cf. ʿAsqalānī, *Bulūgh al-Marām*, p. 14) The Qurʾān states: 'God has permitted trade' (Qurʾān, II:275). The general provision of this verse is that all trade is lawful. However, this verse is specified by many traditions which forbid certain kinds of contract. In one tradition transmitted from Ibn ʿUmar, the Prophet forbids ʿasab al-faḥl (see the chapter about the conditions permitting and prohibiting contracts). (ʿAsqalānī, *Bulūgh al-Marām*, pp. 223–240). The general provision of a ḥadīth may also be specified by the Qurʾān. The Prophet says: 'What is cut from an animal while alive is considered dead' (Narrated by Abū Dāwūd and Tirmidhī. Cf. ʿAsqalānī, *Bulūgh al-Marām*, p. 15). This tradition is specified by the following verse: 'And God has made for you from your homes an abode, and made for you out of the hides of cattle [tents as] dwellings which you find so light when you travel and when you make a sojourn; and of their wool, fur and hair furnishings and articles of convenience, [as a comfort] for a while' (Qurʾān, XVI:80). In another tradition the Prophet says, 'When two Muslims cross each other with swords, the killer and the killed are both in hell.' This tradition is specified by the verse: 'And if two parties or groups among the believers fall into fighting, then make peace between them both, but if one of them rebels against the other, then fight [all] against the one who rebels until he complies with the Command of God' (Qurʾān, XLIX:9). Therefore, those who rebel are excluded from the former tradition. The general provision of a *ḥadīth* may be specified by another *ḥadīth*. The Prophet said about *zakāh* on agricultural products: 'What was watered naturally one tenth.' Another saying of his specifies the first one and excludes products which are less than five *awsuq*: 'There is no ṣadaqa on what is less than five *awsuq*.'

55. Qurʾān, II:275.

56. Qurʾān, II:185

57. Ibn Kathīr, *Tafsīr al-Qurʾān al-ʿAẓīm*, II:363–364, III:657–658, IV:489–491.

58. Qurʾān, II:228.

59. Qurʾān, XXXIII:49.

60. Qurʾān, LXV:4.

61. Qurʾān, V:3.

62. Narrated by Aḥmad Nasāʾī, Abū Dāwūd, Tirmidhī, Ibn Mājah and others from Abū Hurayrah. See ʿAsqalānī, *Bulūgh al-Marām*, p. 9.

63. Such as Sālim in *Tashīl al-Wuṣūl ilā Fahm ʿIlm al-Uṣūl*, p. 41; Qaṭṭān, *Mabāhith fī ʿUlūm al-Qurʾān*, p. 227.

64. Muslim, *Ṣaḥīḥ Muslim*, III:1153 (no. 1513).

65. Sālim in *Tashīl al-Wuṣūl ilā Fahm ʿIlm al-Uṣūl*, p. 41.

66. Qurʾān, XXIV:2.

67. Qurʾān, IV:25.

68. Qurʾān, XXVIII:57.

69. Because Ḥanafīs presume that they are parallel in such cases.

70. The majority of scholars regard this as specification (*takhṣīṣ*), not abrogation.

71. Anṣārī, *Ghāyat al-Wuṣūl*, pp. 80–81; Shaʿbān, *Uṣūl al-Fiqh*, p. 277.

72. Qurʾān, XXIII:1–3.

73. Qurʾān, V:1.

74. Since none of them disagreed on this question, there is consensus (*ijmāʾ*). Shaʿbān, *Uṣūl al-Fiqh*, p. 277.

75. *Ẓihār* is when the husband says to his wife: 'You are to me like the back of my mother [i.e. unlawful for me to approach]'. ʿAssāf, *al-Aḥkām al-Fiqhiyyah*, II:398.

76. Qurʾān, LVIII:2.

77. Ibn Kathīr, *Tafsīr al-Qurʾān al-ʿAẓīm*, IV:408–409.

78. Qur'ān, XXIV:6–7.

79. On this matter the Qur'ān states: 'And those who accuse chaste women, and produce not four witnesses, flog them eighty stripes, and reject their testimony forever, they indeed are the disobedient.' (Qur'ān, XXIV:4)

80. His name was Hilāl ibn Umayyah.

81. Ibn Kathīr, *Tafsīr al-Qur'ān al-ʿAẓīm*, III:355–356.

82. Nasā'ī, *Sunan*, I:100–101 (no.69); Ibn Mājah, *Sunan*, I:136 (no. 386); ʿAsqalānī, *Bulūgh al-Marām*, p. 9.

83. Shaʿbān, *Uṣūl al-Fiqh*, p. 278.

CHAPTER 24

Forms of the Specific (*Khāṣṣ*)

Introduction

Khāṣṣ takes different forms. It may take the form of 1) an absolute (*muṭlaq*) which is not qualified, limited or restricted in its application; 2) it may also be qualified (*muqayyad*); 3) it may appear in the form of a command (*amr*); or 4) in the form of a prohibition (*nahy*).

(1) The Absolute (*al-Muṭlaq*)

The linguistic definition of *muṭlaq*:

Muṭlaq refers to free, unlimited, unrestricted, general, absolute, absolute as opposed to restricted (*muqayyad*).[1]

The technical definition of *muṭlaq*

Āmidī offered for the following definition: '*Muṭlaq* is an indefinite word [*nakirah*] used to convey the positive.'[2] Shawkānī employed several definitions. In one, he calls *muṭlaq* 'what is widespread within its sort.'[3] According to Anṣārī, *muṭlaq* is 'an utterance that indicates an entity as it is in itself'.[4]

Based on these definitions we may formulate the following definition: *muṭlaq* is an utterance that indicates a subject or a group within a larger group (*māhiyyah*) without being specified or restricted by anything that may reduce its commonality. We may construe *muṭlaq* to include only one subject which is not specified or restricted, but not a specified or limited group. This means that *muṭlaq* excludes all words restricted by attribute, condition, place, time, etc. When *muṭlaq* is qualified it becomes *muqayyad*. For example, 'a man' is *muṭlaq*, but 'a wise man' is *muqayyad*.

The difference between *ʿāmm* and *muṭlaq*

As mentioned in the definition, the general (*ʿāmm*) includes everything to which is applicable. On the other hand, an absolute utterance indicates a single common or a common group of a kind or class, and does not include all of them. Like the general, it can also include all of them, but not at one and the same time.

Therefore, *ʿāmm* includes everything (all subjects) to which it is applicable, at once; while *muṭlaq* includes only one thing non-specified of all the subjects to which it is applicable. Saying 'the man'[5] includes at once every human being and is considered *ʿāmm*. Saying, however, 'a man' means any human being. It may not include all human beings at the same time, but all of them (successively) at different times. It is considered *muṭlaq*.

Beside these differences *ʿāmm* and *muṭlaq* have some common characteristics. Both of them are open to interpretation beyond the obvious sense of their provisions, and anything that specifies *ʿāmm* qualifies *muṭlaq*.[6]

Examples of *muṭlaq*[7]

(a) The Qurʾān states: 'So whoever of you sights the month must fast that month, and whoever is ill or on a journey, [should fast] the same number on other days'.[8] The word 'days' is absolute in the sense that it has no restriction, such as succession, either in this verse or in any other authoritative text. Therefore, it remains *muṭlaq* – whoever does not fast during Ramaḍān because of illness or travel must fast the same number of other days, in succession or separately.

(b) The Qurʾān states: 'And those of you who die and leave wives behind, [their wives] shall wait [as regards their marriage] for four months and ten days.'[9] The word 'wives' is an absolute because it has no restriction in the sense of including those with whom the marriage was not consummated. It is not restricted, either in this verse or in any other authoritative text. Therefore, it remains *muṭlaq* and includes any woman whose husband dies, whether or not the marriage was consummated.

(c) The Qurʾān states: '[The distribution of wealth occurs] after the payment of the legacies or debts of the deceased person.'[10] The word 'legacies' is absolute, in the sense that it does not limit the amount. According to this indication someone may give all his property as legacy. However, this was restricted by the tradition where the Prophet forbade one from giving more than one third of one's entire property as a legacy. Therefore, 'legacies' in the verse means one third or less, because this ruling did not remain absolute, but became restricted.

The value of *muṭlaq*

The legal adherence to *muṭlaq* is strictly obligatory in Islamic law, as is the implementation of its absolute meaning. It may not be restricted until a reliable proof[11] suggests a restriction.[12] Therefore, no one can reduce the extent of its indication[13] unless a reliable proof suggests that a specified individual subject is intended. *Muṭlaq* provides a definite indication (*qaṭʿī al-dalālah*), because it represents a form of *khāṣṣ* which is definitive (*qaṭʿī*).

(2) The Qualified (*al-Muqayyad*)

The linguistic definition of *muqayyad*

Muqayyad refers to bound, tied, limited, qualified, restricted, confined.[14]

The technical definition of *muqayyad*

The qualified, or *muqayyad* is opposite to the absolute (*muṭlaq*). Therefore, its technical definition should be opposite to that of *muṭlaq*. Taftāzānī defined *muqayyad* as 'what is excluded from any commonality.[15] Shawkānī defined it as 'what is not widespread within its sort'.[16] According to these definitions, *muqayyad* is a word that indicates a subject or non-specified group of subjects (*māhiyyah*) to which is attached what restricts their commonality – e.g., 'a righteous person', 'righteous person', 'a white book', 'white books', 'a good student', 'good students', etc. Therefore, like *muṭlaq*, *muqayyad* includes only one subject or non-specified group of subjects in a multitude. But unlike *muṭlaq*, the one subject or group is limited by a restriction. These and similar words represent absolute nouns which have a restriction. Therefore, the term applies only to these restricted subjects. This means that *muqayyad* includes all restricted words limited by an attribute, condition, place, time, etc.

Examples of *muqayyad*[17]

(a) The Qur'ān states: 'And whosoever finds [the penance of freeing a slave] beyond his means must fast for two consecutive months in order to seek repentance from God. And God is Ever All-Knowing, All-Wise.'[18] This verse prescribes the penance for a Muslim who unjustly kills another Muslim. The word 'two months' is restricted by 'consecutive'. Because no reliable proof suggests another meaning, it continues to be *qualified* and the penance is for two 'consecutive' months.

(b) The Qur'ān states: 'And he who finds not [the money for freeing a slave] must fast two consecutive month before they touch each other [i.e. husband and wife].'[19] This verse prescribes the penance in cases of *ẓihār*. Like the previous verse it is restricted by 'consecutive'. It remains qualified because no reliable proof suggests otherwise.

(c) The Qur'ān states: 'Forbidden to you [for marriage] are your mothers ... and your step-daughters under your guardianship, born of your wives unto whom you have gone – but you will not sin [to marry the daughters of the women] unto whom you have not gone.'[20] The word 'stepdaughters' has been qualified by 'under your guardianship'. However, this restriction has been cancelled by the statement 'but there is no sin on you if you have not gone unto them'. Therefore, this *muqayyad* has not been implemented because its restriction has been nullified and it has become *muṭlaq*.

Conflict between *muṭlaq* and *muqayyad*[21]

When *muṭlaq* and *muqayyad* pertain to the same issue, there are four possibilities: 1) that they agree on the cause and the ruling; 2) that they agree on the cause and disagree on the ruling; 3) that they disagree on the cause and agree on the ruling; 4) and that they disagree on both the cause and the ruling.

(1) Regarding the first possibility, scholars agree that *muqayyad* prevails over *muṭlaq* and qualifies it. This conflict is illustrated by the following verses. The Qur'ān states: 'Forbidden to you [for food] are the dead animal and blood.'[22] In this verse blood is forbidden for human consumption. The word 'blood' is absolute but one qualified in another verse as 'blood shed forth'.[23] Blood in the second verse is restricted and the restricted sense prevails over the absolute.[24]

(2) In the second possibility, where *muṭlaq* and *muqayyad* agree on the cause[25] and disagree on the ruling,[26] *muqayyad* will not qualify *muṭlaq* and everyone will treat it as it stands. This is illustrated by the verses related to *wuḍū'* and *tayammum*. The Qur'ān states about *wuḍū'*, 'O you who believe! When you stand to offer prayer, wash you faces and your hands [forearms] up to the elbows.'[27] The washing of the hands is restricted to 'up to the elbows'. The same verse does not restrict rubbing the hands in *tayammum*: 'And if you find no water, then perform *tayammum* with clean earth and rub therewith your faces and hands.' Because the two verses pertain to different rulings, the first verse will not qualify the second, and thus in *tayammum* the hands should not be rubbed 'up to the elbows'.[28]

(3) The third possibility is that they disagree on the cause and agree on the ruling. As an example of this possibility we may refer to the following verses. The Qur'ān states: 'And get two witnesses from among your own men.'[29] This verse requires two witnesses in commercial transactions. The word 'men' is absolute because this verse does not qualify it. Another verse also deals with the subject of witnesses. The Qur'ān states: 'And take for witness two just persons from among you.'[30] This verse, however, qualifies

the persons as 'just'. The ruling of these two verses is the same because both require two witnesses. The causes of these rulings, however, are different. In the former the cause is commercial transactions, whereas in the latter it is the revocation of divorce. Since the qualified prevails over the absolute, the latter verse prevails over the former and the ruling is that witnesses in both commercial transactions and the revocation of divorce must be 'just'. This accords with the opinion of Shāfiʿīs, while Ḥanafī scholars do not qualify *muṭlaq* by *muqayyad* in this situation, and every verse operates as it stands.

(4) The fourth possibility is that they disagree on both the cause and the ruling. An example of this may be seen in the verses related to ablution and theft. The Qurʾān states regarding ablution: 'O you who believe! When you stand to offer prayer, wash you faces and your hands [forearms] up to the elbows.'[31] The washing of the hands in this verse is restricted to 'up to the elbows'. In the verse about theft there is no such restriction. The Qurʾān states: 'Cut off the hand of the thief, male or female.'[32] Therefore, it is absolute. Due to the fact that both causes and rulings in these verses are different, there is no conflict between them and each verse operates as it stands.

The precondition for the restriction of *muṭlaq* by *muqayyad*

Before the *muqayyad* can qualify *muṭlaq*, certain conditions must hold, as stipulated by scholars. The most important of these are:[33]

(1) The restriction should be in the form of attributes, where the basics of rulings are already established in both *muṭlaq* and *muqayyad*. If the restriction of the absolute establishes the fundamental ruling in the form of an increase, or an increase in the number of times, the *muqayyad* may not qualify the *muṭlaq*. For example, it is obligatory in *wuḍūʾ* to wash or wipe four parts, while for *tayammum* only two parts. Here, the *muqayyad* may not restrict the *muṭlaq*, since this would lead to the affirmation of a ruling which has not been mentioned, and the restriction may operate in the sphere of attributes only.

(2) The absolute should be of one origin (source). If the absolute alternates between two different restrictions, the restriction will not take place. An example of this condition is the restriction that the inheritance between spouses should take place after regulating legacy and debts.[34] Inheritance has been mentioned in other places in the form of an absolute (*muṭlaq*). Because this *muṭlaq* (the inheritance) and the inheritance mentioned in other places in authoritative texts are all of one and the same origin, it will be restricted, and therefore the inheritance will take place after the legacy and debts are regulated.

(3) That they may not be harmonised (reconciled) except by restriction because implementing their full meaning is better than cancelling some meaning.

(4) That there is not a reliable proof which prevents the restriction from taking place.

(5) That an additional meaning has not been mentioned and joined to the *muqayyad* in a way that may suggest that the restriction has been mentioned because of that additional meaning. If such additional meaning is joined to *muqayyad*, the restriction may not take place.

The value of *muqayyad*

As in the case of *muṭlaq*, the legal adherence to *muqayyad* is obligatory and constitutes the implementation of its restricted meaning. *Muqayyad* also provides a definite indication (*qaṭʿī al-dalālah*), because it represents a form of *khāṣṣ* which is definitive.

(3) The Command (*al-Amr*)

The linguistic definition of *amr*

Amr refers to order, command, instruction, decree, authority. The term occurs in many verses of the Qur'ān in the sense of command.[35]

The technical definition of *amr*

Ibn al-Ḥājib provides the following definition of *amr*: 'Requirement of an act, not abstention, from the position of superiority.'[36] Āmidī quoted a few definitions for *amr* and discussed them. He chose the definition provided by the Shāfiʿīs: '*Amr* is an order, from the position of superiority, to act.'[37] Nasafī defined *amr* simply as an order to act.[38] Based on these definitions we may define *amr* as the provision of an order to act in the future, whenever that order is issued from someone entitled to make such a command.

Forms of *amr*

Amr may be expressed in a variety of forms:[39]

(1) The imperative mood of verbs exemplified in the following verse: 'Then depart (*afīḍū*) from the place whence all the people depart and ask (*istaghfirū*) God for His forgiveness.'[40]

(2) The jussive mood of verbs (imperfect) preceded by the command article '*li*' such as in the verse: 'Then let them complete [*li yaqḍū*] the prescribed duties for them, and perform [*li yūfū*] their vows, and circumambulate [*li yaṭṭawwafū*] the Ancient House.'[41]

(3) The verbs in simple passive voice exemplified in the verses: 'O you who believe! The law of equality in punishment is prescribed upon you in case of murder.'[42] 'O you who believe! Fasting is prescribed upon you.'[43]

(4) The verbal imperative noun exemplified in the verse: 'O you who believe! You are responsible for your own souls.'[44] The word "*'alaykum*' is an imperative verbal noun and is regarded as a form of *amr*.

(5) The verbal noun which is a substitute for the imperative mood of verbs, as in the verse: 'Strike at their necks.'[45] The word '*ḍarb*' is a verbal noun which means striking, hitting. In this verse, however, it acts as a substitute for the imperative mood and means 'strike'.

Besides these forms of *amr*, there are other forms which may give the same indication – explicit mention of the following words: to order (*amara*), to ordain (*faraḍa*), to prescribe (*kataba*), the duty upon (*ḥaqq 'alā*) and similar words. Included here are the provisions that indicate a moral condemnation, threats of punishment, or the expunging of someone's good deeds because of abandoned duties. A sentence that provides information by which an order is intended is illustrated in the verse: 'The mothers suckle [*yurḍi'na*] their children for two whole years.'[46] This information indicates that an order is intended. Some translators took this into consideration and translated the verse as: 'The mothers suckle.'[47]

The primary indication of *amr*[48]

If a form of *amr* is not accompanied by clues or evidences suggesting a kind of request, *amr* implies a definite order. This is the opinion of the majority of Islamic scholars.[49] The following proofs have been offered.

(1) Many Qur'ānic verses include clear explanatory statements: '[God] said: "What prevented you [O Iblīs] from prostrating, when I commanded you?"'[50] 'And when it is said to them: "Bow down [in prayer]!" They bow not down [to offer prayers].'[51] 'And let those who oppose his [the Messenger's] commandment beware, lest some *fitnah* befall them or a painful torment be inflicted on them.'[52] 'It is not for a believer, man or woman, when God and His Messenger have decreed a matter, to have any choice in their decision. And whoever disobeys God and His Messenger has indeed strayed in plain error.'[53]

(2) There is unanimous agreement among the Companions of the Prophet in this matter.

(3) This is the nature of the Arabic language and the scholars of language have agreed upon it.

These proofs are explicit and so strong that, according to Islamic science, no other proofs can refute them.

The absolute and the restricted order[54]

An absolute order (*amr muṭlaq*) must include everything without which it may not be completed. For example, the order to perform prayer must include the order for ablution because the prayer will be invalid without it.[55] This is when there is an absolute order. When we have a restricted order (*amr muqayyad*) such as in the case of alms, which is restricted by the possession of a certain amount of wealth, there is no question of obligation to achieve that. This is because, by achieving it, the order, not the duty and obligation will be completed.[56]

Other usages of *amr*[57]

Amr essentially implies obligation. It may, however, imply other things, depending on the evidence (context and circumstances), which may point away from its original meaning towards other meanings. Other usages of *amr* are:

(1) Recommendation (*nadb*) exemplified by the verse: 'O you who believe! When you contract a debt for a fixed period, write it down.'[58]

(2) Permissibility (*ibāḥah*) as in: 'and eat and drink.'[59]

(3) The threat as in: 'Do what you will.'[60]

(4) Indebtedness as in: 'And eat of the things that God has provided for you.'[61]

(5) Honour and hospitality as in: 'Enter therein [Paradise], in peace and security.'[62]

(6) Deeming powerless as in: 'Then produce a chapter of the like thereof.'[63]

(7) Equalisation as in: 'Endure its heat, and whether you are patient or not, it is all the same.'[64]

(8) Contempt as in: 'Cast down what you want to cast.'[65]

(9) Consultation as in: 'What do you think?'[66]

(10) A call for contemplation as in: 'Look at their fruits when they begin to bear.'[67]

(11) Supplication (*duʿāʾ*), when a request comes from an inferior being to another, as in the verse: 'My Lord forgive me.'[68]

(12) Warning as in: 'But take every precaution for yourselves.'[69]

(13) Insult as in: 'Taste you [this]! Verily, you were [pretending to be] the mighty, the generous.'[70]

(14) Request when a demand comes from an equal or nearly-equal person, as when a student asks a friend: 'Give me the pen.'

The indication of *amr* after *nahy*[71]

In authoritative texts there are rulings which abrogate others and rulings which command the opposite of what has hitherto been prohibited. For example, the Prophet once said: 'I have forbidden you from visiting the graves. Nay, visit them, for it reminds you of the Hereafter.'[72] In these situations we may ask whether the command after prohibition implies obligation or something else. The majority of scholars maintain that it implies permissibility, not obligation.

Single compliance with *amr* or its repetition[73]

Amr may be: a) absolute, b) restricted to a single act of compliance, c) restricted to repetition. When *amr* is restricted it is implemented according to its restrictions, because the qualified has preference over the absolute. Single compliance with it may be illustrated by the verse: 'And *hajj* is a duty that mankind owes to God.'[74] The Prophet was asked if it had to be performed every year, and he replied it should be done once in a lifetime.[75]

An example of repetition is in the verse: 'Cut off the hand of the thief, male or female.'[76] The command in this verse is dependent on an attribute, i.e., theft. Therefore, whenever theft occurs the hand must be severed.[77] The majority of the scholars maintain that when *amr* is absolute it does not imply a single act of compliance or repetition. However, keeping in mind that the obligation may not be fulfilled without a single act of compliance, single compliance becomes necessary, but not because the absolute *amr* itself indicates it.

Some scholars maintain that *amr* implies a single compliance, others that it implies repetition during one's lifetime. The majority opinion and those who maintain that *amr* implies a single act of compliance do not differ in practical terms. The second opinion, however, seems more consistent with the Arabic language.

The time at which *amr* should be performed[78]

Amr may be restricted as to the time of its performance. However, if the *amr* is an absolute, it must be performed immediately[79] because people are generally commanded not to delay the performance of good deeds. Several Qur'ānic verses indicate this: 'And vie one with another for forgiveness from your Lord.'[80] 'Race one with another for forgiveness from your Lord.'[81] 'So vie with one another in good works.'[82] Moreover, bearing in mind the uncertainty of the time of one's death, the immediate performance of *amr* seems more to be an even greater requirement.[83]

Who is addressed by *amr*?[84]

In respect of rationality, human beings may be divided into two groups: those to whom legal or religious obligations (legal awareness) apply and those to whom they do not apply because of immaturity, or temporary or permanent loss of mental capabilities. The legal texts are not addressed to those who do not possess legal awareness. This is a logical conclusion because an order is normally issued to someone who can presumably perform the obligation. Furthermore, the authoritative texts themselves make this clear. The Prophet has said, 'There is no responsibility upon three persons: a sleeping person before he wakes, a youth before puberty (i.e. the legal age of maturity in Islamic law), and a lunatic before he recovers his senses.[85]

The value of *amr*[86]

Amr is better thought of as implying a definite obligation. Therefore, Muslims ought to understand this before setting out in search for clues or evidence which may provide other indications.

(4) Prohibition (*al-Nahy*)

The linguistic definition of *nahy*

Nahy refers to prohibition, ban, a term which occurs in many verses of Qur'ān in the sense of prohibition.[87]

The technical definition of *nahy*

Āmidī held that *nahy* is the opposite of *amr*, and thus an order not to act, from a position of superiority.[88] Nasafī defined *nahy* as an utterance by someone, from a position of superiority, for another not to act.[89] Shawkānī defined *nahy* as: 'The declaration that requires an abstention, from the position of superiority.'[90] According to these definitions we may define *nahy* as a provision that prohibits an act in the future when that prohibition is issued from someone who is entitled to make it.

The forms of *nahy*[91]

Nahy may appear in different forms:

(1) The imperfect preceded by the article *lā* (jussive mood) as in the verses: 'And consume not each other's property unjustly [i.e., illegally]'[92] 'O you who believe! Betray not [*lā takhūnū*] God and His Messenger.'[93]

(2) The explicit mention of a prohibition (*taḥrīm*), and ban (*nahy*), as in the following verses: 'Such a thing is forbidden [*ḥurrima*] to the believers.'[94] 'God does not prohibit you [*lā yanhākum*] from dealing justly and kindly with those who you fought not for religion and who did not drive you out of your homes. Verily, God loves those who deal equitably. He only prohibits you [*yanhākum*] from befriending those who fight against you for religion, drive you out of your homes, and help to drive you out.'[95]

(3) A command that requires the avoidance of something: 'O you who believe! When the call for the prayer is proclaimed on Friday come to the remembrance of God, and put aside [*wa dharū*] trading.'[96] 'So shun [*ijtanibū*] the abomination of idols and shun lying speech.'[97]

(4) Threats against and criticism of those who do commit certain deeds:

'And whoever does this shall receive punishment.'[98] 'And who does more wrong than one who invents a lie against God, while he is being invited to Islam.'[99]

(5) Prescribing penance for certain deeds: 'And whoever kills a believer by mistake must set free a believing slave and give compensation to the deceased's family, unless they remit it.'[100]

(6) The expressions 'you ought not' in the verse: 'And you ought not annoy God's Messenger, or ever marry his wives after him.'[101]

(7) Prescribing a punishment (*hadd*) as a consequence for certain deeds: 'The woman and the man guilty of illegal sexual relations, flog each of them a hundred lashes.'[102]

(8) Moral condemnation of certain conduct as in the verse: 'It is not of righteousness that you enter the houses from the back.'[103]

(9) Description of a deed as corrupt or an act of the devil: 'O you who believe! Intoxicants, gambling, arrows [for seeking luck or a decision] are an abomination of Satan's handiwork.'[104]

(10) Confirmation that God abhors those who falsify the Scriptures; that He will not purify,[105] speak to, or look at them.[106]

(11) In the form of information: for *hajj* the months are well known. So, whoever intends to perform *hajj* – no sexual relations, sin, or unjustifiable dispute during the *hajj*.[107]

Other usages of *nahy*[108]

The forms of *nahy* do not always imply strict prohibition (*tahrīm*). They may imply other rulings too:[109]

(1) Blameworthiness (*karāhah*) – e.g., the Prophet's prohibition of drinking from the neck of a waterskin.[110]

(2) Supplication (*duʿāʾ*) of an inferior to a superior being, as in the verse: 'Our Lord seize us not if we forget or fall into error.'[111]

(3) Guidance (*irshād*) as exemplified in the verse: 'O you who believe! Ask not about things which, if made plain to you, may cause you trouble.'[112]

(4) To explain an end or outcome: 'Think not of those who are killed in God's way as dead. Nay, they are alive, with their Lord, and they have provision.'[113]

The indication of *nahy*[114]

The majority of Islamic scholars maintain that *nahy*, in reality, implies prohibition if a reliable proof does not suggest otherwise. As for whether or not *nahy* necessarily means that whatever is prohibited is corrupt, incorrect, or invalid – and as such produces no legal rights and effects – this needs more explanation.

The prohibited may be twofold:

(1) The prohibited which has never been treated by God as a good or acceptable deed: 'And do not approach the unlawful sexual act.'[115] 'Worship God and join none with Him.'[116] These deeds are prohibited because they are considered intrinsically bad. They are forbidden, corrupt and incorrect, and they result only in things corrupt and incorrect. Thus an illegitimate child will not follow the father in partnership, and an unbeliever will not be rewarded in the Hereafter for his good deeds done in this world.[117]

(2) What is prohibited in one respect, but enjoined in another. It is prohibited for three reasons:

(a) because of its attribute – e.g., prohibition for menstruating woman or a drunk person with respect to the performance of prayers;[118]

(b) because of a matter which necessarily accompanies it – i.e., the prohibition of fasting during the first day of *Eid*, because fasting prevents one from celebrating the feast day;

(c) because of a matter which does not accompany it[119] – e.g., the prohibition to perform ablution with stolen water, to pray on land acquired by unlawful means,[120] or trade after the call for Friday prayer.[121]

Single compliance with or repetition of a *nahy*[122]

Nahy indicates an order to abandon an action forever if it is not restricted. The proof for this lies in the fact that scholars used *nahy* as a permanent proof without restricting it.

The value of *nahy*[123]

The absolute *nahy* implies prohibition, and that the thing prohibited is invalid. Therefore, Muslims should believe that a ban (*nahy*) implies prohibition (*taḥrīm*) before they search for contrary clues or evidence.

NOTES

1. *al-Muʿjam al-Wasīṭ*, II:564; Tahānawī, *Dictionary of the Technical Terms*, pp. 921–924; Wehr, *Arabic-English Dictionary*, p. 567.

2. Āmidī, *al-Iḥkām fī Uṣūl al-Aḥkām*, III:5.

3. Shawkānī, *Irshād al-Fuḥūl*, p. 144.

4. Anṣārī, *Ghāyat al-Wuṣūl*, p. 82.

5. If the definite article is for comprehension (*istighrāq*), and not the specification of a known person (*ʿahd*).

6. Therefore, all specifying proofs which have been mentioned previously may be mentioned here as qualifying proofs.

7. As mentioned, *muṭlaq* may be restricted to make it *muqayyad* (qualified). The first two examples I will mention represent a *muṭlaq* which remains *muṭlaq*; the third example will be of a *muṭlaq* which is qualified to make it *muqayyad*.

8. Qur'ān, II:185.

9. Qur'ān, II:234.

10. Qur'ān, IV:11.

11. As in the previous example.

12. Sha'bān, *Uṣūl al-Fiqh al-Islāmī*, p. 248; 'Uthaymīn, *al-Uṣūl min 'Ilm al-Uṣūl*, p. 58.

13. As in the first and second examples.

14. *al-Mu'jam al-Wasīṭ*, II:769; Wehr, *Arabic-English Dictionary*, p. 804.

15. Taftāzānī, *Sharḥ al-Talwīḥ 'alā al-Tawḍīḥ*, I:63.

16. Shawkānī, *Irshād al-Fuhūl*, p. 144.

17. *Muqayyad* may continue to provide a restricted meaning but may become absolute when a reliable proof suggests such a move. The first two examples mentioned below represent a *muqayyad* which remains *muqayyad*; and the third example represents a *muqayyad* which becomes *muṭlaq*.

18. Qur'ān, IV:92.

19. Qur'ān, LVIII:4.

20. Qur'ān, IV:23.

21. Kalwāzānī, *al-Tamhīd*, II:177–186; Āmidī, *al-Iḥkām fī Uṣūl al-Aḥkām*, III:6–9; Aṣfahānī, *Sharḥ al-Minhāj*, I:432; Anṣārī, *Ghāyat al-Wuṣūl*, pp. 82–83; Shawkānī, *Irshād al-Fuhūl*, pp. 144–146.

22. Qur'ān, V:3.

23. Qur'ān, VI:145.

24. The cause in this example is the consumption.

25. In the following example the cause is the intention to perform the prayer, with a need to make ritual preparation for prayer.

26. In the following example the conflict on the ruling lies in the fact that in *wuḍū'* the obligation is washing the hands with water, and in *tayammum* it is rubbing the hands with earth.

27. Qur'ān, V:6.

28. There is disagreement between *fuqahā'* about this question. Some scholars restricted the verse about *tayammum* by some traditions (Ibn Rushd, *Bidāyat al-Mujtahid*, I:68–70).

29. Qur'ān, II:282.

30. Qur'ān, LXV:2.

31. Qur'ān, V:6.

32. Qur'ān, V:38.

33. Shawkānī, *Irshād al-Fuhūl*, pp. 146–147.

34. Qur'ān, IV:12.

35. *al-Mu'jam al-Wasīṭ*, I:26; EI², I:449; Wehr, *Arabic-English Dictionary*, p. 26.

36. Ījī, *Sharḥ Mukhtaṣar al-Muntahā'*, II:77.

37. Āmidī, *al-Iḥkām fī Uṣūl al-Aḥkām*, II:365.

38. Nasafī, *Kashf al-Asrār*, I:44.

39. These are the forms of *amr* provided there is no contrary evidence. Ash'arī scholars, however, maintain that a command has no forms of wording. This opinion is inconsistent with Arabic language rules, the Qur'ān and the *Sunnah*, and thus entirely rejected (Sālim, *Tashīl al-Wuṣūl ilā Fahm 'Ilm al-Uṣūl*, p. 23).

40. Qur'ān, II:199.

41. Qur'ān, XXII:29.

42. Qur'ān, II:178.

43. Qur'ān, II:183.

44. Qur'ān, V:105.

45. Qur'ān, XLVI:4.

46. Qur'ān, II:233.

47. Khān and Hilālī, *Interpretation of the Meaning of the Noble Qur'ān*, p. 58.

48. Shīrāzī, *al-Lumma*ᶜ, p. 13; Aṣfahānī, *Sharḥ al-Minhāj*, I:314–324; Anṣārī, *Ghāyat al-Wuṣūl*, p. 64; Shawkānī, *Irshād al-Fuḥūl*, p. 83; Kawrānī, *Sharḥ Mukhtaṣar al-Manār fī Uṣūl al-Fiqh*, p. 28; Badrān, *Uṣūl al-Fiqh al-Islāmī*, p. 360.

49. There are other views: a) *amr* is a homonym (*mushtarak*) which imparts all sorts of meanings; b) *amr* imparts only obligation and recommendation; c) *amr* imparts permission to act. According to these views, in order to impart meaning *amr* must be supported by clues or circumstances. Accordingly, it may not imply obligation without additional evidence that suggests this. These opinions and their proofs cannot, in my opinion, oppose the clear proofs of the majority of scholars, who maintain that the basic implication of *amr* is obligation. *Amr* must exhibit additional evidence and clues before it can have other implications (Shīrāzī, *al-Lumma*ᶜ, p. 13; Anṣārī, *Ghāyat al-Wuṣūl*, p. 64; Shawkānī, *Irshād al-Fuḥūl*, p. 83).

50. Qur'ān, VII:12.

51. Qur'ān, LXXVII:48.

52. Qur'ān, XXIV:63.

53. Qur'ān, XXXIII:36.

54. Shīrāzī, *al-Lumma*ᶜ, pp. 17–18.

55. This does not mean that there are no special proofs for this and similar obligations.

56. The rule is: That without which a duty may not be fulfilled is a duty, and that without which the order will not be completed is not obligatory.

57. Shīrāzī, *al-Lumma*ᶜ, p. 12; Aṣfahānī, *Sharḥ al-Minhāj*, I:309–312; Anṣārī, *Ghāyat al-Wuṣūl*, p. 64; Shawkānī, *Irshād al-Fuḥūl*, pp. 85–86.

58. Qur'ān, II:282.

59. Qur'ān, VII:31. This verse is normally mentioned by scholars as an example for permissibility (*ibāḥah*). It seems to me to indicate more an obligation. This opinion is supported by many proofs: a) *amr* originally imparts an obligation; b) eating and drinking is the only way to sustain life and to do so is a strict obligation; c) this is mentioned in conjunction with 'eat and drink but waste not in extravagance; certainly [God] likes not the extravagant'. All agree that extravagance in eating and drinking is forbidden. More appropriate as an example of permissibility is the verse: 'But when you finish the *iḥrām* [great or minor pilgrimage] go hunt' (Qur'ān, V:2). 'Go hunt' (*fa iṣṭādū*) is normally translated as 'you may hunt' because the order here implies permissibility.

60. Qur'ān, XLI:40.

61. Qur'ān, V:88.

62. Qur'ān, XV:46.

63. Qur'ān, II:23.

64. Qur'ān, LII: 16.

65. Qur'ān, X:80.

66. Qur'ān, XXXVII:102.

67. Qur'ān, VI:99.

68. Qur'ān, XXXVIII:35.

69. Qur'ān, IV:71.

70. Qur'ān, XLIV:49.

71. Shīrāzī, *al-Lumma*ᶜ, pp. 13–14; Aṣfahānī, *Sharḥ al-Minhāj*, I:327–329; Anṣārī, *Ghāyat al-Wuṣūl*, p. 65.

72. Tabrizi, *Mishkāt al-Maṣābīḥ*, I:554 (no. 1796).

73. Shīrāzī, *al-Lumma*ᶜ, pp. 14–15; Aṣfahānī, *Sharḥ al-Minhāj*, I:329–335; Anṣārī, *Ghāyat al-Wuṣūl*, p. 65; Shawkānī, *Irshād al-Fuḥūl*, p. 86.

74. Qur'ān, III:97.

75. Ibn Kathīr, *Tafsīr al-Qur'ān al-ᶜAẓīm*, I:512.

76. Qur'ān, V:38.

77. If all conditions for punishment are fulfilled.

78. Shīrāzī, *al-Lumma'*, pp. 15–17; Aṣfahānī, *Sharḥ al-Minhāj*, I:337–342; Anṣārī, *Ghāyat al-Wuṣūl*, p. 65; Shawkānī, *Irshād al-Fuḥūl*, pp. 88–89.

79. The time may sometimes be flexible so that someone who does not fulfil the obligation immediately should not be blamed – as in prayers, for which immediate performance is not strictly required. We may consider the Prophet's delay in performing the pilgrimage in the light of this conclusion. While an absolute order may sometimes be delayed, the requirement to perform it as soon as possible remains in effect, due to the general requirement to perform good deeds at the nearest time available.

80. Qur'ān, III:133.

81. Qur'ān, LVII:21.

82. Qur'ān, II:148.

83. According to someone's ability, because God does not burden a person beyond his capacity (cf. Qur'ān, II:286)

84. Shīrāzī, *al-Lumma'*, pp. 20–23; Kawrānī, *Sharḥ Mukhtaṣar al-Manār fī Uṣūl al-Fiqh*, p. 42; 'Uthaymīn, *al-Uṣūl min 'Ilm al-Uṣūl*, p. 39; the answer provided here is also relevant to *nahy*.

85. Tirmidhī, *al-Jāmi' al-Ṣaḥīḥ*, IV:24 (no. 1423); Nasā'ī, *Sunan*, VI:156 (no. 3432).

86. Anṣārī, *Ghāyat al-Wuṣūl*, p. 65.

87. *al-Mu'jam al-Wasīṭ*. II:960; Wehr, *Arabic-English Dictionary*, p. 1005.

88. Āmidī, *al-Iḥkām fī Uṣūl al-Aḥkām*, II:406.

89. Nasafī, *Kashf al-Asrār*, I:140.

90. Shawkānī, *Irshād al-Fuḥūl*, p. 96.

91. Sālim, *Tashīl al-Wuṣūl ilā 'Ilm al-Uṣūl*, p. 28.

92. Qur'ān, II:188.

93. Qur'ān, VIII:27.

94. Qur'ān, XXIV:3.

95. Qur'ān, LX:8–9.

96. Qur'ān, LXII:9.

97. Qur'ān, XXII:30.

98. Qur'ān, XXV:68.

99. Qur'ān, LXI:7.

100. Qur'ān, IV:92.

100. Qur'ān, XXXIII:53.

102. Qur'ān, XXIV:2.

103. Qur'ān, II:189.

104. Qur'ān, V:90.

105. Qur'ān, II:174.

106. See the following verses: Qur'ān, II:174; Qur'ān, III:77.

107. Qur'ān, II:197.

108. Shīrāzī, *al-Lumma'*, pp. 24–25; Anṣārī, *Ghāyat al-Wuṣūl*, p. 67; 'Uthaymīn, *al-Uṣūl min 'Ilm al-Uṣūl*, pp. 37–39.

109. In fact *nahy* may imply many of the same rulings as *amr*. The difference is that *amr* implies action and *nahy* abstention (Anṣārī, *Ghāyat al-Wuṣūl*, p. 67).

110. See Nawawī, *Riyāḍ al-Ṣāliḥīn*, p. 269.

111. Qur'ān, II:286.

112. Qur'ān V:101.

113. Qur'ān, III:169.

114. Shīrāzī, *al-Lumma'*, p. 25; Aṣfahānī, *Sharḥ al-Minhāj*, I:343, 345–347; Anṣārī, *Ghāyat*

al-Wuṣūl, p. 68; Shawkānī, *Irshād al-Fuḥūl*, pp. 96–98; Kawrānī, *Sharḥ Mukhtaṣar al-manār fī Uṣūl al-Fiqh*, p. 44; ʿUthaymīn, *al-Uṣūl min ʿIlm al-Uṣūl*, p. 36.

115. Qurʾān, XVII:32.

116. Qurʾān, IV:36.

117. According to Islamic belief, non-believers are rewarded for their good deeds in this world.

118. Menstruation and drunkenness are attributes that prohibit one from prayer.

119. That is, there is no relation between the prohibited and this matter.

120. The prohibition here was introduced because of a matter unrelated to what is prohibited. Ablution is prohibited not because the ablution will be incorrect (as in the case of dirty water), but because the water may not be used without the permission of its owner. Therefore, the prohibition is the same whether the stolen water is used for ablution or for something else. Sullied and stolen water differ in their prohibition because of the presence of an intrinsic attribute, and a matter which does not accompany it.

121. Some scholars maintain that the deeds under these circumstances are correct. Other scholars, however, maintain that such deeds are incorrect because the prohibition demands punishment and correctness requires reward, and there may not be a deed for which a person is rewarded and punished at the same time. The latter opinion is preferable because it is supported by strong proofs. The Prophet said that a deed which was not in accordance with his practice would be rejected. His Companions used prohibitions as an argument for the invalidity of a deed – e.g. usurious trading.

122. Aṣfahānī, *Sharḥ al-Minhāj*, I:343–344; Anṣārī, *Ghāyat al-Wuṣūl*, p. 67.

123. ʿUthaymīn, *al-Uṣūl min ʿIlm al-Uṣūl*, p. 36.

PART IV

The Interpretation of Clear and Unclear Words (*Ta'wīl*)

Introduction

Ta'wīl is a major cause of disagreement between Islamic scholars, because many *Sharīʿah* source-texts are susceptible to more than one interpretation. This holds true not only of ambiguous texts but also of those containing more obvious (or apparent) meanings (in both the Ḥanafī and Shāfiʿī schools). Because *ta'wīl* can be abused,[1] Islamic scholars have methods for elaborated and explained scientific *ta'wīl*. In their opinion every *ta'wīl* must be supported by scientific proof. The methods they suggest have helped *mujtahids* in their legal reasoning, and protected them from voicing mere opinions.[2] These methods have focused their attention on the correct practice of *ta'wīl*.

NOTES

1. Many people explain the authoritative texts according to their own inclinations because they merely want to achieve their own objectives. From an orthodox point of view, *ta'wīl* that has no scientific basis is used as an instrument to deform, distort and misrepresent Islamic teachings.

2. The Prophet said: 'He who speaks about the Qur'ān according to his own opinion is wrong even if he says what is right.' Tirmidhī, *al-Jāmiʿ al-Ṣaḥīḥ*, V:183 (no. 2950; Abū Dāwūd, *Sunan*, III:320 (no. 3652).

The Interpretation of Clear and Unclear Words (*Ta'wīl*)

The linguistic definition of *ta'wīl*

Ta'wīl refers to interpretation, construction, explanation.[1] Muthannā said: '*Ta'wīl* is interpretation, reference, source and destiny.'[2]

Although it is often rendered as interpretation, or equated with *tafsīr*, *ta'wīl* more properly signifies interpreting in a manner not according to the letter or overt sense of a text; it is explaining the covert or virtual meaning, and interpreting in a manner beyond the obvious meaning.

Ta'wīl also means 'turning a verse of the Qur'ān from its apparent meaning to a meaning which it bears, or admits, when the latter is agreeable with the Qur'ān and the *Sunnah*.' For instance, in the phrase in the Qur'ān: '*Yukhrij al-ḥayy min al-mayyit*' (VI: 95) if the meaning is 'He produces the bird from the egg' it is *tafsīr*; if the meaning is 'He produces the believer from the unbeliever' or 'the knowing from the ignorant', it is *ta'wīl*. *Ta'wīl* also means 'explaining the meaning of that which is *mutashābih* [or what is equivocal, or ambiguous] – i.e., what is not understood without repeated consideration'.[3]

The meaning of *ta'wīl* for the *Salaf* and the first Islamic scholars[4]

The first Muslims (*salaf*) understood *ta'wīl* to be interpretation in the sense of source and destiny. This is reflected in Ibn Taymiyyah's[5] statement: 'In the tradition of the *salaf* the word *ta'wīl* carries the same meanings God mentions in His Book. These meanings may be exemplified by the following verses: "Do they await only for the final fulfilment [*ta'wīlah*] of it [the Event]? On the Day it [the Event] is finally fulfilled [i.e. the Day of Resurrection], those who neglected it before will say: Verily, the Messengers of our Lord came with the truth."[6]; "That is better and more suitable for final determination [*aḥsan ta'wīl*]"[7]; "And he said: 'O my father!

This is the interpretation [*ta'wīl*] of my dream of old! My Lord has made it come true!"[8]; "Thus will your Lord choose you and teach you the interpretation [*ta'wīl*] of events."[9]; "Then the one of the two who was released, now at length remembered and said: 'I will tell you its interpretation [*ta'wīl*], so send me forth.'[10]

The opinion expressed by Ibn Taymiyyah is supported by many proofs exemplified by the tradition transmitted from Zuhrī, who stated: 'I asked ʿUrwah why ʿĀʾishah completed her prayer while travelling. He said: "She interpreted [*ta'awwalat*][11] like ʿUthmān.'"[12] Because the first Muslims spoke a pure form of Arabic, their understanding of various expressions is accepted as reliable in the interpretation of the Qurʾān, which was revealed in pure Arabic.[13]

Early scholars did not differ from the *salaf* in their understanding of *ta'wīl*. Shāfiʿī understood *ta'wīl* to carry the meanings of interpretation, source and destiny. From the following example, whereby his talent in *ta'wīl* is demonstrated, he sought to reconcile texts which appear to give conflicting meanings.[14]

The Prophet said: 'Start your dawn prayer at daybreak, for [its performance] at that time is the most rewarding for you.'[15] In another tradition, ʿĀʾishah said: 'They, the believing women, were in the habit of performing the dawn prayer with the Prophet; then they went their way in twilight, wrapped in their robes and unrecognised by anyone because of darkness.'[16] According to Shāfiʿī, these two traditions can be reconciled by interpreting one of them beyond its obvious import (*ta'wīl*). He said: 'So whenever traditions are found to be contradictory, we ought to choose the one which has valid reason to make us believe that it is more reliable than others.' When he was asked what that reason could be, he replied, 'That one of the two traditions should be more consistent with [the meaning of] the Book of God, for consistency with the Book of God is evidence [of reliability].'

Shāfiʿī meant that the second tradition is closer to the following verse: 'Guard strictly the prayers, especially the middle prayer.'[17] He added that it is clear that someone who prays at the beginning of the period set for the every prayer is more anxious to perform the prayer at its proper time than he who delays it to the end of the determined period. He explained, 'We have noted that men prefer to perform their obligatory and voluntary prayers as nearly on time as they can, for they are liable to be busy or forgetful or to suffer from other illnesses [which may cause postponement] – these are matters which are understandable.'[18]

Shāfiʿī maintained that the latter tradition agrees with the former in some respect. He said: 'Since the Apostle urged men to perform their prayers at the scheduled time and pointed out that this was meritorious, his [attitude] implied that he was in favour of performing the prayer at the end of daybreak so he said: "Pray at daybreak", by which he meant "just at the time when the dawn begins".' When he was asked if there was any other possible meaning, Shāfiʿī replied: 'Yes. It may mean either what you have held, or an intermediary position between your opinion and mine, or any other meaning that may be implied by [the term] daybreak.' He was asked: 'What makes your opinion preferable to mine?' Shāfiʿī replied: 'That which I have already explained as well as the Prophet's statement: "There are two dawns: the first is like the tail of the wolf [i.e. a false dawn],[19] when [the performance of prayer] is neither prohibited nor permitted; [the other] is daybreak, when the performance of prayer is permitted, but taking the meal is forbidden – that is to say, for he who intends to fast [that day].'[20]

From the previous example it is obvious that Shāfiʿī used the *ta'wīl* of the former tradition as an argument. At the same time he interpreted the latter tradition by saying that it is more consistent with the Book. Elsewhere, Shāfiʿī called the acceptance of one of two meanings 'an interpretation' (*ta'wīl*). He maintained that when a tradition is ambiguous, a scholar is permitted to accept one interpretation in preference to another.[21] Juwaynī defined *ẓāhir* as a provision which is susceptible to two meanings and one of them is clearer. If a less clear meaning is given precedence, based on a proof, it is called *ta'wīl*.[22]

The technical definition of *ta'wīl*

With the evolution of the science of *uṣūl al-fiqh* the meaning of *ta'wīl* became more focused and distinct from *tafsīr*. The scholars' definition of *ta'wīl* falls within the scope of 'abandoning' the apparent meaning of the word for the suspected and non-preferable meaning, by way of a proof which stands in favour of the non-preferable meaning. Because *tafsīr* is an explanation of meaning by authoritative assertion, while *ta'wīl* is based on supposition and uncertainty, some hold that although one may produce a *ta'wīl* based on personal opinion, one may not do so in *tafsīr*.[23]

Ghazālī defined *ta'wīl* as 'a possibility backed by a proof, which allows conjecture to prevail over the apparent meaning.'[24] Naṣafī defined *ta'wīl* as 'what becomes most probable and preferable of a homonym's indications'.[25] This definition may be criticised from different angles: 1) The homonym has equal meanings, and in case of *ta'wīl* we must have an apparent meaning and other likely meanings. Therefore, *mushtarak* has nothing to do with *ta'wīl*. 2) The suspected meaning which is given precedence over the apparent meaning of an utterance must be supported by a reliable proof, not personal opinion. No *ta'wīl* based on personal opinion is acceptable.

Taftāzānī defined *ta'wīl* as: 'Disclosure that a proof should be taken into account by which a meaning becomes more probable than the apparent meaning.'[26] A similar definition was offered by Bādshāh.[27] Shawkānī's definition: 'Giving the precedence to a non-preferable meaning over the apparent meaning, relying on a proof which makes the non-preferable meaning preferable.'[28]

Whenever *ta'wīl* is mentioned without comparison it is meant to be the acceptable reading. Some scholars like Āmidī, Taftāzānī, and Shawkānī distinguished *ta'wīl*, which is acceptable by Islamic law, from that which is not. Āmidī defined acceptable *ta'wīl* as: 'Interpretation of the word by its non-apparent meaning, relying on a proof which supports interpretation without entirely dismissing its apparent meaning.'[29] Non-acceptable *ta'wīl* is not supported by proof.

From these definitions one may conclude that *ta'wīl* in the science of *uṣūl al-fiqh* consists in turning from the word's essential, literal and apparent meaning towards another, possible meaning based on a proof, which suggests that it is like adopting a particular meaning from the general, or so-called *takhṣīṣ*. Therefore, unlike *tafsīr*, which aims to explain authoritative texts within the limits of literal meanings, *ta'wīl* goes beyond the literal meaning and reads hidden meanings into texts.[30]

Is *ta'wīl* acceptable as a way of interpreting source texts?

As we have seen, the majority of scholars maintain that *ta'wīl* can be a rigorously rational part of *ijtihād*, useful in interpreting the source-texts when its preconditions are fulfilled. Therefore, they accept it under certain conditions. On the opposite side, the Ẓāhirī *madhhab* eschews all interpretation beyond the obvious meaning. Dāwūd al-Ẓāhirī and his followers[31] rejected *ta'wīl* entirely. They adhere only to the apparent meaning of the Qur'ān and the *Sunnah*, which in their general meanings provide answers for everything. If they find no such a proofs in either of them, the Ẓāhirīs refer to *ijmāʿ*.[32] They also reject analogy. They maintain that all source-texts are clear and therefore need no interpretation beyond their obvious sense. They do not abandon an apparent meaning unless another apparent meaning from the Qur'ān, *Sunnah* or *ijmāʿ* suggests otherwise, because language is created by God as a way of conveying meanings. Languages consist merely of words attached to certain meanings.[33] Ibn Ḥazm, the most prominent scholar among Ẓāhirīs, held that *ta'wīl* 'transfers the word from its apparent and literal indication to another meaning'.[34] According to him *ta'wīl* is correct if the 'transferer' is obedient to God and his Prophet. Otherwise the *ta'wīl* is invalid and as such rejected.

The sphere of *ta'wīl*

When we examine any expression with an open mind, in order to interpret it in as many ways as possible, we will find that almost every expression is capable of numerous interpretations. At worst, this could mean that people do not fully understand each other and that they cannot meaningfully convey what is in their minds. On the other hand, if our understanding is based on certain grounds of interpretation, we could make ourselves better understood. If someone denies this understanding, we may contest this and provide them with personal evidence to the contrary.

In every language there are rules for comprehension. These rules were at first unwritten. With the development of language they were collected and systematised. Nowadays, these rules help us to understand others, both from the past and the present. One of the most important benefits of these rules is that they prevent misinterpretation for preconceived purposes. This is extremely important when the *Sharīʿah* source-texts are in question. Since these rules are known, one has to ask what the sphere of *ta'wīl* is?

Islamic scholars acknowledge that authoritative expressions cannot always be interpreted according to their apparent meaning.[35] At the same time they have felt a moral obligation to interpret the *Sharīʿah* source-texts according to the intention of the Lawgiver. The predominant method is to refer to the rules of the language. They also insist that it is unacceptable to interpret source-texts according to personal whim. This attitude towards the *Sharīʿah* source-texts is the principal reason why Islamic thought has escaped distortion. While there are clearly many divisions among the followers of Islam, the fact remains that Muslims agree on matters where disagreement is impossible.

The implementation of the apparent meaning

All the imams of the main legal schools agree that the basic method for deriving legal rulings is non-*ta'wīl*. In this view, the implementation of the apparent meaning is an indisputable obligation (*wājib*), and no one is allowed to avoid the apparent meaning without a proof requiring such a move. Therefore, a general expression should be interpreted in a general sense until particularisation emerges. Unrestricted expression must be interpreted in that sense until restriction emerges, and the command will be interpreted as an undisputed obligation until that which directs it towards another meaning emerges. Therefore, the apparent meaning of an expression, which strikes the listener in the manner of a spontaneous understanding, is counted as the true meaning of an expression, and is consequently implemented. Avoiding the apparent meaning is not allowed except because of reliable proof. This is confirmed by all Islamic scholars.

About the orders of prohibition which are consistent with previous orders in certain matters, Shāfiʿī mentioned a tradition where the Prophet said: 'When the sun first rises, Satan's horns are associated with it;[36] when it is up, they are separated; when it is at the meridian they join it; when it begins to descend, they are separated; when it approaches its setting, they join it again; and when it disappears, they are separated.' The Prophet has forbidden the performance of prayer during these hours (when Satan's horns are associated with the sun).[37] Shāfiʿī stated that this text may be interpreted in different ways. He concluded: 'Since the two meanings [are permissible], it is obligatory for the learned not to become attached to the particular – as distinct from the general – meaning, unless there is a specifying indication in the *Sunnah*, or an agreement among scholars who do not agree on any matter contrary to the *Sunnah*. Other traditions of the Apostle should be accepted as explicitly general unless there is a contrary indication, or unless Islamic scholars have agreed to specify that their meaning is implicit, not explicit (literal), and that it is particular, not general. In either cases, people are advised to obey them.'[38] Elsewhere in his *Risālah*, he said: 'Thus every explicitly general statement in the *Sunnah* of the Apostle should be accepted as such unless another reliable tradition from the Apostle indicates that only part of that explicitly general statement was intended to be general, as I have already explained regarding this and other similar points.'[39]

Shāfiʿī's statement is based on the fact that the Qur'ān is revealed in pure Arabic. This implies that Qur'ānic injunctions are apparent and general. No one has the right to deny or restrict the apparent meaning without a reliable proof, because this would violate linguistic rules, and violate the intention of the text.

Other scholars agree entirely with Shāfiʿī on this matter.[40] The famous commentator of the Qur'ān, Ṭabarī, states that: 'One is not allowed to leave a comprehensive apparent meaning and incline towards the hidden for which there is no proof of validity.'[41] In his commentary on the verse: 'When He decrees a matter, He only says to it: "Be!" – and it is',[42] Ṭabarī explained that 'it is general in everything that God has decreed and created, because its apparent meaning is general. One is not allowed to turn the apparent meaning into hidden meaning by *ta'wīl* without a proof'.[43]

Although the basic method of deriving legal rulings is the interpretation of texts according to the obvious and apparent meaning – non-*ta'wīl* – one may conclude that the majority of authoritative texts related to command injunctions (*aḥkām taklīfiyyah*) can be interpreted beyond their obvious sense. This includes all ambiguous texts (*khafī*, *mushkil*, *mujmal*, and *mutashābih*),[44] whereas the clear (*wāḍiḥ*) includes only *ẓāhir*.[45] Because of this fact, *ta'wīl* can easily be misused if scientific rules are not followed in *ijtihād*. If the person interpreting the Qur'ān has no fear of reprisals from God, he is liable to interpret the intended meaning according to his fictions, imagination or desires. In this way he could change the meanings and injunctions entirely.[46] However, it is not enough for the person interpreting the Qur'ān for legal rulings to be God-fearing. He must also have knowledge of all the Islamic sciences relevant to interpretation and legal reasoning (*ijtihād*).

Preconditions (*shurūṭ*) for *ta'wīl*[47]

Islamic scholars have affirmed that the basic method of textual interpretation accords with the obvious meaning. In order to prevent misinterpretation of the Qur'ān and the *Sunnah*, Islamic scholars have suggested preconditions for *ta'wīl*. These preconditions were reached after an examination of various cases in the spirit of Islam. If the following preconditions are fulfilled, *ta'wīl* will be accepted; but if any one is lacking, the *ta'wīl* is invalid and therefore rejected:

(1) A person who exercises *ta'wīl* (i.e. *ijtihād*) must be qualified for this task to ensure that the interpretation is consistent with the rules of the language, customary and juridical usage and the spirit of Islam and its general rules.[48]

(2) A word or text must be open to different interpretations.[49]

(3) A meaning given precedence over the apparent meaning of a word must be probable.[50] Therefore, adopting a particular meaning from the general (*ḥaml al-ʿāmm ʿalā al-khāṣṣ*) is correct if supported by a reliable proof, because the general meaning in reality assumes possible specification and restriction. Adopting a metaphor (*majāz*) is correct if supported by a reliable proof, because the words are open to metaphorical meaning. For example, if 'transaction' (*bayʿ*) is transferred from its apparent meaning to mean gift, because a proof suggests that this particular operation was in fact a transfer of ownership free of charge, this would be correct a *ta'wīl*, because the word *bayʿ* is open to that interpretation.

If the word, however, does not support such a meaning, and in no way indicates it, this *ta'wīl* will be incorrect and unacceptable in Islamic law. Therefore, if someone interprets sheep to mean camel or horse, this *ta'wīl* will be incorrect because this is not how the Legislator uses words and it is not His customary practice.

(4) The interpretation beyond the obvious import has to be supported by a correct and reliable proof, i.e. there has to be reliable evidence which gives precedence to a non-preferable meaning in relation to the apparent meaning. That reliable proof can be another authoritative text, consensus of opinion (*ijmāʿ*), analogy (*qiyās*), or another principle of Islamic law. This precondition is by virtue of the fact that the Lawgiver's expressions have apparent meanings.[51] Therefore, the implementation of the apparent mean-

ing is an indisputable obligation until a reliable proof suggests otherwise. This means that something commanded (*amr*) implies a strict obligation and cannot be regarded merely as a praiseworthy action (*mandūb*) without sufficient proof. Prohibition (*nahy*) means strict prohibition and cannot be turned into something disliked (*makrūh*), until a reliable proof suggests such an interpretations. If *ta'wīl* is not based at least on one reliable proof it is invalid.

If *ta'wīl* rests on this basis, it constitutes a valid basis for judicial decisions and becomes a strong rational part of *ijtihād*. This is very useful in the interpretation of source-texts and thus in the deduction of legal rulings. This kind of *ta'wīl* is generally accepted in Islam, and from the *ṣaḥābah* to later Islamic scholars, all have applied it while exercising *ijtihād*.

Kinds of *ta'wīl* according to their likelihood[52]

(1) Close interpretation of meaning. This kind of *ta'wīl* refers to the interpretation that accepts the non-preferable yet possible meaning, when supported by minimal proof, instead of the apparent meaning. For example, the Qur'ān states: 'O you who believe! When you get up [intending] to offer a prayer, wash your faces and hands up to the elbows, rub [by passing wet hands over] your heads, and [wash] your feet up to the ankles.'[53] 'Get up' is interpreted not in its apparent sense (getting up) but according to the possible (non-preferable) meaning – namely, the 'intention' to perform prayer. This can be proved by the following three points:

(a) This meaning represents a spontaneous understanding of the verse.

(b) The Lawgiver did not order the ablution after the prayer begins, but before. He made this a precondition without which no valid prayer can be performed; therefore, this precondition must be fulfilled before the prayer.

(c) 'Get up' applies before the commencement of prayer; no scholar maintained that ablution is obligatory before intending the prayer.

Likewise the interpretation of: 'And not to show off their adornment except that which is apparent.'[54] It is a well-recorded view among the majority of scholars that 'that which is apparent' may be interpreted as a reference to the face and hands.[55] This interpretation is supported by the tradition narrated by 'Ā'ishah that her sister Asmā' entered the room wearing thin clothes in the presence of the Prophet. He lowered his gaze and said: 'O Asmā'! When a woman begins menstruation [reaches puberty] it is not right to see her [body] except this and that' – and he pointed to his face and hands.[56] Because the non-preferred meaning is quite possible, this kind of *ta'wīl* is given precedence even if the proof is not strong.

(2) Remote interpretation of meaning.[57] This kind of *ta'wīl* refers to an

acceptance of a non-preferable meaning which is far from possible, instead of the apparent meaning. Because such a meaning is hardly possible, it needs strong proof in order to be acceptable.

This is illustrated in the interpretation of the following verse of the Qur'ān: 'O you who believe! When you intend to offer prayer, wash your faces and hands up to elbows, rub [by passing wet hands over] your heads, and your feet (*arjulakum* or *arjulikum*) up to the ankles.'[58] For 'your feet', two[59] different but correct readings (declensions) were transmitted (in the accusative *arjulakum* and in the genitive *arjulikum*).[60] If the *mujtahid* relies on the genitive declension, he can interpret this verse in two different ways. The first indicates that the feet should be washed, the second that wiping the feet with wet hands is sufficient. The majority of Islamic scholars maintain that this interpretation is far from possible. They maintained that 'your feet' is coupled with 'your hands'. The latter is accusative. Therefore, what is coupled to it must also be in the accusative, due to the Arabic rule that what follows the conjunction '*waw*' takes the same case as that to which it is joined.[61] They supported their opinion with various proofs from both linguistic usage and *ṣaḥīḥ* traditions.

(3) Impossible interpretation. This is where an expression does not accept a certain interpretation by any method of analysis, and so the *ta'wīl* is invalid and unacceptable. Ghazālī said, 'Every interpretation which removes and eliminates a *naṣṣ* or its part is invalid.'[62]

Kinds of *ta'wīl* according to the proofs supporting it[63]

Ta'wīl may be based on authoritative source-texts, or any secondary sources.[64] The source-texts are the strongest foundation for *ta'wīl*. An example of this is found with respect to the ruling on the legitimacy of using the skin of a dead animal. The Qur'ān states: 'Forbidden to you are dead animals.'[65] This statement apparently indicates that using the skin of a dead animal is forbidden under all circumstances, whether the skin is tanned or not. This indication is derived from the general meaning of the word 'the dead'. But it is possible that the tanned hide is not meant by this general meaning, since the prohibition relates to 'the dead'. This, in the Lawgiver's customary expression, indicates that eating is forbidden, and since the hide is not normally eaten, the general meaning does not include the use of the leather. This conclusion, deduced through *ta'wīl*, is supported by the following *ḥadīth* source-texts.

In a tradition narrated by Ibn ʿAbbās, the Prophet said: 'When any skin is tanned it becomes clean.'[66] In its apparent general meaning, this tradition includes the skin of a dead animal. In another tradition related to a dead sheep granted to the freed slave of Maymūnah, the Prophet said: 'Why have you not taken its skin, tanned it and benefited from it.' They answered that it was dead. He replied: 'What is forbidden is to eat it.'[67]

These two authoritative texts clearly indicate that tanned skin is not forbidden. Therefore they stand in support of *ta'wīl* indicating that leather is excluded from the general meaning of the verse.[68] Similarly, there is the ruling related to the prohibition of blood in the same verse: 'Forbidden to you are dead animals and blood.'[69] In its general meaning this verse includes blood, whether shed or not. This general meaning, however, has been interpreted beyond its obvious sense. Through *ta'wīl*, unshed blood is excluded, based on another verse which restricts the general meaning of 'blood': 'Say [O Muḥammad]: In what has been inspired to me I find nothing forbidden to be eaten by one who wishes to eat it, unless it is a dead animal or blood poured forth.'[70] The latter verse explains that prohibited 'blood' in the former verse means blood that has been shed. In that way the latter verse supports *ta'wīl* of the former verse whereby the blood that has not been shed is excluded from the general meaning of the verse.[71]

Analogy is often a strong proof in *ta'wīl*. This is illustrated in the question of feeding the poor as a penance for wrongful killing. The Qur'ān does not mention feeding as a way of expiation in case of manslaughter.[72] Moreover, this kind of penance apparently means that it is not an obligatory duty. According to those who accept the analogy in this field, feeding as penance for manslaughter may be extended by analogy to *ẓihār*[73] and the deliberate breaking of the fast,[74] because all penances are God's rights (*ḥuqūq Allāh*). The penance for manslaughter is similar to *ẓihār* and the penance for breaking the fast.

The Lawgiver's intention or the wisdom behind the legislation are reasons for *ta'wīl*, and the proof on which it relies. An example of this kind is the understanding of *zakāt* in the Ḥanafī *madhhab*. The Prophet said, "For every forty grazing sheep one is due.'[75] The apparent meaning of this tradition is that one sheep would have to be given, but Ḥanafī scholars maintained that the monetary value of sheep may also be given instead. They argue that the wisdom behind the legislation of the *zakāt* is to benefit the poor. That goal can be reached by giving either a sheep or money. Moreover, the value of the sheep may even be more useful to the poor than the animal itself.

External evidences may serve as proof which supports *ta'wīl*. The Prophet once said: 'A bad example is not for us to follow. He who retrieves his gift is like a dog that swallows vomit.'[76] This tradition apparently means that retrieving a gift is not forbidden because it is not forbidden for a dog to swallow its vomit. However, the beginning of the tradition gives clear evidence that it is a 'bad example' denounced by the Lawgiver. Consequently, it is forbidden for a giver to take back a gift he has granted to someone.

The value of *ta'wīl*

It is obligatory to adhere to the meaning determined through proper *ta'wīl*. However, this adherence should not be unquestionable and conclusive. The reason for this is that *ta'wīl* is established through opinion[77] which can contain oversight and error, and therefore cannot be certain. If someone, for example, finds water, he must use it for ablution if his dominant opinion is that it is clean, with only a possibility that it is unclean. If it transpires that the water is not clean, he must renew his ablution and prayer.[78]

NOTES

1. Ba'labakī, *al-Mawrid*, p. 265.
2. Muthannā, *Majāz al-Qur'ān*, I:87. Ṭabarī gave the same linguistic definition (*Jāmi' al-bayān 'an Ta'wīl Āy al-Qur'ān*, VI:204).
3. *al-Mu'jam al-Wasīṭ*, I:33; Lane, *Arabic-English Lexicon*, I:1257, II:2397; EI², I:275, I:412, I:1039.
4. Practical examples of *ta'wīl* when the Prophet's tradition is in question may be seen in the book *al-Ta'wīl Dirāsah Mawḍū'iyyah fī al-Aḥādīth al-Nabawiyyah* by Sa'īd.
5. Ibn Taymiyyah, *Muwāfaqāt Ṣarīḥ al-Ma'qūl li Ṣaḥīḥ al-Manqūl*, I:119–120.
6. Qur'ān, VII:53.
7. Qur'ān, IV:59.
8. Qur'ān, XII:100.
9. Qur'ān, XII:6.
10. Qur'ān, XII:45.
11. He meant that she interpreted the ruling related to the traveller's prayer in the same way 'Uthman did when in Mina, during the *ḥajj*, when he did not shorten his prayers, though one is permitted to do so. There are two possible explanations for this: the first is that, he had been married from Mecca and he thought that the people of Mecca were not permitted to shorten their prayers in Mina; second, he was afraid that some Bedouin might be confused when they watched him pray less *rak'ats*, and so he did not shorten his prayers.
12. Ibn al-Athīr, *al-Nihāyah*, I:51.
13. The Qur'ān states: 'Which the trustworthy Rūḥ [Gabriel] has brought down upon your heart that you may be [one] of the warners, in the clear Arabic language.' (Qur'ān, XXVI:193–5)
14. Shāfi'ī, *al-Risālah*, pp. 212–217.
15. Tirmidhī, *al-Jāmi' al-Ṣaḥīḥ*, I:289–291 (no. 154).
16. Bukhārī, *al-Jāmi' al-Ṣaḥīḥ*, I:144 (9:27); Muslim, *Ṣaḥīḥ Muslim*, V:143–144.
17. Qur'ān, II:238.
18. Shāfi'ī, *al-Risālah*, p. 215.
19. Lane, *Arabic-English Lexicon*, p. 1345.
20. Bayhaqī, *al-Sunan al-Kubrā*, IV:215; Suyūṭī, *al-Durr al-Manthūr*, I:200.
21. Shāfi'ī, *al-Risālah*, p. 277.
22. Maḥallī, *Sharḥ al-Waraqāt*, p. 18.
23. Taftāzānī, *Sharḥ al-Talwīḥ 'alā al-Tawḍīḥ*, I:125.

24. Ghazālī, *al-Mustaṣfā*, p. 196.

25. Nasafī, *Kashf al-Asrār*, I:204.

26. Taftāzānī, *Sharḥ al-Talwīḥ ʿalā al-Tawḍīḥ*, I:125.

27. Badshāh, *Taysīr al-Taḥrīr*, I:137.

28. Shawkānī, *Irshād al-Fuḥūl*, p. 154.

29. Āmidī, *al-Iḥkām fī Uṣūl al-Aḥkām*, III:50.

30. It may be noted that at no time were *tafsīr* and *ta'wīl* so clearly distinguished. Some scholars made no distinction at all. In our time, however, it seems that scholars tend to use *tafsīr* and *ta'wīl* with these two distinctive meanings.

31. Ibn Ḥazm was Dāwūd's most famous follower. He revived the Ẓāhirī *madhhab* and himself became the leader of this *madhhab*. Khuḍarī, *Tārīkh al-Tashrīʿ al-Islāmī*, pp. 267–268; Madkūr, *Tārīkh al-Tashrīʿ al-Islāmī wa Maṣādiruh*, pp. 194–195.

32. They accept only the *ijmāʿ* of the Prophet's Companions, which is based on a proof provided by the Prophet.

33. Ibn Ḥazm, *al-Iḥkām fī Uṣūl al-Aḥkām*, III:41.

34. Ibn Ḥazm, *al-Iḥkām fī Uṣūl al-Aḥkām*, III:42.

35. The Ẓāhirī *madhhab* rejected *ta'wīl* entirely and maintained that every *Sharīʿah* source-text had to be interpreted according to its obvious sense.

36. Scholars entertained different opinions about the meaning of Satan's horns (*qarn al-shayṭān*). Some maintained that it means the proximity (*muqāranah*) of the devil to the sun, while others accepted literally that the sun rises between the two horns of the devil (Suyūṭī, *Tanwīr al-Ḥawālik Sharḥ Muwaṭṭa' Mālik*, I:220).

37. Mālik, *al-Muwaṭṭa'*, I:145.

38. Shāfiʿī, *al-Risālah*, p. 231.

39. Shāfiʿī, *al-Risālah*, p. 238.

40. See *ẓahir* and *ʿāmm* in both Shāfiʿī and Ḥanafī works.

41. Ṭabarī, *Jāmiʿ al-Bayan ʿan Ta'wīl āy al-Qur'ān*, II:15.

42. Qur'ān, II:117.

43. Ṭabarī, *Jāmiʿ al-Bayan ʿan Ta'wīl āy al-Qur'ān*, II:546.

44. *Mutashābih* texts are unrelated to commandments, and Muslims are not obliged to search for their meanings (see interpretation of seventh verse of sūra *Āl ʿImrān*).

45. When deriving legal rulings from the *Sharīʿah* source-texts, many kinds of interpretative outcomes are possible. Some are: adopting the particular from the general (*ḥaml al-ʿāmm ʿalā al-khāṣṣ*), adopting a metaphor instead of real meaning (*ḥaml al-ḥaqīqah ʿalā al-majāz*), adopting one of a homonym's meanings (*ḥaml al-mushtarak ʿalā aḥad maʿnayayn*), adopting a command which is not obligatory (*wājib*), adopting a prohibition which is not strictly forbidden (*ḥarām*), etc.

46. This is why Islamic scholars stipulate that the commentator of the Qur'ān and the *mujtahid* must be righteous and honest Muslims (*ʿadl*).

47. Āmidī, *al-Iḥkām fī Uṣūl al-Aḥkām*, III:50; Shawkānī, *Irshād al-Fuḥūl*, p. 156; Shaʿbān, *Uṣūl al-Fiqh al-Islāmī*, pp. 288–289.

48. This precondition is stipulated for two reasons: a) no-one is allowed to speak about the Qur'ān without knowledge; b) no *muqallid* is allowed to follow someone ignorant.

49. Only certain types of words are open to *ta'wīl* – the apparent (*ẓāhir*) and explicit (*naṣṣ*) according to the Ḥanafī *madhhab*, the explicit (*naṣṣ*) according to the Shāfiʿī *madhhab*, or the general (*ʿāmm*) and the absolute (*muṭlaq*) according to both. If a word does not accept *ta'wīl*, such as the thing explained (*mufassar*) and what is firm (*muḥkam*), its interpretation beyond obvious sense will be invalid.

50. The preferable meaning has to be indicated either by the literal apparent meaning (*manṭūq*) or the implicit meaning (*mafhūm*). On the other hand, the non-preferable meaning

must be consistent with the Arabic language, even by way of metaphor, customary usage or the method of the Lawgiver.

51. In relation to proof, *ta'wīl* can be: a) acceptable, if a proof is strong enough to support a non-preferable meaning in relation to the apparent meaning; b) unacceptable, if a proof is not strong enough to support a non-preferable meaning in relation to the apparent meaning; c) when the apparent and non-preferable meanings are equal. In this case more proof to support one of the meanings is needed.

52. Ghazālī, *al-Mustaṣfā*, p. 196; Shawkānī, *Irshād al-Fuḥūl*, p. 156.

53. Qur'ān, V:6.

54. Qur'ān, XXIV:31.

55. Ibn Kathīr, *Tafsīr al-Qur'ān al-ʿAẓīm*, III:379.

56. Ibn Kathīr, *Tafsīr al-Qur'ān al-ʿAẓīm*, III:379.

57. Shāfiʿī scholars usually mention, when speaking about this kind of interpretation, some examples of interpretations provided by the Ḥanafīs. They claim that the latter's interpretations are quite remote (Ghazālī, *al-Mustaṣfā*, p. 197–202; Āmidī, *al-Iḥkām fī Uṣūl al-Aḥkām*, III:51–60).

58. Qur'ān, V:6.

59. That is, they are among the seven methods of recitation (*qirā'āt sabʿah*) transmitted from the Prophet and regarded as *mutawātir*.

60. Ibn Kathīr, *Tafsīr al-Qur'ān al-ʿAẓīm*, II:36–40.

61. Qabash, *al-Kāmil fī al-Naḥw wa al-Ṣarf*, p. 190.

62. Ghazālī, *al-Mustaṣfā*, p. 198.

63. Islamic scholars disagree on the strength of some legal proofs and their reliability for interpretation beyond the obvious sense. For example, whether analogy or the narration of one Companion only (*khabar al-wāḥid*) should be used to restrict a general meaning to yield a particular indication (*ḥaml al-ʿāmm ʿalā al-khāṣṣ*) or to restrict the absolute (*ḥaml al-muṭlaq ʿalā al-muqayyad*).

64. Among secondary sources are *ijmāʿ*, *qiyās*, *istiṣḥāb*, *istiḥsān*, *istiṣlāḥ*.

65. Qur'ān, V:3.

66. Muslim, *Ṣaḥīḥ Muslim*, I:277 (no. 366).

67. Bukhārī, *al-Jāmiʿ al-Ṣaḥīḥ*, VI:231 (72:30).

68. Kāsānī, *Badā'iʿ al-Ṣanā'iʿ*, I:85. There are other views on this question. Ibn Rushd, *Bidāyat al-Mujtahid*, I:78–79; Ibn Qudāmah, *al-Mughnī*, I:66.

69. Qur'ān, V:3.

70. Qur'ān, VI:145.

71. This *ta'wīl* is supported by many traditions (Ibn Kathīr, *Tafsīr al-Qur'ān al-ʿAẓīm*, II:11–12).

72. Qur'ān, IV:92.

73. Marghīnānī, *al-Hidāyah*, II:19; Ibn Rushd, *Bidāyat al-Mujtahid*, II:111.

74. Marghīnānī, *al-Hidāyah*, I:124–125; Ibn Rushd, *Bidāyat al-Mujtahid*, I:301–303.

75. Bukhārī, *al-Jāmiʿ al-Ṣaḥīḥ*, II:124 (24:38). (See: ʿAsqalānī, *Bulūgh al-Marām*, p. 168).

76. Bukhārī, *al-Jāmiʿ al-Ṣaḥīḥ*, III:142–143 (51–30).

77. Therefore, if someone denies it he cannot be considered an unbeliever.

78. Sarakhsī, *Uṣūl al-Sarakhsī*, I:163; Nasafī, *Kashf al-Asrār*, I:205.

Conclusion

During my studies of the linguistic principles of *uṣūl al-fiqh* and their effect on legal reasoning in Islamic law, I have come to the following conclusions. Some of these conclusions are general and some specific.

General conclusions:

(1) All the Islamic sciences are close to each other and none can be entirely isolated.' For example, a jurist of Islamic law needs to know all the other sciences, without which he cannot reach the level of *mujtahid*.

(2) The Arabic language is an inseparable part of Islamic law. The decline of Arabic is thus detrimental to the sciences of Islamic law. It is a collective obligation (*farḍ kifāyah*) upon the Muslim *ummah* to have scholars knowledgeable in Arabic who can maintain this knowledge.

(3) Only the scientific approach to the sources of Islamic law guarantees their proper use.

(4) In Islamic law there are certain principles which are considered unchangeable, e.g. certain prohibitions mentioned in the Qur'ān. Despite the fact that some laws are bound to change with changing circumstances, any alterations must remain consistent with the immutability of the above principles.

Specific conclusions:

(1) A thorough knowledge of the linguistic principles found in the source methodology of Islamic jurisprudence is essential to a proper understanding of the authoritative texts from which the legal rulings of Islamic law are deduced.

(2) These principles are based on the rules of the Arabic language.

Therefore, knowledge of the Arabic language is necessary for any Islamic jurist in the field of legal reasoning (*ijtihād*).

(3) The source methodology (*uṣūl*) and the particulars (*furū'*) of Islamic law are inseparably connected. Knowledge of this link and the application of the source methodology in legal reasoning is the safest way of conducting *ijtihād*.

(4) These principles facilitate the legal reasoning of *mujtahids*, because they help them distinguish between speculative and definite meanings. They allow them to categorise these meanings so that the clearer ones may be given precedence in case of conflict.

(5) It is necessary to understand the language and the environment in which the Qur'ān was revealed: this knowledge helps us better understand the authoritative texts.

(6) Legal reasoning in Islamic law cannot be properly carried out without the implementation of these linguistic principles.

(7) Understanding the authoritative texts and their interpretation is a major cause of disagreement between Islamic jurists (*fuqahā'*).

(8) The linguistic principles are only one step in the process of legal reasoning in Islamic law. Before a *mujtahid* reaches this step he must examine the authenticity of the texts used in the process of *ijtihād*.

(9) Some disagreements regarding method among Islamic scholars are of a technical nature.

(10) An authoritative text cannot be interpreted in isolation from other authoritative texts, because authoritative texts explain each other.

(11) An interpretation beyond the obvious meaning of the texts (*ta'wīl*) must be used with great care and by strict adherence to strict rules. Any other approach may lead to the misinterpretation of authoritative texts.

(12) Knowledge of linguistic principles may help to provide a better understanding of legislation in Islam and of Islamic law in general.

NOTES

1. Even sciences which study nature are a part of Islam and may be considered 'Islamic'. This is because every true knowledge, according to Islam, comes from one source, God, and every true knowledge leads to Him by His way.

Selected Biographical Notes

ʿABD AL-JABBĀR, al-Hamadhānī al-Asdābādī (d. 415AH/1025CE). He was the most prominant of *Muʿtazilī* scholars and held the title Qāḍī al-Quḍāt (Judge of Judges). Among his books are: *Tanzīh al-Qurʾān ʿan, al-Maṭāʿin, al-Amālī, Sharḥ al-Uṣūl al-Khamsah, al-Mughnī fī Abwāb al-Tawḥīd wa'l-ʿAdl, Tathbīt Dalāʾil al-Nubuwwah, Mutashābih al-Qurʾān.* (*al-Aʿlām*, III:273.)

ʿABDULLĀH IBN ʿUMAR, (d. 73AH/692CE) A companion of the Prophet and son of the second caliph. He gave *fatwās* for a period of 60 years. Books of *ḥadīth* record his 2630 *ḥadīth*. (*Tahdhīb al-Asmāʾ wa'l-Lughāt,* I:278; *Ṭabaqāt Ibn Saʿd* IV:105-138; *Ḥulyat al-Awliyāʾ wa-Ṭabaqāt al-Aṣfiyāʾ,* I:292; *al-Aʿlām,* IV:108.)

ʿABDULLĀH IBN AL-ZUBAYR, (d. 73AH/692CE). The first child born in Medina after the *Hijrah.* He became caliph in 64 AH, after the death of Yazīd b. Muʾāwiyah, and held that post for nine years. (*al-Aʿlām,* IV:87.)

ABŪ ḤANĪFAH, al-Nuʿmān b. Thābit, (d. 150AH/767CE). The founder of the Ḥanafī *madhhab* and a prominent *mujtahid.* One of four *imāms* of Ahl al-Sunnah. Among his works are: *al-Musnad, al-Makhārij, al-Fiqh al-Akbar.* (*Tārīkh Baghdād,* XIII:323-423; *al-Bidāyah wa'l-Nihāyah.* X:107; *al-Aʿlām,* VIII:36.)

ABŪ HURAYRAH, ʿAbd al-Raḥmān b. Ṣakhr al-Dawsī, (d. 59AH/679CE). A companion of the Prophet and one of the most prolific narrators of *ḥadīth.* In all, 5,374 *ḥadīth* were transmitted from him. (*Tahdhīb al-Asmāʾ wa'l-Lughāt,* II:270; *Ṣifat al-Ṣufwah* I:285; *al-Aʿlām.* III:308.)

ABŪ YŪSUF, Yaʿqūb b. Ibrāhīm al-Anṣārī al-Kūfī (d. 182AH/798CE). The famous student of Abū Ḥanīfah and a great scholar *of fiqh.* Among his books are: *al-Kharāj, al-Āthār, al-Nawādir, Ikhtilāf al-Amṣār, Adab al-Qāḍī, al-Amālī fi al-Fiqh.* (*al-Aʿlām,* VIII:191.)

ʿĀʾISHAH, bint Abī Bakr al-Ṣiddīq (d. 58AH/678CE). Wife of the Prophet. In her time, the most knowledgeable Muslim woman in law and literature. She transmitted 2,210 *ḥadīth* from the Prophet. (*Ṭabaqāt Ibn Saʿd*, VIII:399; *Ḥulyat al-Awliyāʾ wa-Ṭabaqāt al-Aṣfiyā*, III:43; *al-Aʿlām*, III:240.)

ʿALĪ IBN ABĪ ṬĀLIB (d. 40AH/661CE). Cousin and son–in–law of the Prophet. The fourth 'righteous caliph'. He was the second person to accept Islam after Khadījah, the Prophet's first wife. In the year 35AH/656CE he became caliph. He was assassinated in 40AH/661CE. He transmitted 586 traditions. (*Ṣifat al-Ṣufwah*, I:118; *Tārīkh al-Umam wa'l-Mulūk*, VI:83; *al-Aʿlām*, IV:295.)

AL-ĀMIDĪ, Abū al-Ḥasan Sayf al-Dīn ʿAlī al-Taghlibī, (d. 631AH/1233CE). Authority on *kalām* and jursiprudence. He wrote more than twenty books, among which are: *al-Iḥkām fī Uṣūl al-Aḥkām, Abkār al-Afkār, Lubāb al-Albāb, Daqāʾiq al-Ḥaqāʾiq, al-Mubīn fī Sharḥ al-ʿUlamāʾ wa'l-Mutakallimīn*. (*al-Aʿlām*, IV:332.)

AL-ANṢĀRĪ, Abū Yaḥyā Zakariyyā al-Sanakī al-Miṣrī al-Shāfiʿī, (d. 926AH/1520CE). He was *shaykh al-islām*, a judge, *mufassir* and *ḥāfiẓ* of the traditions. Among his books are: *Ghāyat al-Wuṣūl Sharḥ Lubb al-Uṣūl, Fatḥ al-Raḥmān (tafsīr), Tuḥfat al-Bārī ʿalā Ṣaḥīḥ al-Bukhārī, Asnā al-Maṭālib Sharḥ Rawḍ al-Ṭālib (fiqh)*. (*al-Kawākib al-Sāʾirah fī Aʿyān al-Miʾah al-ʿĀshirah*, I:196; *al-Aʿlām* III:46.)

AL-AṢFAHĀNĪ, Shams al-Din Maḥmūd Abū al-Thanāʾ (d. 749AH/1394CE). Scholar in *fiqh, tafsīr* and philosophy. Among his works are: *Tafsīr, Sharḥ al-Minhāj li'l-Bayḍāwī, Sharḥ Kāfiyat li-Ibn al-Ḥājib*. (*Bughyat al-Wuʿāt*, p. 388; *Shudhurāt al-Dhahab*, V:165; *al-Aʿlām*, VI:176.)

AL-BALKHĪ, Aḥmad b. Sahl (d. 322AH/934CE). A prominent scholar of *Sharīʿah*, philosophy and literature. Among his books are: *Aqsām al-ʿUlūm, Sharāʾiʿ al-Adyān, Kitāb al-Siyāsah al-Kabīr, Akhlāq al-Umam, Naẓm al-Qurʾān*. (*al-Aʿlām*, I:134.)

AL-BAṢRĪ, Muḥammad b. ʿAlī (d. 436AH/1044CE). A Muʿtazilī leader. His best known books are: *al-Muʿtamad fī Uṣūl al-Fiqh, Sharḥ al-Uṣūl al-Khamsah*. (*Wafayāt al-Aʿyān*, I:482; *Tārīkh Baghdād*, III:100; *al-Aʿlām*, VI:275.)

AL-BAYḌĀWĪ, ʿAbdullāh b. ʿUmar (d. 685AH/1286CE). Prominent scholar, judge and commentator on the Qurʾān. Among his books are: *Anwār al-Tanzīl wa-Asrār al-Taʾwīl, Minhāj al-Wuṣūl ilā ʿIlm al-Uṣūl, Ṭawāliʿ al-Anwār*. (*al-Bidāyah wa'l-Nihāyah*. XIII:309; *Bughyat al-Wuʿāt*, p. 286; *al-Aʿlām*, IV:110.)

AL-BAZDAWĪ, Fakhr al-Islām ʿAlī b. Muḥammad (d. 482AH/1089CE). A prominent scholar in *fiqh* and *uṣūl al-fiqh*, he was a follower of the Ḥanafī school. Among his books are: *al-Mabsūṭ, Kanz al-Wuṣūl* (known as *Uṣūl al-Bazdawī*), *Tafsīr al-Qurʾān, Ghināʾ al-Fuqahāʾ*. (*al-Aʿlām*, IV:328.)

AL-BUKHĀRĪ, ʿAbdul-ʿAzīz b. Aḥmad, (d. 730AH/1330CE). A renowned Ḥanafī jurist knowledgeable in *uṣūl al-fiqh*. Among his books are: *Kashf al-Asrār: Sharḥ Uṣūl al-Bazdawī, Sharḥ al-Muntakhab al-Ḥusāmī*. (*al-Aʿlām*, IV:13.)

AL-DABŪSĪ, Abū Zayd ʿAbdullāh b. ʿUmar b. ʿAbdul ʿAzīz (d. 430AH/1039CE). A jurist whose books include: *Taʾsīs al-Naẓar, al-Asrār, Taqwīm al-Adillah*. (*al-Aʿlām*, IV:109.)

AL-ḌAḤḤĀK, Abū Unays b. Qays al-Fihrī (d. 65AH/684CE). A prominent *tābʿī*; Muʿāwiyah appointed him first as governor of Kūfah then as governor of Damascus. (*al-Aʿlām*, III:214.)

FĀṬIMAH BINT QAYS, al-Qurashiyyah (d. circa 50AH/670CE). One the first women companions of the Prophet to choose *hijrah* to Medina. (*al-Aʿlām*, V:131.)

AL-GHAZĀLĪ, Muḥammad Abū Ḥāmid (d. 505AH/1111CE). Recognised as the greatest theologian-mystic of Islam, he wrote more than 200 books among which are: *Iḥyāʾ ʿUlūm al-Dīn, Tahāfut al-Falāsifah, al-Iqtiṣād fiʾl-Iʿtiqād, al-Muṣṭaṣfā min ʿIlm al-Uṣūl, al-Mankhūl min ʿIlm al-Uṣūl*. (*Wafayāt al-Aʿyān*, I:463; *Shudhurāt al-Dhahab*, IV:10; *al-Aʿlām*, VII:22.)

AL-ḤASAN AL-BAṢRĪ, (d. 110AH/728CE). The most famous of the *tābiʿūn*. Born in Medina he moved to Baṣrah and became an *imām* in and a prominent scholar during the reign of Muʿāwiyah. (*al-Aʿlām*, II:226.)

AL-ḤASAN IBN ʿALĪ, (d. 50AH/670CE). Grandson of the Prophet and considered the fifth 'righteous calif'. The people of Iraq appointed him as caliph in 40 AH and asked him to fight Muʿāwiyah. He was reluctant to fight his brothers in Islam. He resigned as caliph and retired to Medina, where he died. (*al-Aʿlām*, II: 199.)

AL-HINDĪ, Abū ʿAbdullāh Ṣafiyyuddīn Muḥammad b. ʿAbdurrāhīm (d. 715AH/1315CE). A scholar of *fiqh* and *uṣūl al-fiqh*. Among his books are: *Nihāyat al-Wuṣūl ilā ʿIlm al-Uṣūl, al-Fāʾiq, al-Zubdah*. (*al-Aʿlām*, VI:200.)

AL-ḤUSAYN IBN ʿALĪ, (d. 61AH/680CE). Grandson of the Prophet. He was killed in Karbalāʾ on Friday, 10th Muḥarram 61 AH. (*al-Aʿlām*, II:243.)

IBN ʿABBĀS, ʿAbdullāh (d. 68AH/687CE). He was a prominent companion renowned for his learning. He transmitted many traditions from the Prophet. Bukhārī and Muslim record 1,660 *hadīths* from him. (*Ḥulyat al-Awliyāʾ wa-Ṭabaqāt al-Aṣfiyāʾ*, I:314; *al-Iṣābah fī Tamyīz al-Ṣaḥābah*, no. 4772; *al-Aʿlām*, IV:95.)

IBN AL-ʿARABĪ, Abū Bakr Muḥammad b. ʿAbdullāh al-Maʿāfirī (d. 543AH/1148CE). A prominent judge and scholar of *hadīth*. He wrote on all the major fields of Islamic science. Among his books are: *al-ʿAwāṣim min al-Qawāṣim, Aḥkām al-Qurʾān, al-Nāsikh waʾl-Mansūkh, al-Inṣāf fī Masāʾil al-Khilāf*. (*al-Aʿlām*, VI:230.)

IBN AL-ATHĪR, Majīd al-Dīn Abū'l Saʿādāt al-Mubārak (d. 606AH/ 1210CE). A famous scholar of the Arabic language, *uṣūl al-fiqh* and *ḥadīth*. Among his books are: *al-Nihāyah fī Gharīb al-Ḥadīth wa'l-Āthār, Jāmiʿ al-Uṣūl fī Aḥādīth al-Rasūl, al-Inṣāf fī al-Jamʿ bayn al-Kashf wa'l-Kashshāf.* (*al-Aʿlām*, V:271.)

IBN AL-ḤĀJIB, ʿUthmān b. ʿUmar b. Abī Bakr al-Mālikī (D. 646AH/ 1249CE). A famous scholar in *fiqh* and Arabic language, he was a follower of the Mālikī *madhhab*. Among his books are: *Muntahā al-Sawl wa'l-Amal fī ʿIlm al-Uṣūl wa'l-Jadal, al-Kāfiyah fī'l-Naḥw.* (*Wafayāt al-Aʿyān*, I:314; *Ghāyat al-Nihāyah fī Ṭabaqāt al-Qurrā'*, I:508; *al-Aʿlām*, IV:211.)

IBN ḤAZM, Abū Muḥammad ʿAlī b. Aḥmad b. Saʿīd, (d. 456AH/1064CE). A famous scholar, poet, and theologian in Andalusia. He was a prominent exponent of the Ẓāhirī school of law. Among his books are: *al-Fiṣal fī'l-Milal wa'l-Ahwā' wa'l-Niḥal, al-Muḥallā, al-Iḥkām fī Uṣūl al-Aḥkām.* (*Irshād al-Arīb ilā Maʿrifat al-Adīb*, V:86–97; *Lisān al-Mīzān*, IV:198; *al-Aʿlām*, IV:254.)

IBN HUMĀM, Muḥammad b. ʿAbd al-Wāḥid (d. 861AH/1457CE). One of the most famous of the Ḥanafī scholars. Among his books are: *al-Fatḥ al-Qadīr, al-Taḥrīr, Zād al-Faqīr, Mukhtaṣar fī Furūʿ al-Ḥanafiyyah.* (*al-Aʿlām*, VI:255.)

IBN KAʿB, ʿUbayy (d. 21AH/642CE). A *ṣaḥābī* from Medina who had been a famous Jewish scholar before he embraced Islam. He was one of the companions who committed the Qur'ān to writing. He transmitted 164 *ḥadīth*. (*al-Aʿlām*, I:82.)

IBN AL-MUNDHIR, Abū Bakr Muḥammad b. Ibrāhīm al-Naysābūrī, (d. 319AH/931CE). A famous jurist, *mujtahid*, and *shaykh* of the Ḥaram in Mecca. Among his books are: *al-Mabsūṭ, al-Awsaṭ fī al-Sunan wa-Ijmāʿ wa-Ikhtilāf al-ʿUlamā', Tafsīr al-Qur'ān.* (*al-Aʿlām*, V:294.)

IBN AL-MUSAYYAB, Saʿīd b. al-Musayyab al-Makhzūmī al-Qurashī (d. 94AH/713CE). One of the prominent *tābiʿūn* and one of the seven jurists (*fuqahā'*) of Medina. (*Ḥulyat al-Awliyā' wa-Ṭabaqāt al-Aṣfiyā'*, II:161; *al-Aʿlām*, III:101.)

IBN QUDĀMAH, Muwaffaq al-Dīn ʿAbdullāh b. Aḥmad b. Muḥammad (d. 620AH/1223CE). A prominent *faqīh* and among the greats of the Hanbalī *madhhab*. Among his books are: *al-Mughnī, Rawḍat al-Nāẓir wa-Jannat al-Manāẓir, al-Muqniʿ.* (*al-Bidāyah wa'l-Nihāyah*, XIII:99; *Shudhurāt al-Dhahab*. V:88; *al-Aʿlām*, IV:76.)

IBN AL-RĀHAWAYH, Abū Yaʿqūb Isḥāq b. Ibrāhīm al-Ḥanẓalī al-Marwazī (d. 238AH/853CE). A renowned scholar whose students included Aḥmad b. Ḥanbal, Bukhārī, Muslim, Tirmidhī and Nasā'ī. Among his books are: *al-Musnad, al-Ḥāshiyah* (*al-Aʿlām*, I:292.)

IBN ṢĀMIT, Aws (no dates). A companion of the Prophet who took part in the battle of Badr and most of the other military campaigns. (*Usud al-Ghābah fī Tamyīz al-Ṣaḥābah*, I: 146.)

IBN TAYMIYYAH, Aḥmad (d. 728AH/1328CE). A famous theologian and a *mujtahid*. He was imprisoned many times in Cairo, Alexandria and Damascus and died in prison in Damascus. He wrote more than three hundred works among which are: *al-Siyāsah al-Sharʿiyyah, al-Fatāwī, al-Īmān, al-Jamʿ Bayn al-Naql wa'l-ʿAql, al-Furqān Bayn Awliyā' Allāh wa Awliyā' al-Shayṭān.* (*al-Aʿlām*, I:144.)

AL-ĪJĪ, ʿAḍud al-Dīn ʿAbdurraḥmān b. Aḥmad (d. 786AH/1355CE). A scholar of *uṣūl al-fiqh* and Arabic language. Among his books are: *al-Mawāqif, al-ʿAqā'id al-ʿAḍudiyyah, Sharḥ Mukhtaṣar Ibn al-Ḥājib.* (*Bughyat al-Wuʿāt fī Ṭabaqāt al-Lughawiyyīn wa'l-Nuḥḥāt*, p. 296; *Miftāḥ al-Saʿādah wa-Miṣbāḥ al-Siyādah*, I: 196; *al-Aʿlām*, III:295.)

ʿIKRIMAH IBN ʿABDULLĀH, (no dates). A prominent *tābiʿī*. He was knowledgeable in *tafsīr*. (*al-Aʿlām*, IV:244.)

AL-JAṢṢĀṢ, Abū Bakr Aḥmad b. ʿAlī al-Rāzī (d. 370AH/980CE). A prominent Ḥanafī scholar. Among his books are: *Aḥkām al-Qur'ān, al-Fuṣūl fī Uṣūl al-Fiqh.* (*al-Jawāhir al-Muḍiyyah fī Ṭabaqāt al-Ḥanafiyyah.* I:84; *al-Aʿlām*, I:171.)

AL-JUBBĀ'Ī, Abū al-Ḥasan ʿAlī b. Muḥammad al-Anṣārī al-Ishbīlī (d. 663AH/1265CE). He was a prominent judge in Andalusia and Morocco. (*al-Aʿlām*, IV:331.)

AL-KARKHĪ, Abū al-Ḥasan ʿAbdullāh b. al-Ḥusayn (d. 340AH/952CE). The last of the famous Ḥanafī jurists of Iraq. Among his books are: *Risālah fī al-Uṣūl, Sharḥ al-Jāmiʿ al-Ṣaghīr, Sharḥ al-Jāmiʿ al-Kabīr.* (*al-Aʿlām*, IV:191.)

KHAWLAH BINT THAʿLABAH, al-Khazrajiyyah (no dates). A companion of the Prophet. An incident concerning her and her husband was a reason for the revelation of the verses of *ẓihār* (*Tahdhīb al-Tahdhīb*, XII:314.)

AL-KHUDRĪ, Saʿd b. Mālik al-Khazrajī (d. 64AH/666CE). A prominent companion of the Prophet and a leader of the *Anṣār*. (*Mashāhīr ʿUlamā' al-Amṣār wa-Aʿlām Fuquhā'al-Aqṭār*, p. 30.)

AL-MĀWARDĪ, Abū al-Ḥasan ʿAlī b. Muḥammad (d. 450AH/1058CE). A prominent scholar and judge. Among his books are: *Adab al-Dunya wa'l-Dīn, al-Aḥkām al-Sulṭāniyyah, al-Nukat wa'l-ʿUyūn, al-Ḥāwī, Naṣīhat al-Mulūk, Aʿlām al-Nubuwwah.* (*al-Aʿlām*, IV:327.)

MAYMŪNAH, bint al-Ḥārith b. Ḥuzn al-Hilāliyyah (d. 51AH/671CE). The last woman to marry the Prophet, and the last of his wives to die. (*Ṭabaqāt Ibn Saʿd*, VIII:94-100; *Usud al-Ghābah fī-Tamyīz al-Ṣaḥābah*, V:550; *al-Aʿlām*, VII:342.)

MUʿĀDH IBN JABAL, al-Awsī al-Khazrajī, (d. 18AH/639CE). A prominent companion of the Prophet. He transmitted 157 *ḥadīth*. (*al-Aʿlām*, VII:258.)

MUJĀHID IBN JABR, Abū al-Ḥajjāj al-Makkī (d. 104AH/722CE). One of the *tābiʿūn* and a renowned *muffasir*. He was taught *tafsīr* by Ibn ʿAbbās. (*Mīzān al-Iʿtidāl*, III:9; *Ḥulyat al-Awliyā' wa-Ṭabaqāt al-Aṣfiyā'*, III:279; *al-Aʿlām*, V:278.)

MUTHANNĀ, Abū ʿUbaydah Maʿmar b. al-Muthannā al-Baṣrī (d. 209AH/824CE). A prominent scholar in Arabic language and literature. He wrote more than two hundred books, among which are: *Naqā'd Jarīr wa'l-Farazdaq*, *Majāz al-Qur'ān*, *Ma'āthir al-ʿArab*, *al-Insān*, *Ṭabaqāt al-Shiʿr*. (*al-Aʿlām*, VII:272.)

AL-NAKHAʿĪ, Abū ʿImrān Ibrāhīm b. Yazīd al-Kūfī (d. 96AH/815CE). A prominent narrator of *ḥadīth* from the second generation of Muslims; also a *mujtahid* with his own *madhhab*. (*Ṭabaqāt Ibn Saʿd*, VI: 188–199; *Ḥulyat al-Awliyā' wa-Ṭabaqiāt al-Aṣfiyā'*, IV:219; *al-Aʿlām*, I:80.)

AL-NASAFĪ, Ḥāfiẓ al-Dīn Abū al-Barakāt ʿAbdullāh b. Aḥmad (d. 710AH/1310CE) He was knowledgeable in *fiqh* and *tafsīr* and was the author of many works among which are: *Madārik al-Tanzīl*, *Kanz al-Daqā'iq*, *Kashf al-Asrār*, *al-Wāfī*. (*al-Aʿlām*, IV:67.)

AL-QARRĀFĪ, Abū al-ʿAbbās Shihāb al-Dīn Aḥmad b. Idrīs (d. 684AH/1285CE). A Malikī scholar. Among his books are: *al-Dhakhīrah*, *Sharḥ Tanqīḥ al-Fuṣūl*, *Nafā'is al-Uṣūl*. (*Shajarat al-Nūr al-Zakiyyah*, p. 188; *Muʿjam al-Maṭbūʿāt*, p. 1501; *al-Aʿlām* I:94.)

AL-RĀZĪ, Fakhr al-Dīn (d. 606AH/1210CE). A famous theologian, philosopher, scholar of *uṣūl al-fiqh* and *tafsīr*. Among his books are: *Mafātiḥ al-Ghayb*, *al-Maḥṣū fī ʿIlm al-Uṣūl*, *al-Masā'il al-Khamsūn fī ʿIlm al-Kalām*. (*Wafayāt al-Aʿyān*, I:474: *Lisān al-Mīzān*, IV:426; *al-Aʿlām*, VI:311.)

SAʿD IBN ʿUBĀDAH, al-Khazrajī, (d. 14AH/635CE) One of the companions of the Prophet and the leader of the Khazraj. He took part in many battles with the Prophet. (*al-Aʿlām*, III:85.)

SĀLIM IBN ʿABDULLĀH, b. ʿUmar b. al-Khaṭṭāb (d. 106AH/725CE). Grandson of ʿUmar ibn al-Khaṭṭāb and one of the prominent *tābiʿūn*. He was one of seven famous jurists of Medina. (*al-Aʿlām*, III:71.)

SAMURAH, b. Jundub b. Hilāl al-Fazārī (d. 60AH/679CE). A prominent companion of the Prophet. He transmitted some traditions from the Prophet. (*al-Aʿlām*. III:139.)

AL-SARAKHSĪ, Abū Bakr Shams al-A'immah Muḥammad b. Aḥmad (d. 483AH/1090CE) He was a judge, prominent Ḥanafī scholar and *mujtahid*. Among his books are: *al-Mabsūṭ* (which he dictated to his students while confined in the Well of Ozjand in Farghānah), *Uṣūl al-Sarakhsī*, *Sharḥ al-Jāmiʿ al-Kabīr li'l-Imām Aḥmad*. (*al-Jawāhir al-Muḍiyyah fī Ṭabaqāt* al-Ḥanafiyyah, II:28; *Miftāḥ al-Saʿādah wa-Miṣbāḥ al-Siyādah*, II:55; *al-Aʿlām*, V:315.)

AL-SHĀFIʿĪ, Muḥammd b. Idrīs (d. 204AH/820CE). The founder of the Shāfiʿī *madhhab* and one of the four *imāms* of Ahl al-Sunnah. Among his books are: *al-Umm, al-Musnad, Aḥkām al-Qur'ān, al-Risālah.* (*Tadhkirat al-Ḥuffāẓ*, I:329; *Tahdhīb al-Tahdhīb*, IX:25; *Tārikh Baghdād*, II:56-73; *al-Aʿlām*, VI:26.)

AL-SHĀṬIBĪ, Ibrāhīm b. Mūsā (d. 790AH/1388CE). A famous scholar in *uṣūl al-fiqh* from Granada and a leader in the Mālikī school. Among his books are: *al-Muwāfaqāt, al-Iʿtiṣām, al-Maqāṣid al-Shāfiyah fī Sharḥ Khulāṣat al-Kāfiyah.* (*Nayl al-Ibtihāj bi-Taṭrīz al-Dībāj*, pp. 46-50; *al-Aʿlām*, I:75.)

AL-SHAWKĀNĪ, Muḥammad b. ʿAlī (d. 1250AH/1834CE). A prominent jurist and a *mujtahid* from Yemen. He maintained that *taqlīd* is forbidden. He wrote 114 books, including: *Nayl al-Awṭār Sharḥ Muntaqā al-Akhbār, Irshād al-Fuḥūl, Fatḥ al-Qadīr.* (*al-Badr al-Ṭāliʿ bi-Maḥāsin man baʿd al-Qarn al-Tāsiʿ*, II:214-225; *al-Aʿlām*, VI:298.)

AL-SHAYBĀNĪ, Muḥammad b. Ḥasan (d. 189AH/804CE). He was an *imām* in both *fiqh* and *uṣūl al-fiqh*. He transmitted and spread the *fiqh* of Abū Ḥanīfah. His most famous books are: *al-Mabsūṭ, al-Ziyādāt, al-Jāmiʿ al-Kabīr, al-Jāmiʿ al-Ṣaghīr, al-Siyar al-Kabīr, al-Siyar al-Ṣaghīr.* (*al-Bidāyah wa'l-Nihāyah*, I:202; *Lisān al-Mīzān*, V:121; *al-Aʿlām*, VI:80.)

AL-SHĪRĀZĪ, Ibrāhīm b. ʿAlī al-Fayrūzābādī (d. 476AH/1083CE) A prominent scholar and *muftī*. Among his books are: *al-Tanbīh, al-Muhadhdhab, al-Tabṣirah, al-Lummaʿ, Ṭabaqāt al-Fuqahā'.* (*Ṭabaqāt al-Shāfiʿiyyah al-Kubrā*, III:88; *Wafayāt al-Aʿyān, al-Aʿlām*, I:51.)

SUFYĀN AL-THAWRĪ, (d. 161AH/778CE). Renowned for his piety, he was a leading *ḥadīth* scholar. Among his books are: *al-Jāmiʿ al-Kabīr, al-Jāmiʿ al-Ṣaghīr, al-Farā'iḍ.* (*Ṭabaqāt Ibn Saʿd*, VI:257; *al-Fahrasat*, I:225; *Tahdhīb al-Tahdhīb*, IV:111-115; *al-Aʿlām*, III:104.)

AL-ṬABARĪ, Muḥammad b. Jarīr (d. 310AH/923CE). A prominent historian and *mufassir*. His books include: *Akhbār al-Rusul wa'l-Mulūk* (known as *Tārikh al-Ṭabarī*), *Jāmiʿ al-Bayān fī Tafsīr al-Qur'ān* (known as *Tafsīr al-Ṭabarī*), *Ikhtilāf al-Fuqahā', al-Qirā'āt.* (*al-Aʿlām*, VI:69.)

AL-ṬŪSĪ, Abū al-Maḥāsin Shihābuddīn (d. 515AH/1122CE). He was a minister at the time of sultan Shanjar Shāh al-Saljūqī. His teacher was Imām al-Ḥaramayn al-Juwaynī. He died in Naysābūr. (*al-Aʿlām*, III:352.)

ʿUMAR IBN AL-KHAṬṬĀB, (d. 23AH/644CE). The second caliph and the first to be given the title *amīr al-mu'minīn*. Under his reign, the Islamic state rapidly extended. He transmitted 537 *ḥadīth*. (*Ḥulyat al-Awliyā' wa-Ṭabaqāt al-Aṣfiyā'*, I:38; *Ṣifat al-Ṣufwah*, I:101; *al-Aʿlām*, V:45.)

ʿURWAH IBN AL-ZUBAYR, (d. 93AH/712CE). Brother of ʿAbdullāh ibn al-Zubayr and one of the seven main jurists of Medina. (*Ṣifat al-Ṣufwah*,

II:47; *Ḥulyat al-Awliyā' wa-Ṭabaqāt al-Aṣfiyā'*, II:176; *al-Aʿlām*, IV:226.)

'UTHMĀN IBN ʿAFFĀN, (d. 35AH/656CE). He was the third of the righteously-guided caliphs. He completed the collection of the Qur'ān. He transmitted 146 *ḥadīth*. (*Ḥulyat al-Awliyā' wa-Ṭabaqāt al-Aṣfiyā'* I:55; *Ṣifat al-Ṣufwah*. I:12; *al-Aʿlām*, IV:210.)

AL-ẒĀHIRĪ, Dāwūd b. ʿAlī b. Khalaf, (d. 270AH/884CE). An *imām* and *mujtahid*. He and his followers were called Ẓāhirīs because they followed the apparent meaning (*ẓāhir*) of the authoritative texts. They rejected *ta'wīl* and *qiyās*. Dāwūd was the first to express these opinions. (*Wafayāt al-Aʿyān*, I:175; *Tadhkirat al-Ḥuffāẓ* II:136; *Lisān al-Mīzān*, II:422; *al-Aʿlām*, II:331)

AL-ZUHRĪ, Abū Muḥammad ʿAbdullāh b. ʿUmar (d. 252AH/866CE). A judge and *ḥadīth* scholar who hailed from Aṣbahān. (*al-Aʿlām*, IV:109.)

Glossary

Aḥād: solitary *ḥadīth* reported by a single person or a limited number of persons.

Aḥkām ʿaqliyyah: rational judgements.

Aḥkām ḥissiyyah: rulings reached through the senses.

Aḥkām sharʿiyyah: rulings reached through authoritative texts.

Aḥkām taklīfiyyah: commandment rulings.

Ahl al-kitāb: lit. the People of the Book; non-Muslims who believe in the holy scriptures, Christians and Jews.

ʿĀmm: general, unspecified; a technical term normally referring to general meaning.

Amr (pl. *awāmir*): command, matter, affair.

Amr muqayyad: restricted command.

Amr muṭlaq: absolute command.

ʿAqīdah: Islamic beliefs.

ʿAql: reason, intellect, rationality.

Ashʿarīs: the school of *ʿilm al-kalām* named after al-Ashʿarī.

Aṣl (pl. *uṣūl*): lit. root, essence, base; that upon which something else is built. Technically, the sources of law or the principles of jurisprudence.

Bāṭil: invalid, null and void, without any effect.

Bayʿ: sale transaction.

Bayʿ al-gharar: deception sale.

Bayān qaṭʿī: definite explanation and clarification.

Ḍaʿīf: weak; also used for traditions with weak chains of narration.

Dalālāt (sing. *dalālah*): meaning, implication of words.

Dalālāt al-alfāẓ: verbal indications.

Dalālāt al-īmāʾ: gesture, meanings of a given text which is borne out by the text's gesture.

Dalālāt al-iqtiḍāʾ: required meanings of a given text; a technical term which normally refers to a meaning of the text necessarily presumed and on which the correctness of that text and its validity in *Sharīʿah* depend.

Dalālāt al-mafhūm: implied meanings of a given text; a technical term which normally refers to an implicit meaning reached by way of inference and not indicated by the word's apparent indication.

Dalālāt al-manṭūq: pronounced meanings of a given text; a technical term which normally refers to a text's indication for a ruling mentioned in the text and pronounced by complete correspondence (*muṭābaqah*), by partial inclusion (*taḍammun*) or by a necessary idea attached to the meaning in the mind (*iltizām*).

Dalālāt al-naṣṣ: inferred or implied meanings of a given text; a technical term normally mening that the indicated ruling is valid for another incident, because both incidents share an effective cause (*ʿillah*).

Faḥwā al-khiṭāb: superior meaning.

Farʿ: lit. a branch or sub-division, and (in the context of *qiyās*) a new case and a new subject.

Farḍ: obligatory, obligation, precept of the divine law.

Fiqh: lit. understanding, the science of Islamic law or jurisprudence.

Fuqahā' (sing. *faqīh*): legal scholars, jurists, those who are learned in *fiqh*.

Furūʿ (sing. *farʿ*): branches or subsidiaries, such as the branches of *fiqh* as opposed to its roots and sources (*uṣūl al-fiqh*).

Ghālib al-ẓann: prevailing speculative indication.

Ghāyah: the extent of application.

Ghayr al-ṣarīḥ: unclear, latent, unpronounced, ambiguous, equivocal.

Ghubār: dust (normally associated with *tayammum*).

Ḥadd (pl. *ḥudūd*): lit. limit; prescribed punishment; a specific, fixed penalty.

Ḥadīth: narratives and reports of deeds and utterances of the Prophet as recounted by his Companions.

Ḥāl: circumstantial expression, status, linguistic form.

Ḥalāl: what is allowed, a permissible act or an article one is permitted to consume.

Ḥanafī: Sunnī school of law which developed in Kūfa, Iraq, named after Abū Ḥanīfah

Ḥanbalī: the Sunni school of law named after Aḥmad b. Ḥanbal.

Ḥaqīqī: original, real, literal (as opposed to metaphorical).

Ḥaqq: the right cause, right of God or public right.

Ḥarām: forbidden, a forbidden act or an article forbidden to consume.

Ḥayḍ: menstruation.

Ḥiss: intuition.

Ḥudūd: see *ḥadd*.

Ḥujjah: legal proof or evidence.

Ḥukm (pl. *aḥkām*): as in *ḥukm sharʿī* or the injunction of the *Sharīʿah*.

Ḥukm juz'ī: partial ruling or injunction.

Ibāḥah: allowance, permissibility.

'Ibārat al-naṣṣ: explicit meaning of a given text.

Iḍāfah: genitive construction in Arabic.

'Iddah: the waiting period during which a woman cannot remarry following dissolution of marriage by divorce or death. The legal rights and obligations of the spouses are not wholly extinguished during this period.

Ijmāʿ: consensus, a source of Islamic jurisprudence, unanimous opinion of the Muslim scholars on any matter of faith after the death of the Prophet.

Ijtihād: lit. exertion; exertion of effort by a qualified scholar or group of qualified scholars to discover the Islamic point of view on a certain issue through the application of knowledge.

Ikhtilāf: lit. disagreement, normally associated with jurist disagreement.

'Illah: effective cause of a certain injunction (in the original sources of the *Sharīʿah*) which provides justification for assimilating a derived case to a basic case in the process of analogy (*qiyas*). A legal principle established by an original case is extended to cover new cases on the grounds that they possess a common *'illah*.

'Ilm al-kalām: scholastic theology.

Iltizām: a necessary idea attached to a meaning in the mind, e.g. a human being indicates a being capable of knowledge.

Indhār: warning, legal notice.

Iqtiḍā' al-naṣṣ: the required meaning of a given text.

Irshād: guidance.

Ishārat al-naṣṣ: the alluded meaning that can be detected in a given text.

Istiʿārah badīʿah: rhetoric metaphor.

Istighrāq: inclusion by one concept of many others.

Istiḥsān: to deem something good, a discursive evidence used by some jurists whereby preference is given to a rule other than the one reached by the more obvious form of analogy. It is in this context that *istiḥsān* has sometimes been translated as 'jurists' preference'. It is used only in cases not regulated by authority of the Qur'ān, *ḥadīth* or *ijmāʿ*.

Iṣṭilāḥ: convention.

Istinbāṭ al-aḥkām: juridical deduction, deduction of legal rulings.

Istiṣḥāb: presumption of continuity, or of continuation of the *status quo ante*; a methodological principle whereby the welfare and well-being of both the individual and society are deemed paramount in reaching a legal judgement.

Istiṣlāḥ: a methodological principle whereby the welfare and well-being of both the individual and society are deemed paramount in reaching a legal judgement.

Istithnā' muttaṣil: attached exception.

I'tibār: a calling for contemplation, admonition; something consequential.

Jāhiliyyah: ignorance, a term used to refer to the period before the advent of the Prophet and the final revelation.

Janābah: the state of ritual impurity of a person after sexual discharge or contact, whether intentional or not.

Jarḥ wa taʿdīl: the criteria by which to appraise narrators of *ḥadīth* – rejection (*jarḥ*) or acceptance (*taʿdīl*).

Jihād: lit. striving for the sake of God, self-exertion and struggle for the sake of establishing truth and justice in a situation of imbalance.

Jins: kind, type, generic type.

Jumhūr: dominant majority of Muslim scholars.

Kalām: words; normally refers to scholastic theology.

Kanz: accumulated money from which *zakāt* is not paid.

Karārah: blameworthy, abhorrence, abomination.

Khabar wāḥid: a solitary tradition narrated by a limited number of narrators.

Khafī: hidden, obscure; also refers to a category of unclear words.

Khalaf: the latter generation of the Muslim community.

Khāṣṣ: specific, a word or a text which conveys a specific meaning.

Khilāf al-aṣl: opposite to the basic, original and approved status.

Khulʿ: release or redemption, a form of divorce by mutual agreement, a dissolution of the marriage bond by an utterance of this word or its derivatives, and for which the wife pays or promises to pay some/part of the dowry given to her.

Lafẓ ʿāmm: general word.

Laḥn al-khiṭāb: parallel meaning.

Liʿān: lit. imprecation, cursing, a form of irrevocable dissolution of marriage whereby the husband affirms four times under oath that his wife committed adultery and invokes the curse of God on himself should he be telling a lie; the woman then affirms four times under oath that her husband is telling a lie, and invokes on herself the curse of God should he be telling the truth. Also called *mulāʿanah*.

Madhhab (pl. *madhāhib*): classical juridical/theological schools of legal thought.

Mafhūm: notion, concept, implicit meaning.

Mafhūm al-mukhālafah: divergent meaning, an interpretation which diverges from the obvious meaning of a given text.

Mafhūm al-muwāfaqah: agreed meaning, an interpretation which agrees with the obvious meaning of a given text.

Maḥdhūf: omitted.

Mahr: also called *ṣadāq*, dowry, sum of money or other property payable by the husband to the wife to effect the marriage.

Makrūh: blameworthy, abominable, reprehensible.

Mālikī: a Sunni school of law developed in Medina and named after Mālik b. Anas.

Manāṭ al-ḥukm: effective cause.

Mandhūr: vow made to God.

Mandūb: praiseworthy, a desirable cause which does not cause blame if left unperformed.

Manṭūq: pronounced.

Maqīs: subsidiary new case in *qiyās*.

Maqīs ʿalayhi: original case in *qiyās*.

Marjūḥ: non-preferable opinion.

Mashhūr: a well-known tradition of the Prophet.

Mashrūṭ: stipulated.

Mashūrah: consultation.

Maskūt ʿanh: not mentioned, concealed, unpronounced rulings.

Maʿṣūm: infallible, immune from making errors (normally refers to the Prophet).

Mawlā (pl. *mawālī*): a homonym that means both the freer (the master) and the freed (the slave).

Mayyitah: dead animal; cattle or beast not slaughtered according to the requirements of Islamic law.

Mu'awwal: interpreted beyond the obvious meaning of the text.

Mubayyan: determined and explained words.

Mubham: ambiguous and unclear words.

Muḍārabah: speculation; a profit and loss-sharing contract by which one party provides capital and the other party manages the enterprise. In case of loss, the supplier of capital bears the financial loss while the agent-partner loses the return for his labour. Both parties share in the profit in agreed proportions.

Muḍmar: concealed, implicit words in a given text.

Muḥkam: firm; technical term normally referring to a word or text which is susceptible neither to *ta'wīl* nor abrogation.

Mujmal: inconclusive, ambivalent, ambiguous; a technical term which normally refers to a category of unclear words.

Mujtahid: a qualified person who exercises *ijtihād*.

Mufassar: explained, clarified; a technical term which normally refers to a category of explained and clarified words.

Mukallaf: a person who has reached maturity and is in full possession of his faculties and is therefore morally responsible.

Mukhaṣṣiṣ (pl. *mukhaṣṣiṣāt*): articles which offer specification, proofs of specification.

Muqaṭṭaʿāt: individual (abbreviated) letters in the Qur'an.

Muqayyad: confined, qualified; a technical word which normally refers to a word that indicates a subject or non-specified group of subjects (*māhiyyah*), to which is attached what restricts their commonality.

Muqtaḍā: required indication of a given text without which the meaning of the text would be incomplete.

Muqtarin: joined and associated.

Mushkil: difficult; a technical term which normally refers to a provision which cannot be easily understood.

Mushtarak: homonym; a technical term which normally refers to a word or phrase imparting more than one meaning.

Mustaqill: independent.

Mutawāṭi': a specified personal meaning.

Mutawātir ḥadīth: a tradition which has a sufficiently large number of independent chains of authority to guarantee its authenticity.

Muṭābaqah: complete correspondence.

Mut'ah: lit. pleasure, temporary marriage recognised only by the Shī'ah school, and considered illegal by the Sunnis.

Mutakallimūn: theologians of *uṣūl al-fiqh*.

Mutashābihāt (sing. *mutashābih*): verses of the Qur'ān which are beyond human comprehension.

Muṭlaq: absolute, unqualified; a technical term which normally refers to a word indicating a subject or a group in a multitude (*māhiyyah*) without being specific or restricted by anything that may reduce its commonality.

Muṭlaq ṣīghat al-amr: absolute imperative (jussive).

Muṭlaq ṣīghat al-nahy: absolute prohibition (jussive).

Nadb: recommendation.

Nafl: supererogatory worship.

Najāsah: impurity, uncleanness, dirt, filth.

Nahy: prohibition.

Nakirah: indefinite noun, unknown person.

Naskh: abrogation, cancellation, deletion or substitution of one text or its injunction by another.

Naṣṣ: text; an explicit provision of the Qur'ān or Sunnah, a clear injunction, an explicit textual ruling.

Nifās: women's menstrual period after giving birth.

Niṣāb: wealth up to a determined minimum value, normally the amount which makes the owner responsible for paying *zakāt*.

Niyyah: intention; in Islam actions are valued according to their intention.

Qadhf: slanderous accusation of illicit sexual relations.

Qadr: amount.

Qarīnah: evidence, context or circumstantial evidence.

Qaṣr: limitation.

Qaṭʿī: definitive, decisive, free of speculative content.

Qaṭʿi al-dalālah: the definite meaning.

Qawāʿid fiqhiyyah: rules extracted from Islamic law by the *fuqahā'* to form a general rule or maxim.

Qinṭār: measuring unit. One *qinṭār* has 100 *raṭls*(1 *raṭl*=407.5 gms).

Qiyās: the process of forming Islamic judgements through logical deduction based on the original sources of the *Sharīʿah*.

Qiyās awlā: analogy of the superior; logical deduction based on an original source when the cause (*ʿillah*) in a new case is more evident than in the original case.

Qiyās jalī: clear analogy; logical deduction based on an original source when the cause in a new case is more evident than in the original case.

Qiyās musāwī: analogy of equals; logical deduction based on an original source when the cause is equally evident in both the new case and the original case.

Qur' (pl. *qurū'*): a homonym that means both the menstrual period and the period between two menstrual cycles.

Rājiḥ: preferable, used for a variant juristic opinion which is deemed to be a more correct view.

Ribā': usury, interest on a capital loan.

Riwāyah: narration, transmission of *ḥadīth*.

Rukn (pl. *arkān*): basic element, pillar, essential ingredient, essential requirement.

Sabab al-nuzūl: the specific reason and circumstances for the revelation of certain verses of the Qur'ān.

Ṣadaqah: alms and voluntary almsgiving, charity.

Ṣaḥābah (sing. *ṣaḥābī*): Prophet's Companions.

Ṣaḥīḥ: valid and effective; authentic tradition.

Ṣaʿīd: earthy soil, dust.

Salaf: the first generations of Muslims.

Ṣalāh: lit. call, invocation, supplication (*duʿā'*); the special obligatory prayers required by Islam.

Ṣarīḥ: clear, plain, open, frank, unambiguous, unequivocal.

Ṣīghah mujmalah: ambivalent mood.

Ṣīghat al-jumūʿ: mood of general meaning.

Ṣifah: attribute.

Ṣiyām: fasting; abstaining from everything which may invalidate the fast, from the first light of dawn to sunset.

Shāfiʿī: Sunni schools of law named after Muḥammad b. Idrīs al-Shāfiʿī. In *uṣūl al-fiqh*, *Shāfiʿī* school of law includes: Shāfiʿī, Mālikī, Ḥanbalī and Zāhirī.

Sharīʿah: the divine law of Islam.

Sharṭ (pl. *shurūṭ*): condition.

Shirk: polytheism, idolatry; worshipping someone or something other than God, or associating something or someone with Him.

Shubuhāt: suspicions.

Shumūl: comprehension.

Shūrā: consultation.

Sunnah: traditions attributed to the Prophet; the way of the Prophet which Muslims consider relevant to religious guidance, usually divided into verbal utterances, acts of the Prophet and the tacit assent of the Prophet. After the Qur'ān, it is the second most important source for Islamic law.

Taʿabbud: piety, devotion, worship, obedience to God.

Taʿadhdhur: impossibility of doing something.

Tabaʿiyyah: subsequently, afterwards, consequently.

Tābiʿūn: next generation of Muslims after the *ṣaḥābah*.

Taḍamum: partial inclusion.

Tafsīr: explanation, normally refers to commentaries on the Qur'ān.

Tafsīr qaṭʿī: definitive explanation.

Ṭahārah kubrā: the complete ablution, washing the entire body with water after ritual impurity.

Tahdīd: threat.

Ṭāhir: pure.

Taḥrīm: prohibition or rendering something *ḥarām*.

Taʿjīz: to deem powerless.

Takbīr: saying *Allāh Akbar* (God is Most-great).

Takhṣīṣ: specifying the general provision.

Talāzum: correlation between two meanings or ideas.

Taʿlīl: justification, ratiocination, search for the effective cause of a ruling.

Tamyīz: specification of a meaning or subject.

Taʿqīb: continuation.

Targhīb: invitation, attraction.

Tarhīb: intimidation, threatening.

Tashdīd: intensification, strengthening; intensified pronunciation, doubling of a consonant, doubling sign over a consonant.

Taswiyah: equalisation between two things.

Taṭhīr: purification.

Tawātur: continuous recurrence, continuous testimony, impeccable plurality of narrators which continue from one generation to another; normally describes the narration of the Qur'ān or *ḥadīth*.

Tawḥīd: the belief in the oneness of God; the science of Islamic beliefs.

Ta'wīl: interpretation beyond the obvious sense of a given text; allegorical interpretation.

Tayammum: ablution by rubbing the hands with clean earth where no water is available.

Tayyibāt: all good things.

Taʿzīr: lit/ deterrence; non-fixed punishment, discretionary penalty determined by a judge (*qāḍī*).

Ṭuhr: purity; normally the period between two menstrual cycles.

Turāb: dust.

ʿUlamā' (sing. *ʿālim*): scholars.

ʿUlūm al-ḥadīth: the sciences of *ḥadīth*.

ʿUlūm al-Qur'ān: the sciences of understanding the Qur'ān.

Ummah: the community of Islam, a generation of Muslims which includes all those considered in the faith of Islam.

ʿUmūm al-muqtaḍā: a technical term which normally refers to the generalisation of the required meaning.

ʿUrf qawlī: verbal customs and habits prevalent in society.

Uṣūl al-fiqh: source methodology of Islamic jurisprudence.

Uṣūlīyūn: the scholars of *uṣūl al-fiqh*.

Wāḍiḥ: clear, lucid, plain, distinct, obvious, manifest; a technical term which normally refers to clear words.

Wājib: obligatory, strict obligation which Muslims must observe.

Wāqifiyyah: a name applied to a number of Muslim groups or sects who 'halt' to give their legal opinion about certain questions.

Waqt: time.

Wijāʿ: cutting; in *ḥadīth* refers to protection against sin.

Wuḍū': ablution with clean water.

Ẓāhir: apparent, manifest; a technical term which normally refers to the apparent meaning of a text.

Ẓāhirī: a school of Islamic law based on the principle of relying exclusively on the literal meaning (*ẓāhir*) of authoritative texts.

Zakāh: a religious obligation on Muslims to pay annually a predetermined percentage of the value of their assets to the Islamic state, to be distributed to certain categories of people.

Zakāt al-fiṭr: obligatory donation of foodstuffs or money required at the end of Ramaḍān, the month of fasting.

Ẓannī: indefinite, speculative, doubtful; the legal value attached to the results of juristic reasoning.

Ẓannī al-dalālah: indefinite meaning.

Ẓarf makān: place adverb.

Ẓarf zamān: time adverb.

Ẓihār: refers to what husbands once said to their wives when divorcing them: 'You are to me like the back of my mother' (i.e. unlawful for me to approach).
Zinā': adultery, fornication.
Ẓulm: oppression, injustice.
Ẓunūn: indefinite meanings.

Bibliography

ʿAbd al-Bāqī, Muḥammad Fuʾād, *Al-Muʿjam al-Mufahras li-Alfāẓ al-Qurʾān al-Karīm*, Beirut: Dār Iḥyāʾ al-Turāth al-Islāmī, n.d.

ʿĀbidīn, Muḥammad ʿAlāʾuddīn, *Al-Hadiyyah al-ʿAlāʾiyyah*, 3rd edn, 1398/1978.

Abū Dāwūd, al-Sijistānī, *Sunan*, ed. Muḥammad Muḥyiddīn ʿAbdul Ḥamīd, Beirut: al-Maktabah al-ʿAṣriyyah, n.d.

Abū Ḥātim, Muḥammad b. Hibbān, *Mashāhīr ʿUlamāʾ al-Amṣār wa-Aʿlām Fuqahāʾ al-Aqṭār*, ed. Marzūq ʿAlī Ibrāhīm, Beirut: Muʾassasat al-Kutub al-Thaqāfiyyah, 1408/1987.

Abū Zahrah, Muḥammad, *Uṣūl al-Fiqh*, Cairo: Maṭbaʿat Mukhaymir, n.d.

Abughosh, Bassam Sulayman and Waffa Zaki Shaqra, *A Glossary of Islamic Terminology*, London: Ta Ha Publishers, 1992.

ʿAjlūnī, Ismāʿīl, *Kashf al-Khafāʾ wa-Muzīl al-Ilbās ʿammā Ishtahara min al-Aḥādīth ʿalā Alsinat al-Nās*, Maṭbaʿat al-Qudsī, 1351 AH.

Āl-ʿAbd al-Laṭīf, ʿAbd al-Laṭīf, *Ṭarīq al-Rushd ilā Takhrīj Aḥādīth Bidāyat Ibn Rushd*, Medina: Islamic University of Medina, n.d.

Al-ʿAlāʾī, Khalīl, *Talqīḥ al-Fuhūm fī Tanqīḥ Ṣiyagh al-ʿUmūm*, ed. ʿAbd Allāh b. Muḥammad b. Isḥāq al-Shaykh, 1403/1983.

Al-Albānī, Muḥammad Nāṣir al-Dīn, *Irwāʾ al-Ghalīl fī Takhrīj Aḥādīth Manār al-Sabīl*, 10 vols., al-Maktab al-Islāmī, 1399/1979.

Al-ʿAlwānī, Ṭāhā Jābir, *Source Methodology in Islamic Jurisprudence*, 2nd edn, Herndon (VA): The International Institute of Islamic Thought, 1415/1994.

Al-Āmidī, Sayf al-Dīn, *Al-Iḥkām fī Uṣūl al Aḥkām*, 2 vols., Beirut: Dār al-Kutub al-ʿIlmiyyah, 1405/1985

Anderson, Norman, *Law Reform in the Muslim World*, London: The Athlone Press, 1976.

Al-Anṣārī, ʿAbd al-ʿĀlī Muḥammad, *Fawātiḥ al-Raḥamūt*, printed on the margin of *al-Mustaṣfā*, Cairo: al-Maṭbaʿah al-Amīriyyah, 1334 AH.

Al-Anṣārī, Shams al-Islām Abū Yaḥya, *Ghāyat al-Wuṣūl Sharḥ Lubb al-Uṣūl*, Indonesia, n.d.

Arberry, Arthur J., *The Koran Interpreted*, Oxford: Oxford University Press, 1964.

Al-Aṣfahānī, Aḥmad b. ʿAlī, *Ḥulyat al-Awliyā' wa-Ṭabaqāt al-Aṣfiyā*, Cairo, 1351 AH.

Al-Aṣfahānī, Shams al-Dīn Maḥmūd, *Sharḥ al-Minhāj*, Riyadh: Maktabat al-Rushd, 1410 AH.

Al-ʿAsqalānī, Aḥmad b. Ḥajar, *al-Iṣābah fī Tamyīz al-Ṣaḥābah*, Cairo, 1358/1937.

——*Bulūgh al-Marām*, Kuwait: Revival of Islamic Heritage Society, 1994.

——*Fatḥ al-Bārī*, Cairo: al-Maṭbaʿah al-Amīriyyah, 1301 AH.

——*Lisān al-Mīzān*, Haydarabad, 1331 AH.

Al-Baʿalabakī, *Al-Mawrid*, 4th edn, Beirut: Dār al-ʿIlm li'l-Malāyīn, 1992.

Badrān, Abū al-ʿAynayn, *Uṣūl al-Fiqh al-Islāmī*, Alexandria: Mu'assasat Shabāb al-Jāmiʿah, 1404/1984.

Bādshāh, Muḥammad Amīn al-Ḥusaynī, *Taysīr al-Taḥrīr*, 2 vols., n.p., n.d.

Al-Baghdādī, al-Khaṭīb, *Tārīkh Baghdād*, Cairo, 1349 AH.

Al-Bardīsī, Muḥammad Zakariyyā, *Uṣūl al-Fiqh*, 2nd edn, Cairo: Maṭbaʿat Dār al-Ta'līf, 1381 AH.

Al-Baṣrī, Abū al-Ḥusayn Muḥammad, *Al-Muʿtamad fī Uṣūl al-Fiqh*, Damascus: The French Institute for Islamic Studies, 1384/1964.

Al-Bayhaqī, Aḥmad b. al-Husayn, *Al-Sunan al-Kubrā*, 10 vols., Hyderabad: Maṭbaʿat Dār al-Maʿārif al-ʿUthmāniyyah, 1356/1937.

Al-Bazdawī, Fakhr al-Islām ʿAlī, *Uṣūl Fakhr al-Islām al-Bazdawī*, printed on the margin of *Kashf al-Asrār ʿan Uṣūl Fakhr al-Islām al-Bazdawī*, Cairo: Dār al-Kitāb al-Islāmī, n.d.

Bell, Richard, *Bell's Introduction to the Qur'ān*, Edinburgh: Edinburgh University Press, 1977.

Al-Bukhārī, ʿAlā' al-Dīn, *Kashf al-Asrār ʿan Uṣūl Fakhr al-Islām al-Bazdawī*, 2 vols., Cairo: Dār al-Kitāb al-Islāmī, n.d.

——*Al-Tawḍīḥ fī Ḥalli Ghawāmiḍ al-Tanqīḥ*, Printed together with *Sharḥ al-Talwīḥ ʿalā al-Tawḍīḥ* of Taftāzānī.

Al-Bukhārī, Muḥammad b. Ismāʿīl, *Al-Jāmiʿ al-Ṣaḥīḥ*, Istanbul: al-Maktabah al-Islāmiyyah, n.d.

Al-Bunānī, ʿAbd al-Raḥman, *Ḥāshiya ʿalā Sharḥ al-Maḥallī ʿalā Jamʿ al-Jawāmiʿ*, 2 vols., 2nd edn, Cairo: Muṣṭafā al-Bābī al-Ḥalabī, 1386 AH.

Coulson, N. J., *A History of Islamic Law*, Edinburgh: Edinburgh University Press, 1978.

Al-Dabbūsī, ʿAbd Allah, *Al-Asrār fī'l-Uṣūl wa'l-Furūʿ fī Taqwīm Adillat al-Sharʿ*, Ph.D. thesis presented at al-Azhar University, Cairo, by Maḥmūd Tawfīq al-ʿAwāṭilī al-Rughāʿī.

Al-Dārimī, ʿAbd Allāh, *Sunan*, Beirut: Dār Iḥyā' al-Sunnah al-Nabawiyyah, n.d.

Al-Dassūqī, Muḥammad, *Ḥāshiyat al-Dassūqī ʿala al-Sharḥ al-Kabīr*, 4 vols., Cairo: ʿĪsā al-Bābī al-Ḥalabī, n.d.

Al-Dhahabī, Muḥammad, *Tadhkirat al-Ḥuffāẓ*, Hyderabad, 1333–1334 AH.

——*Mīzān al-Iʿtidāl fī Naqd al-Rijāl*, Dār al Fikr al-ʿArabī, n.d..

Al-Dimashqī, Abū Zakariya Yaḥyā, *Riyāḍ al-Ṣalihīn*, Kuwait: Revival of Islamic Heritage Society, 1414/1994.

Al-Dimashqī, ʿImād al-Dīn Ismāʿīl, *al-Bidāyah wa'l-Nihāyah*, Cairo, 1351–1358 AH.

Doi, Abdurrahman I., *Sharīʿah: the Islamic Law*, London: Ta Ha Publishers, 1404/1984.

Donzel, E. van, *Islamic Desk Reference*, Leiden: E. J. Brill, 1994.

Encyclopedia of Islam, 8 vols. and supplement (1913–1938), Leiden: E.J. Brill, 1987.

——*Encyclopedia of Islam*, new edn, Leiden: E.J. Brill, 1960–.

Esposito, John L., *Modern Islamic World*, 4 vols., Oxford: Oxford University Press, 1995.

Fārūqī, Ḥārith Sulaymān, *Fārūqī's Law Dictionary*, 2nd edn, Beirut: Librairie du Liban, 1983.

Al-Fayrūzabādī, Majd al-Dīn Muḥammad, *al-Qāmūs al-Muḥīṭ*, 4 vols., 5th edn, Cairo: Muṣṭafā Maḥmūd, 1373 AH.

Al-Ghazālī, Abū Ḥāmid Muḥammad, *al-Mustaṣfā fī ʿIlm al-ʿUsūl*, Beirut: Dār al-Kutub al-ʿIlmiyyah, 1413/1993.

Al-Ghazzī, Najm al-Dīn, *al-Kawākib al-Sā'irah fī Aʿyān al-Mi'ah al-ʿĀshirah*, Beirut: al-Maktabah al-Amrīkiyyah, 1945.

Gibb, H. A. R., *Mohammedanism*, 2nd edn, Oxford: Oxford University Press, 1953.

Gibb, H. A. R. & Kramers, J. H., *Shorter Encyclopedia of Islam*, Leiden: E. J. Brill, 1974.

Glasse, Cyril, *The Concise Encyclopedia of Islam*, London: Stacey International, 1989.

Al-Ḥafnāwī, Muḥammad, *al-Taʿāruḍ wa'l-Tarjīḥ*, 2nd edn, Manṣūrah: Dār al-Wafā', 1408/1987.

Al-Ḥamawī, Abū ʿAbdullāh Yāqūt, *Irshād al-Arīb ilā Maʿrifat al-Adīb*, Cairo: Maṭbaʿat Marghilyūth, 1907.

Al-Ḥanbalī, Abū al-Falāḥ ʿAbd al-Ḥayy, *Shudhurāt al-Dhahab fī Akhbār man Dhahab*, Beirut: al-Maktabah al-Tijāriyyah li'l-Ṭibāʿah wa'l-Nashr, n.d.

Harris, P., *An Introduction to Law*, 2nd edn, London: Weidenfeld and Nicolson, 1984.

Al-Ḥasan, Khalīfah, *Takhṣīṣ al-Nuṣūṣ bi'l-Adillah al-Ijtihādiyyah ʿinda al-Uṣūliyyīn*, Cairo: Maktabat Wahbah, 1413/1993.

Haywood, L. A. & Nahmad, H. M., *A New Arabic Grammar*, London: Lund Humphries, 1993.

Hilālī, Muḥammad Taqiyuddīn & Khān, Muḥammad Muḥsin, *Tafsīr Maʿānī al-Qurʾān al-Karīm*, 4th edn, Maktabat Dār al-Salām, 1994.

Ibn Abī al-ʿIzz, ʿAlī, *Sharh al-ʿAqīdah al-Ṭaḥāwiyyah*, Beirut: Muʾassasat al-Risālah, n.d.

Ibn ʿĀbidīn, Muḥammad Amīn, *Ḥāshiyat Radd al-Muḥtār ʿalā al-Durr al-Mukhtār* (known as *Ḥāshiyat ibn ʿĀbidīn*), 5 vols., Egypt: Maṭbaʿat Būlāq, 1282 AH.

Ibn Amīr al-Ḥājj, Muḥammad, *Al-Taqrīr waʾl-Taḥbīr*, 3 vols., 2nd edn, Egypt: al-Maṭbaʿah al-ʿUthmāniyyah, 1311 AH.

Ibn al-ʿArabī, Abū Bakr Muḥammad, *Aḥkām al-Qurʾān*, 4 vols., Cairo: ʿĪsā al-Bābī al-Ḥalabī, 1376–1378 AH.

Ibn al-Athīr, Majd al-Dīn Muḥammad, *Al-Nihāyah fī Gharīb al-Ḥadīth waʾl-Āthār*, Egypt: al-Maṭbaʿah al-ʿUthmāniyyah, 1311 AH.

Ibn al-Ḥājib, Jamāl al-Dīn ʿUthmān, *Sharh Mukhtaṣar al-Muntahā*, printed with *Sharh al-ʿAḍud maʿā Mukhtaṣar al-Muntahā*, 2 vols., Cairo: Maṭbaʿat al-Kulliyyah al-Azhariyyah, Cairo, 1406/1986.

Ibn Ḥanbal, Aḥmad, *Musnad*, ed. Aḥmad Muḥammad Shākir, Cairo: Dār al-Maʿārif, Cairo: 1377.

Ibn Ḥazm, ʿAlī b. Aḥmad, *al-Muḥallā*, Beirut: Dār al-Āfāq al-Jadīdah, n.d.

——*al-Iḥkām fī Uṣūl al-Aḥkām*, 8 vols., Cairo: Maṭbaʿat al-Saʿādah, 1935.

——*al-Fiṣal fī al-Milal waʾl-Aḥwāl waʾl-Niḥal*, 5 vols., Maktabat al-Salām al-ʿĀlamiyyah, n.d.

Ibn al-Humām, al-Kamāl, *Fath al-Qādir Sharh al-Hidāyah*, 8 vols., Cairo: al-Maṭbaʿah al-Amīriyyah, 1315 AH.

Ibn al-Jawzī, Abū al-Faraj Jamāl al-Dīn, *Ṣifat Ṣufwah*, Hyderabad, 1355 AH.

Ibn Kathīr, ʿImād al-Dīn, *Tafsīr al-Qurʾān al-ʿAẓīm*, Kuwait: Revival of Islamic Heritage Society, 1414/1994.

Ibn Khalkān, Aḥmad, *Wafayāt al-Aʿyān wa-Anbāʾ Abnāʾ al-Zamān*, Cairo, 1310 AH.

Ibn Mājah, Muḥammad, *Sunan Ibn Mājah*, ed. Muḥammad Fuʾād ʿAbd al-Bāqī, Istanbul: al-Maktabah al-Islāmiyyah, n.d.

Ibn al-Nadīm, Muḥammad b. Isḥāq, *Al-Fahrasa (Fahrasat Ibn Nadīm)*, Leipzig, 1871.

Ibn Nujaym, Zayn al-ʿĀbidīn, *Al-Ashbāh waʾl-Naẓāʾir*, Cairo: Muʾassasat al-Ḥalabī, 1387/1968.

Ibn Qudāmah, Abū Muḥammad ʿAbdullāh, *Al-Kāfī*, 4 vols., 2nd edn, Beirut: al-Maktab al-Islāmī, 1399/1979.

——*Al-Mughnī*, 9 vols., Riyadh: Maktabat al-Riyāḍ al-Ḥadīthah, n.d.

Ibn Rushd, Muḥammad, *Bidāyat al-Mujtahid*, 2 vols., 7th edn, Beirut: Dār al-Maʿrifah, 1405/1985.

Ibn Taymiyyah, Taqī al-Dīn Aḥmad, *Al-Muqaddimah fī Uṣūl al-Tafsīr*, ed. ʿAdnān Zarzūr, 2nd edn, Beirut: Dār al-Qurʾān al-Karīm, 1979.

Al-Ījī, ʿAbd al-Raḥmān, *Mukhtaṣar al-Muntahā*, 2 vols., Cairo: Maktabat al-Kulliyyah al-Azhariyyah, 1403/1983.

Al-Isnawī, Jamāl al-Dīn, *Nihāyat al-Sawl*, printed on the margin of *al-Taqrīr waʾl-Taḥbīr* of Ibn Amīr al-Ḥājj, 3 vols., 2nd edn, Beirut: Dār al-Kutub al-ʿIlmiyyah, 1403/1983.

——*al-Tamhīd fī Takhrīj al-Furūʿ ʿalā al-Uṣūl*, ed. Muḥammad Ḥusayn Hītu, 3rd edn, Beirut: Muʾassasat al-Risālah, 1404/1984.

Jabbūrī, Ḥusayn Khalaf, *al-Aqwāl al-Uṣūliyyah liʾl-Imām Abī al-Ḥasan al-Karkhī*, 1409/1989.

Al-Jaṣṣāṣ, Abū Bakr Aḥmad, *Aḥkām al-Qurʾān*, 3 vols., Cairo: Maṭbaʿat al-Awqāf al-Islāmiyyah, 1335 AH.

Al-Jawziyyah, Ibn Qayyim, *Iʿlām al-Muwaqqiʿīn ʿan Rabb al-ʿĀlamīn*, 4 vols., Cairo: Maṭbaʿat al-Saʿādah, n.d.

Al-Jazarī, Muḥammad, *Ghāyat al-Nihāyah fī Ṭabaqāt al-Qurrāʾ*, Cairo, 1351 AH.

Al-Kalwazānī, Maḥfūz b. Aḥmad, *al-Tamhīd fī Uṣūl al-Fiqh*, ed. Mufīd Maḥmūd Abū ʿAmshah, Mecca: Umm al-Qurā University, 1406/1985.

Al-Kāsānī, Abū Bakr b. Masūd, *Badāiʿ al-Ṣanāiʿ fī Tartīb al-Sharīʿah*, Beirut: al-Maktabah al-Islāmiyyah. n.d.

Al-Kawrānī, Ṭāhā b. Aḥmad, *Sharḥ Mukhtaṣar al-Manār fī Uṣūl al-Fiqh*, ed. Shaʿbān Muḥammad Ismāʿīl, Dār al-Salām, 1408/1988.

Khallāf, ʿAbd al-Wahhāb, *ʿIlm Uṣūl al-Fiqh*, Cairo: Maktabat al-Daʿwah al-Islāmiyyah, n.d.

Al-Khaṭīb, Muḥammad ʿUjāj, *Lamaḥāt fī al-Maktabah waʾl-Baḥth waʾl-Maṣādir*, 14th edn, Beirut: Muʾassasat al-Risālah, 1412/1991.

Al-Khaṭīb, Shams al-Dīn Muḥammad, *Mughnī al-Muḥtāj ilā Maʿrifat Maʿānī Alfāẓ al-Minhāj*, 4 vols., Cairo: Muṣṭafā al-Bābī al-Ḥalabī, 1377 AH.

Khuḍarī, Muḥammad b. ʿAfīfī, *Tārīkh al-Tashrīʿ al-Islāmī*, Cairo, n.d.

——*Uṣūl al-Fiqh*, Beirut: Dār al-Fikr, 1409/1988.

Lane, E. W., *Arabic-English Lexicon*, Cambridge: Islamic Texts Society, 1984.

Al-Lubnānī, Salīm Rustum, *Sharḥ al-Majallah*, 3rd edn, Beirut: Dār Iḥyāʾ al-Turāth al-ʿArabī, 1406/1986.

Madkūr, Muḥammad Salām, *Tārīkh al-Tashrīʿ al-Islāmī wa-Maṣādiruh wa-Naẓratuh liʾl-Amwāl waʾl-ʿUqūd*, 2nd edn, Cairo, 1955.

Al-Maḥallī, Jalāl al-Din Muḥammad, *Sharḥ al-Waraqāt*, Riyadh: Maktabat Riyāḍ al-Ḥadīthah, n.d.

Majmaʿ al-Lughah al-ʿArabiyyah, *al-Muʿjam al-Wasīṭ*, 2nd edn, Cairo: Dār Iḥyāʾ al-Turāth al-ʿArabī, 1380/1960.

Mālik, b. Anas, *Al-Muwaṭṭaʾ*, ed. Muḥammad Fuʾād ʿAbd al-Bāqī, 2nd edn, Cairo: Dar al-Nafāʾis, 1951.

Mallat, Chibli, *The Renewal of Islamic Law*, Cambridge: Cambridge University Press, 1993.

Al-Marghīnānī, Burhān al-Dīn, *Al-Hidāyah*, 2 vols., al-Maktabah al-Islāmiyyah, n.d.

Al-Mawdūdī, Abū al-ʿAlā, *Islamic Law and Constitution*, 8th edn, Lahore: Islamic Publications Ltd, n.d.

Mayhawī, Mulla Jiyūn b. Abī Saʿīd, *Sharḥ Nūr al-Anwār ʿalā al-Manār*, printed on the margin of *Kashf al-Asrār Sharḥ al-Muṣannif ʿalā al-Manār*, 2 vols., Mecca: Dār al-Bāz, 1406/1986.

Muṣleḥuddin, Muḥammad, *Islamic Jurisprudence and the Rule of Necessity and Need*, Jeddah: Abūl Qasim Bookstore, n.d.

Muslim, Abū al-Ḥusayn b. al-Ḥajjāj, *Ṣaḥīḥ Muslim*, Cairo: Dār Iḥyāʾ al-Kutub al-ʿArabiyyah, n.d.

Al-Muthanna, Abū ʿUbaydah, *Majāz al-Qurʾān*, 1374 AH.

Al-Naṣafī, ʿAbd Allāh, *Kashf al-Asrār Sharḥ al-Muṣannif ʿalā al-Manār*, 2 vols., Mecca: Dār al-Bāz, 1406/1986.

Al-Nasāʾī, Aḥmad, *Al-Mujtabā* (known as *Sunan al-Nasāʾī*), Aleppo: Maktabat al-Maṭbūʿāt al-Islāmiyyah, n.d.

Naṣir, Jamāl, *The Islamic Law of Personal Status*, 2nd edn, London: Graham & Trotman, 1990.

Al-Nawawī, Abū Zakariyyā Yaḥyā, *Sharḥ Ṣaḥīḥ Muslim*, 18 vols., Cairo: Muḥammad ʿAlī Ṣubayḥ, n.d.

——*Tahdhīb al-Asmāʾ waʾl-Lughāt*, Cairo, n.d.

Pickthall, M. Marmaduke, *The Meaning of the Glorious Koran*, New Delhi: Taj Company, 1989.

Qabash, Aḥmad, *Al-Kāmil fī al-Naḥw waʾl-Ṣarf*, 6th edn, Dār al-Rashīd, 1986.

Qalʿajī, Muḥammad Rawwās, *Muʿjam Lughat al-Fuqahāʾ*, Beirut: Dār al-Nafāʾis, 1985.

Al-Qarāfī, Shihāb al-Dīn Aḥmad, *Sharḥ Tanqīḥ al-Fuṣūl*, Cairo: Dār al-Fikr, 1393/1973.

Al-Qurashī, ʿAbd al-Qādir b. Muḥammad, *Al-Jawāhir al-Muḍiyyah fī Ṭabaqāt al-Ḥanafiyyah*, Hyderabad, 1332 AH.

Al-Qurṭubī, Muḥammad b. Aḥmad, *Al-Jāmiʿ li-Aḥkām al-Qurʾān*, 20 vols., Dār al-Kitāb al-ʿArabī, n.d.

Ramić, Šukri H., *Taʿāruḍ mā Yukhill biʾl-Fahm wa-Atharuh fī al-Aḥkām al-Fiqhiyyah*, Dār al-Andalus al-Khadrāʾ 1ˢᵗ edn, Jaddah, 1421/2000.

Al-Rāzī, Fakhr al-Dīn, *Al-Maḥṣūl*, 6 vols., ed. Ṭāhā Jābir Fayyāḍ al-ʿAlwānī, Riyadh: Muḥammad Ibn Saʿūd Islamic University, 1399/1979.

Saʿd, Maḥmūd Tawfīq Muḥammad, *Dalālat al-Alfāẓ*, Cairo: Maṭbʿat al-Amānah, 1407/1987.

Saʿīd, Muḥammad Raʾfat, *Al-Taʾwīl Dirāsah Mawḍūʿiyyah fī al-Aḥadīth al-Nabawiyya*, Doha: Maktabat al-Aqṣā, 1994.

Ṣāliḥ, Muḥammad Adīb, *Tafsīr al-Nuṣūṣ*, 3rd edn, Beirut: al-Maktaba al-Islāmī, 1404/1984.

Al-Ṣanʿānī, Muḥammad, *Subul al-Salām*, 2 vols., 2nd edn, Cairo: Muṣṭafā al-Bābī al-Ḥalabī, 1369 AH.

Al-Sarakhsī, Shams al-Dīn Muḥammad, *Uṣūl al-Sarakhsī*, ed. Abū Wafāʾ al-Afghānī, 2 vols., Beirut: Dār al-Maʿrifah, n.d.

——*Al-Mabsūṭ*, 30 vols., Beirut: Dār al-Maʿrifah, 1406/1986.

Shaʿbān, Zakiyy al-Dīn, *Uṣūl al-Fiqh al-Islāmī*, Cairo: Dār al-Kitāb al-Jāmiʿī, 1983.

Al-Shāfiʿī, Muḥammad b. Idrīs, *Al-Risālah fī Uṣūl al-Fiqh*, trans. M. Khadduri, 2nd edn, Cambridge: The Islamic Texts Society, 1987.

——*Al-Umm*, 7 vols., Cairo: al-Maṭbaʿah al-Amīriyyah, 1321–1325 AH.

——*Al-Musnad*, ed. Muḥammad ʿĀbid al-Sindī, Cairo, 1369/1950.

Al-Shahrastānī, Muḥammad ʿAbd al-Karīm, *Al-Milal wa'l-Niḥal*, printed on the margin of Ibn Ḥazm's work of the same title, Cairo: al-Maṭbaʿa al-Adabiyyah, 1317 AH.

Al-Shawkānī, Muḥammad b. ʿAlī, *Nayl al-Awṭār Sharḥ Muntaqā al-Akhbār*, 8 vols., 2nd edn, Cairo: Muṣṭafā al-Bābī al-Ḥalabī, n.d.

——*Irshād al-Fuḥūl*, Mecca: Dār al-Bāz, n.d.

——*al-Badr al-Ṭāliʿ bi-Maḥāsin man baʿd al-Qarn al-Tāsiʿ*, Cairo, 1348 AH.

Al-Shīrāzī, Abū Isḥāq Ibrāhīm, *Al-Lummaʿ*, Beirut: Dār al-Kutub al-ʿIlmiyyah, 1405/1985.

——*Al-Muhadhdhab*, 2 vols., Cairo: Maṭbaʿat Muṣṭafā al-Bābī al-Ḥalabī, n.d.

Al-Subkī, Tāj al-Dīn, *Ṭabaqāt al-Shāfiʿiyyah al-Kubrā (Ṭabaqāt al-Subkī)*, Cairo, 1324 AH.

Al-Suyūṭī, Jalāl al-Dīn, *Lubāb al-Nuqūl fī Asbāb al-Nuzūl*, 2nd edn, Cairo: Muṣṭafā al-Bābī al-Ḥalabī, n.d.

——*Bughyat al-Wuʿāt fī Ṭabaqāt al-Lughawiyyīn wa'l-Nuḥḥāt*, Cairo, 1326 AH.

——*Tanwīr al-Ḥawālik Sharḥ Muwaṭaʾ Mālik*, Beirut: Dār al-Nadwah al-Jadīdah, n.d.

——*Al-Durr al-Manthūr*, Cairo, 1314/1897.

——*Al-Ashbāh wa'l-Naẓāʾir*, Cairo: Maṭbaʿat Muṣṭafā Muḥammad, n.d.

Al-Ṭabarī, Abū Jaʿfar Muḥammad, *Jāmiʿ al-Bayān ʿan Tafsīr Āy al-Qurʾān*, 30 vols., Cairo: Maṭbaʿat Būlāq, 1329 AH. Also edition of Maḥmūd Shākir, Cairo: Dār al-Maʿārif, n.d.

——*Tārīkh al-Umam wa'l-Mulūk*, Cairo, 1326 AH.

Al-Ṭabrīzī, Muḥammad b. ʿAbd Allāh, *Mishkāt al-Maṣābīḥ*, ed. Muḥammad Nāsir al-Dīn al-Albānī, 3 vols., 2nd edn, Beirut: al-Maktab al-Islāmī, 1399/1979.

Al-Taftazānī, Masʿūd b. ʿUmar, *Sharḥ al-Talwīḥ ʿalā al-Tawḍīḥ*, Beirut: Dār al-Kutub al-ʿIlmiyyah, n.d.

——Ḥāshiyat al-Taftazānī, printed with Sharḥ al-ʿAḍud maʿa Mukhtaṣar al-Muntahā, 2 vols., Cairo: Maṭbaʿat al-Kulliyyah al-Azhariyyah, 1406/1986.

Al-Tahānawī, Muḥammad, Dictionary of the Technical Terms, Calcutta, 1862.

Al-Ṭaḥāwī, Abū Jaʿfar Aḥmad, Sharḥ Maʿānī al-Āthār, 2 vols., 1302 AH.

——Mushkil al-Athār, 4 vols., Hyderabad, 1333 AH.

——Mukhtaṣar al-Ṭaḥawī, ed. Abū al-Wafā’ al-Afghānī, Beirut: Dār Iḥyā’ al-ʿUlūm, 1406/1986.

Al-Tanbaktī, Aḥmad Bābā, Nayl al-Ibtihāj bi-Ṭaṭrīz al-Dībāj, printed on the margin of al-Dībāj al-Mudhahhab, Cairo, 1329 AH.

Al-Tilmisānī, Abū ʿAbdullāh Muḥammad, Miftāḥ al-Wuṣūl ilā Binā’ al-Furūʿ ʿalā al-Uṣūl, Tunis: al-Maṭbaʿah al-Ahliyyah, 1346 AH.

Al-Tirmidhī, Abū ʿĪsa Muḥammad, Al-Jāmiʿ al-Ṣaḥīḥ, 5 vols., ed. Aḥmad Muḥammad Shākir, Beirut: Dār al-Kutub al-ʿIlmiyyah, n.d.

——An Introduction to the Exegesis of the Qur’ān, trans. Muḥammad ʿAbdul-Ḥaq Anṣārī, Riyadh: Muḥammad Ibn Saʿūd Islamic University, 1409/1989.

Wehr, Hans, Arabic-English Dictionary, ed. J. M. Cowan, 3rd edn, London: Harrap, 1976.

Wensinck, A. J., al-Muʿjam al-Mufahras li-Alfāẓ al-Ḥadīth al-Nabawī, Leiden: E. J. Brill, 1965.

Zādah, Aḥmad b. Muṣṭafā, Miftāḥ al-Saʿādah wa-Miṣbāḥ al-Siyādah, Hyderabad, 1329 AH.

Al-Zamakhsharī, Maḥmūd, Al-Kashshāf ʿan Ḥaqā’iq Ghawāmiḍ al-Tanzīl wa-ʿUyūn al-Aqāwīl fī Wujūh al-Ta’wīl, Beirut: Dār al-Maʿrifah, n.d.

Zander, Michael, The Law-Making Process, 2nd edn, London: Weidenfeld and Nicolson, 1985.

Al-Zariklī, Khayruddīn, al-Aʿlām, 6th edn, Beirut: Dār al-ʿIlm li’l-Malāyīn, 1984.

Zaydān, ʿAbd al-Karīm, al-Madkhal li-Dirāsat al-Sharīʿah al-Islāmiyyah, Baghdad: Maṭbaʿat al-ʿĀnī, 1967.

Al-Zaylaʿī, Muḥammad b. ʿAbd Allāh, Naṣb al-Rāyah fī Takhrīj Aḥādīth al-Hidāyah, 4 vols., Cairo: Maṭbaʿat Dār al-Maʿmūm, 1357 AH.

Zuhrī, Muḥammad b. Saʿd, Ṭabaqāt Ibn Saʿd, Leiden, 1321 AH.

Index